Lloyd J. Ogilvie General Editor

THE
PREACHER'S
COMMENTARY

DANIEL

Sinclair B. Ferguson

THOMAS NELSON PUBLISHERS
Nashville

THE PREACHER'S COMMENTARY SERIES, Volume 21: *Daniel.* Copyright ©
1988 by Word, Inc.

Published in Nashville, Tennessee, by Thomas Nelson, Inc

Library of Congress Cataloging in Publication Data

The preacher's commentary (formerly The communicator's commentary).

  Includes bibliographical references.
  Contents: v. 21. Daniel/Sinclair B. Ferguson
  1. Bible. O.T.—Commentaries. I. Ogilvie, Lloyd John. II. Ferguson, Sinclair
B., 1948—

BS1151.2.C66 1986   221.7'7   86–11138
ISBN 13: 978-0-7852-4795-1

Printed in the United States of America

HB 11.04.2024

To
Eric and Greta Alexander
and
Jennifer and Ronald

CONTENTS

EDITOR'S PREFACE

God has called all of His people to be communicators. Everyone who is in Christ is called into ministry. As ministers of "the manifold grace of God," all of us—clergy and laity—are commissioned with the challenge to communicate our faith to individuals and groups, classes and congregations.

The Bible, God's Word, is the objective basis of the truth of His love and power that we seek to communicate. In response to the urgent, expressed needs of pastors, teachers, Bible study leaders, church school teachers, small group enablers, and individual Christians, the Preacher's Commentary is offered as a penetrating search of the Scriptures of the Old and New Testament to enable vital personal and practical communication of the abundant life.

Many current commentaries and Bible study guides provide only some aspects of a communicator's needs. Some offer in-depth scholarship but no application to daily life. Others are so popular in approach that biblical roots are left unexplained. Few offer impelling illustrations that open windows for the reader to see the exciting application for today's struggles. And most of all, seldom have the expositors given the valuable outlines of passages so needed to help the preacher or teacher in his or her busy life to prepare for communicating the Word to congregations or classes.

This Preacher's Commentary series brings all of these elements together. The authors are scholar-preachers and teachers outstanding in their ability to make the Scriptures come alive for individuals and groups. They are noted for bringing together excellence in biblical scholarship, knowledge of the original Hebrew and Greek, sensitivity to people's needs, vivid illustrative material from biblical, classical, and contemporary sources, and lucid communication by the use of clear outlines of thought. Each has been selected to contribute to this series because of his Spirit-empowered ability to help people live in the skins of biblical characters and provide a "you-are-there" intensity to the drama of events of the Bible which have so much to say about our relationships and responsibilities today.

The design for the Preacher's Commentary gives the reader an overall outline of each book of the Bible. Following the introduction, which reveals the author's approach and salient background on the book, each chapter of the commentary provides the Scripture to be exposited. The New King James Bible has been chosen for the Preacher's Commentary because it combines with integrity the beauty of language, underlying Hebrew and Greek textual basis, and thought-flow of the 1611 King James Version, while replacing obsolete verb forms and other archaisms with their everyday contemporary counterparts for greater readability. Reverence for God is preserved in the capitalization of all pronouns referring to the Father, Son, or Holy Spirit. Readers who are more comfortable with another translation can readily find the parallel passage by means of the chapter and verse reference at the end of each passage being exposited. The paragraphs of exposition combine fresh insights to the Scripture, application, rich illustrative material, and innovative ways of utilizing the vibrant truth for his or her own life and for the challenge of communicating it with vigor and vitality.

It has been gratifying to me as editor of this series to receive enthusiastic progress reports from each contributor. As they worked, all were gripped with new truths from the Scripture—God-given insights into passages, previously not written in the literature of biblical explanation. A prime objective of this series is for each user to find the same awareness: that God speaks with newness through the Scriptures when we approach them with a ready mind and a willingness to communicate what He has given; that God delights to give communicators of His Word "I-never-saw-that-in-that-verse-before" intellectual insights so that our listeners and readers can have "I-never-realized-all-that-was-in-that-verse" spiritual experiences.

The thrust of the commentary series unequivocally affirms that God speaks through the Scriptures today to engender faith, enable adventuresome living of the abundant life, and establish the basis of obedient discipleship. The Bible, the unique Word of God, is unlimited as a resource for Christians in communicating our hope to others. It is our weapon in the battle for truth, the guide for ministry, and the irresistible force for introducing others to God.

A biblically rooted communication of the gospel holds in unity and oneness what divergent movements have wrought asunder. This commentary series courageously presents personal faith, caring for individuals, and social responsibility as essential, inseparable dimensions of biblical Christianity. It seeks to present the quadrilateral gospel in its fullness which calls us to unreserved commitment to Christ, unrestricted self-esteem in His grace, unqualified love for others in personal evangelism, and undying efforts to work for justice and righteousness in a sick and suffering world.

A growing renaissance in the church today is being led by clergy and laity who are biblically rooted, Christ-centered, and Holy Spirit-empowered. They have dared to listen to people's most urgent questions and deepest needs and then to God as He speaks through the Bible. Biblical preaching is the secret of growing churches. Bible study classes and small groups are equipping the laity for ministry in the world. Dynamic Christians are finding that daily study of God's Word allows the Spirit to do in them what He wishes to communicate through them to others. These days are the most exciting time since Pentecost. The Preacher's Commentary is offered to be a primary resource of new life for this renaissance.

I am pleased to introduce to you the author of this superb volume in the Preacher's Commentary series, Dr. Sinclair B. Ferguson, Professor of Systematic Theology at Westminster Seminary in Dallas. Dr. Ferguson, who is quite familiar to readers from Great Britain, studied in Scotland, receiving his Ph.D. from the University of Aberdeen. Prior to moving to the United States, Dr. Ferguson worked for many years as a pastor. Today, he is becoming increasingly known as a fine teacher and author of outstanding Christian literature.

I am certain that this commentary on Daniel will extend Dr. Ferguson's well-deserved reputation for excellence in biblical scholarship. He proposes to "maintain the balance between exposition and illustration and application," and does so in an exemplary fashion. Thus he illustrates the essence of the Preacher's Commentary series while adding his own particular strengths.

You will feel a solidness as you use this commentary. Dr. Ferguson has melded detailed examination of the text of Daniel with a systematic theologian's ability to give an ordered elucidation of theological content. You will appreciate Dr. Ferguson's guidance through the often-complicated maze of Daniel's life and thought, for he dialogues not only with contemporary biblical scholarship but equally with the great theologians of the Protestant and Reformed traditions.

This volume excels not only academically but pastorally as well. Sinclair Ferguson's years in pastoral ministry are reflected in his rich illustrations and down-to-earth applications. He allows Daniel to speak to us: theologically, pastorally, profoundly.

You will find in this commentary a most refreshing and helpful approach to the Book of Daniel. Dr. Ferguson avoids the apocalyptic guessing games that plague many contemporary uses of the prophet. Rather he allows Daniel to speak with his own voice and perspective. "It should be part of the task of expounding Daniel," Dr. Ferguson writes, "to help people see the big picture before attempting to explain the details." Daniel's big picture portrays graphically the sovereignty of God over all of history—and over all of our lives. From this perspective we are propelled, not into end-time speculations, but into "a life of holy obedience." Correct interpretation of Daniel, Dr. Ferguson contends, places the central focus of the book not in our current events, but "in the incarnation, death, resurrection, and ascension of Christ."

Dr. Ferguson hopes that his work may "encourage others to see how important it is to communicate the message of the Book of Daniel today." It will surely do so by highlighting this message anew with commendable faithfulness to Daniel's original intent. Dr. Ferguson helps us to respond with deeper understanding, heartier communication, and truer obedience.

—LLOYD J. OGILVIE

AUTHOR'S PREFACE

In commentaries, as in other things, "one man's meat is another man's poison." The old Latin proverb is also true: *de gustibus non disputandum est* ("you cannot argue about taste"). My personal taste is for studies that are suggestive rather than exhaustive (or exhausting). I do not want someone to do for me what I should be doing for myself. Nor do I want someone to tell me only what I know already. Therefore, in this study I have tried to maintain the balance between exposition and illustration and application. I have avoided the temptation to produce an exposition that could be "lifted off the page" and carried into the pulpit or classroom. On the other hand, I have tried to suggest lines of application and illustration that may act as catalysts for fellow teachers and preachers. If these pages encourage others to see how important it is to communicate the message of the Book of Daniel today, I shall be well satisfied.

It is always a privilege to be asked to expound sacred scripture. I am indebted therefore to the general editor of the Preacher's Commentary, Dr. Lloyd J. Ogilvie, for his gracious invitation to share in this series. My wife and children merit special appreciation for their long-suffering. They know now why Daniel's window opened toward Jerusalem.

—SINCLAIR B. FERGUSON
Westminster Theological Seminary
Dallas, Texas

INTRODUCTION

To open the Book of Daniel is to enter a strange but brave new world. We are in Babylon in the sixth century before Christ. The experience, however, is not seen through the eyes of a recognized prophet: an Isaiah, with his words of comfort and hope, a Jeremiah with his dark words of judgment, or an Ezekiel, with his bright visions of God. Rather these eyes are those of an exile in Babylon, a statesman whose personal experiences are breathtaking in their heroism and triumph. Yet we are not in the world of a calculating politician. For while the first half of Daniel (chs. 1—6) describes his political activities as a man of faith and prayer, the second half (chs. 7—12) explains his public energy. He knew God intimately, and God revealed His secrets to him (cf. Amos 3:7).

Daniel was a visionary, a man who received revelations of the future in a form that is always dramatic and at times almost grotesque in its unveiling of the bestial nature of evil. What impresses the reader above everything else, however, is how God-centered Daniel is and how God-centered is his view of the political stage on which he plays his part.

A genuinely God-centered worldview is something to which we are little accustomed today. On a recent vacation I read the extensive published version of the diary of a British cabinet minister. It was a vivid illustration of the psalmist's words: "God is in none of his thoughts" (Ps. 10:4). It was not simply that he did not mix religion and politics; God was completely absent from his entire perspective on life. He had "no need for that hypothesis." In sharp contrast, there is something thrilling about the "diary" of a "chief of staff" (Dan. 2:48) whose perspective on life is so biblical.

The Book of Daniel—Its Date and Setting

The life of Daniel is set in Babylon in the sixth century B.C. It begins with the siege of Jerusalem by Nebuchadnezzar in "the third year of the reign of Jehoiakim" (Dan. 1:1), that is, 605 B.C.

The final date mentioned is "the third year of Cyrus king of Persia" (Dan. 10:1), namely, 537 B.C. We thus are exposed to a span of some seventy years of Daniel's life, from his captivity as a young man (Dan. 1:3–6) until he is well into his ninth decade.

Unlike modern books, the author's name was not written on the dust jacket of Daniel. In the closing chapters, however, most of the material is written in the first person singular ("I saw in my vision" [7:2]; "a vision appeared to me—to me, Daniel" [8:1]; "in the first year of his reign I, Daniel, understood . . ." [9:2]; "in those days, I, Daniel . . ." [10:2]). Much of the book therefore claims an autobiographical authorship. This in itself does not exclude the work of other hands in the sections written in the third person. There are, however, good reasons for believing that the book came from one hand, a fact recognized even by some who believe Daniel was written in the second century B.C. If such unity exists, we are certainly led in the direction of seeing Daniel himself as the author of the book that bears his name. It is called Daniel not only because it is about him (in fact, it is about God), but because it was also written by him.

This view of Daniel, which accepts a sixth-century dating, runs contrary to the trends of contemporary critical scholarship. Many scholars date the latest sections in the book in the second century B.C. Several reasons are advanced for this view including technical historical and linguistic arguments. These arguments have been faithfully dealt with by competent conservative scholars over the decades.[1] Sadly, they have been almost entirely ignored by the critical scholarly community, as a glance at the bibliographies of critical commentaries on Daniel will underline. Without doubt the principal argument for a late dating lies in the extended description of future events contained in Daniel 11. Here we find an outline of historical events between the days of Daniel (the sixth century B.C.) and those of the Syrian ruler Antiochus IV (the second century B.C.). It is inconceivable to the critical mind that such an outline could have been revealed to a man in sixth-century Babylon. It is akin to suggesting that Martin Luther could forecast the flow of world history from the time of the Reformation up through the Second World War.

It would be wrong to tar all critical scholars with the same brush. Some would argue that this is not so much the issue for them as the fact that the Book of Daniel as a whole breathes the spirit of a genre of literature that was characteristically pseudonymous. The book is set in the sixth century B.C. but its author did not expect any of his readers to believe it was written then, any more than the author of a historical novel written in the first person would expect his readers to think that his book was written at the time of the hero or heroine.

In contrast to this view the rest of Scripture views the content of the Book of Daniel as historical. The references to Daniel 3 and 6 in Hebrews 11:33–34 and our Lord's description of him as a prophet (Matt. 24:15) point in this direction. Nor is there any evidence that the earliest readers of the book regarded it as a work of fiction.

We should not tone down how contrary to human expectation and experience the visions in Daniel actually are. We need to ask ourselves: Do we seriously believe that our God gave such a remarkable revelation? In the final analysis, the great issue may be one that surfaces in Daniel itself, in the questions: Do we have a God who knows and rules the future? Do we have a God who reveals His secrets to His people? Do we have a God who delivers men from burning furnaces? Or is this world a closed system—a place where God is essentially the stranger who set it all in motion, providing at best an endowment fund of natural and moral laws which, if broken, will lead to disaster? Lurking behind the denial of the possibility of predictive prophecy is a deistic rather than a Christian and biblical view of God.

Our Approach to Studying and Expounding Daniel

The exposition of Daniel that follows is designed for a "communicator's" commentary. One of the first questions an expositor must ask of a biblical book is: What kind of book is this? The answer will in part determine the way in which its teaching should be presented.

Daniel contains historical material, but it is not simply a history book. Nor does Daniel seem to be only a book of prophecy. True, other prophetic books contain biographical details (think of Isaiah, Jeremiah, Ezekiel, Hosea), but perhaps it is significant that in the Hebrew Bible Daniel was placed not among the Prophets but in the group known as the Writings. Daniel is not distinguished by the presence of the biographical so much as by the presence of what is usually called apocalyptic: visions of the future describing the course of world history in terms of nonhuman symbols—similar to those in Revelation (or the Apocalypse). For this reason, Daniel is often referred to as an example of the apocalyptic literary genre.

We must not make the mistake of too narrowly defining what this means. Daniel contains apocalyptic elements. Its style is not in its entirety apocalyptic. We are dealing here with a literary genre that developed over several centuries—rather like the novel, a genre usually dated from the eighteenth century only, yet having literary forebears stretching back through the years.

From one point of view, this style of communication seems far removed from the early twenty-first century; it describes an alien world in colorful, dramatic, and sometimes grotesque pictures. Yet it is this element—the pictorial and visual—that may make the message of Daniel easier rather than more difficult to communicate to twenty-first-century people.

Like the Book of Revelation, the visionary sections of Daniel contain God's picture book. We should read and expound them as though the Lord were saying: "Come and see this!" That is why sometimes children see the basic message of the books of Daniel and Revelation more immediately than their parents! They do not get sidetracked by the details, failing to see and feel the general impact. It should be part of the task of expounding Daniel to help people to see the big picture before attempting to explain the details.

There is a biblical reason for adopting this procedure. It was the only procedure open to Daniel himself. For all the wisdom and insight he was given, it is clear that he did not fully understand his own visions (Dan. 12:8). How then could he benefit from them? Apparently he was able to see the various portrayals of God's sovereignty woven into the tapestry of his visions. He did not need to understand fully the details in order to see and hear the encouragement God wanted to give him.

The Structure of Daniel

The Book of Daniel breaks down into two halves: Chapters 1 through 6 are clearly biographical in nature, tracing Daniel's witness in the royal court of Babylon. Chapters 7 through 12 contain a record of his visions of God's purposes for the future. The actual structure of the book, however, is more complex. For one thing (as the footnote in NKJV will indicate to those who do not have access to the original text of Daniel), Daniel 2:4b—7:28 is written in Aramaic.

Aramaic was an international language as early as the ninth or eighth century B.C. An interesting (if not to say amusing) illustration of this appears in 2 Kings 18:20. It has therefore been suggested that the section in Daniel of special significance to those who were not Jews was written in the international language. It is important, however, to notice that the Aramaic section does not neatly dovetail with the simplest division of the book into biography and apocalypse (chaps. 1—6, 7—12). In fact, rather than separate them, it links them together. It has been suggested that by doing so, it is made clear that chapters 2—7 represent the core of the book. If this is correct, a further pattern may be traced in this central section:

Chapters 2 and 7 present the four world empires;
Chapters 3 and 6 present narratives of mighty deliverance;
Chapters 4 and 5 describe God's judgment on world rulers.

If this pattern reflects the intention of the author, then we also see the significance of the opening and closing sections of the book: Chapter 1 sets the scene in Babylon for what follows. Chapters 8—12 expound the earlier pattern of world history in detail but from the viewpoint of God's people in particular, and with a view to explaining God's purposes for them.

Many of us have a tendency to prefer things to start at the beginning, continue without interruption, and finish at the end. It is often said, with good reason, that this is a distinctively Western mind-set (perhaps, indeed, the product of the influence of Aristotle and his logic). We must unlearn this straight-line view of things if we are to feel the full force of the Book of Daniel (and also, it should be said, the Book of Revelation and Jesus' discourses in Matt. 24 and 25 and Mark 13). Here we encounter a structure that can be described variously. It has been called "progressive parallelism": a style of presentation in which the author takes us from the beginning to the end of a sequence of events and then returns to the beginning to describe them again, this time in different terms or from another perspective. One might liken the structure to a spiral staircase, turning around the same central point on more than one occasion, yet rising higher and higher at the same time.

Thus in the Book of Daniel we keep returning to the same general outline of world history (compare, for example, chs. 2 and 7). Yet we are presented with different viewpoints, or the material is presented through different imagery, or our attention is focused on a particular cross section (for example, 9:20–27). This explains what may seem to some readers a certain monotony in the message of the book. It says the same thing over and over in different ways. That is something the expositor has to recognize in order to focus on each new perspective presented on the central theme.

The Approach to the Book of Daniel

The exposition of Daniel involves handling material calculated to stir the hearts of God's people. It also involves expounding passages that Daniel himself clearly did not understand (12:8). There are few expositors who are prepared to say: "I honestly do not understand what this means." We should not be ashamed of such an admission. In this study the admission is made more by silence than by confession.

One admission, however, demands to be made. The general approach adopted in this volume sees the central focus of Daniel's prophecies in the incarnation, death, resurrection, and ascension of Christ. He is the stone who breaks the kingdoms of this world in pieces and becomes a mountain that fills the whole earth. His kingdom has already come. It awaits final consummation when a final antichrist will be revealed and be overwhelmed by the coming again of Christ at the end of a time of unparalleled tribulation for God's people.

Little interest is expressed in the course of the exposition to detailed identification of Daniel's prophecies. Why this is so will appear in the course of the exposition itself. Here it will suffice to quote from the earliest biblical theologian of the postapostolic church, Irenaeus of Lyons: "It is . . . more certain, and less hazardous to await the fulfillment of the prophecy, than to be making surmises, and casting about for names that may present themselves."[2] Irenaeus was thinking in particular of Revelation and the number of the mark of the beast (666), but his words have a wider application.

The chief reason for this focus is that this is the correct way to grasp the message of Daniel. It is not a book of history written in advance. When it has been treated as such, there has been a tendency for the reader to engage in speculation rather than to be stimulated to a life of holy obedience. Yet such obedience is clearly the whole motive for writing this great book.

The Message of Daniel

What then is the message Daniel brings? It is multifaceted. His visions bring both counsel and encouragement. Their view of the history of the church is that it will always be marked by trial and suffering, by the attacks of seductive powers and malignant forces.

Daniel himself was a man who felt the force of the kingdom of darkness and stood in the evil day, receiving rich blessings from his God. His book not only tells others to stand; it shows us what it means to stand for the Lord and to keep ourselves from idols of every kind (1 John 5:21).

The spiritual decline of the days in which Daniel lived are well indexed in the plaintiff words of Psalm 137:

> By the rivers of Babylon
> There we sat down, yea we wept when we remembered
> Zion.
> We hung our harps
> Upon the willows in the midst of it.
> For there those who carried us away captive asked of us
> a song,
> And those who plundered us requested mirth,
> Saying, "Sing us one of the songs of Zion!"
> How shall we sing the LORD's song in a foreign land?
>
> —*Psalm 137:1–4*

That is the great question. How can the Christian, whose citizenship is in heaven (Phil. 3:20), sing the Lord's song as an exile here (1 Pet. 1:1)? The principles that governed Daniel's life—grace, faith, Scripture, prayer, fellowship, obedience, hope—provide the answer. The narratives of the book put flesh and blood on them for us.

The heart of the book's message is, of course, the good news of the kingdom of God. Nations and empires, thrones and dominions will rise and fall, but the city of God will endure. His kingdom will last forever, and the gates of hell shall not withstand it. The stone cut without hands will break into pieces the idols of man's creation and ultimately grow into a mountain that will fill the whole earth (Dan. 2:34–35). The great hope of the resurrection will one day be fulfilled (Dan. 12:1–3). "The kingdoms of this world will become *the kingdoms* of our Lord and of His Christ, and He shall reign forever and ever!" (Rev. 11:15).

The Christian who sees and believes this will soon learn how to sing the Lord's song in whatever foreign land He places us.

NOTES

1. See, e.g. (in order of publication): R. D. Wilson, *Studies in the Book of Daniel: A Discussion of the Historical Questions* (New York: G. P.

Putnam's Sons, 1917); idem, *Studies in the Book of Daniel: Second Series* (New York: Fleming H. Revell Co., 1938); E. J. Young, *A Commentary on Daniel* (Grand Rapids: Eerdmans, 1949); D. J. Wiseman, ed., *Notes on Some Problems in the Book of Daniel* (London: Tyndale Press, 1965); Joyce G. Baldwin, *Daniel: An Introduction and Commentary* (Downers Grove: InterVarsity Press, 1978).

2. Irenaeus, *Against All Heresies*, 5.30.3.

AN OUTLINE OF DANIEL

I. By the Rivers of Babylon: 1:1–21
   A. Man Proposes, God Disposes: 1:1–2
   B. Brainwashing: 1:3–7
   C. A Purpose Firm: 1:8–16
   D. God Honors Faithfulness: 1:17–21
II. Bad Dreams: 2:1–49
   A. Humanity's Basic Insecurity: 2:1–13
   B. Knocking at Heaven's Door: 2:14–30
   C. A Kingdom that Cannot Be Shaken: 2:31–49
III. The Inquisition: 3:1–30
   A. Totalitarianism: 3:1–7
   B. Obeying God Rather than Men: 3:8–18
   C. Through Fiery Trials: 3:19–25
   D. Impressed Once More: 3:26–30
IV. Signs and Wonders: 4:1–37
   A. Night Visions: 4:1–18
   B. Warnings from God: 4:19–27
   C. The Kingdom Departs: 4:28–33
   D. Reason Restored: 4:34–37
V. The Writing on the Wall: 5:1–31
   A. The Moving Finger Writes: 5:1–9
   B. Weighed in the Balances of God: 5:10–31
VI. In the Lions' Den: 6:1–28
   A. Kingdom Against Kingdom: 6:1–9
   B. Faithful unto Death: 6:10–17
   C. Shut Your Mouth!: 6:18–28
VII. Apocalypse!: 7:1–28
   A. Jungle Book: 7:1–8
   B. The Vision of God: 7:9–14
   C. The Everlasting Kingdom: 7:15–28
VIII. The Ram, the Goat, and the Little Horn: 8:1–27
   A. The Ram with Two Horns: 8:1–4, 15–20
   B. The Goat with the Horn between His Eyes: 8:5–8, 21–22
   C. The Little Horn: 8:9–14, 23–27

CHAPTER ONE—BY THE RIVERS OF BABYLON
DANIEL 1:1–21

Scripture Outline
> Man Proposes, God Disposes (1:1–2)
> Brainwashing (1:3–7)
> A Purpose Firm (1:8–16)
> God Honors Faithfulness (1:17–21)

When I was a very small boy, perhaps four or five years old, I sometimes crawled into the warmth of my parents' bed after they had risen. Although scarcely able to read, I would search through my grandmother's thick-paged, small-print Bible. There were two stories for which I searched. One was the life of Joseph, which I knew was at the beginning somewhere. The other always took me ages to find. It was the story of Daniel.

I have sometimes wondered why I was so fascinated by the story of Daniel's life. I imagine that I was drawn by the two factors that appealed to a young boy: Daniel's story begins when he was himself a child (1:3, 4), and he was a hero. He was the young man who, almost above all others, epitomized what a Christian should be. No wonder in later years at Sunday school I enjoyed singing:

> Dare to be a Daniel,
> Dare to stand alone,
> Dare to have a purpose firm.
> Dare to make it known.

Daniel's heroism and that of his three companions (Shadrach, Meshach, and Abed-Nego) are briefly celebrated in the New Testament: They "stopped the mouths of lions, [and] quenched the violence of fire" (Heb. 11:33–34). No wonder as a youngster I found the story of their heroism so stirring.

23

Such heroism does not develop overnight, nor is it created in a vacuum. It is the mature fruit of lives and characters that have been forged by experience, by the tests and trials of the providence of God, and by faithfulness and obedience to Him. Present heroism cannot be explained apart from past faithfulness. For this reason, Daniel and his companions do not appear full blown on the scene of history, as it were, but as young disciples, set in adverse circumstances and unpromising conditions for the service of God.

The first chapter of Daniel tells us of their early beginnings. Without those early steps of faithfulness to their Lord there would be no record of their later heroism. Scripture does not give us these details of their early years accidentally. It does so in order to teach us that growth in grace and usefulness in God's service does not begin in the world of our dreams but in the context of life's harsh, historical realities. So it was for Daniel; so it will be also for the Daniels of today.

MAN PROPOSES, GOD DISPOSES

1:1 In the third year of the reign of Jehoiakim king of Judah, Nebuchadnezzar king of Babylon came to Jerusalem and besieged it. **2** And the Lord gave Jehoiakim king of Judah into his hand, with some of the articles of the house of God, which he carried into the land of Shinar to the house of his god; and he brought the articles into the treasure house of his god.

—Daniel 1:1–2

The Book of Daniel opens with two succinct statements about the siege of Jerusalem by Nebuchadnezzar, the king of Babylon. The first describes the event in terms of secular history, the second in terms of biblical theology. These two perspectives are woven together throughout the book. Man is active in history: *"Nebuchadnezzar . . . came to Jerusalem and besieged it"* (v. 1). Yet God is also active in the same historical events: *"And the Lord gave Jehoiakim . . . into his hand"* (v. 2).

Here we have clearly stated a principle that runs through the whole of Scripture, even when it is not stated. There are two ways of looking at life. It can be viewed simply in terms of what occurs. That is what we popularly call "history." Christians, however, can never be interested in human life merely to discover the "when" or the "who" or the "what." They are always concerned to know the answer to the question "why" in order to relate their answer to the biblical teaching on the purposes of God.

The viewpoint of history. The end of the seventh century and the beginning of the sixth century B.C. saw the ascendancy of Babylon in the ancient Near East. Jerusalem was attacked as part of a Babylonian expansionist policy, and the city's fall occurred over a three-stage period spanning the years 605, 597, and 587 B.C. (The story is recorded in 2 Kings 24:1—25:1, ending with the summary statement, "Thus Judah was carried away captive from its own land.")

The siege recorded here in Daniel 1 took place in the first of those stages. The apparent victory of the Babylonian gods over the God of the people of Jerusalem was sealed by the removal of some of the sacred furniture to the shrine of Nebuchadnezzar's deity. The humiliation could not have been more patent. Humanly speaking this was a time when God's glory was discounted, and His people were not a testimony to His great name (a situation that has been repeated countless times since). This event was seen by the author as part of a larger whole. No event in history can be isolated from its predecessors. The siege of Jerusalem by the Babylonians was no exception. It is simply a cross section of a conflict that runs through the whole of history: the conflict between the people of God and the people of the world. It can be traced back in Scripture to the prototype of totalitarianism, in the building on the plains of Shinar of a city whose tower would reach up to the heavens and bring fame and fortune (Gen. 11:1–4). It is the conflict of the world against what Augustine of Hippo called "the city of God." It is the same conflict that John Bunyan saw in more personal terms in the efforts of the inhabitants of the "City of Destruction" and "Vanity Fair" to prevent Christian's completing his journey to the "heavenly city."

An age-old conflict lies behind the simple descriptive words, *"Nebuchadnezzar king of Babylon came to Jerusalem and besieged it"*(v. 1). This conflict can be traced back, ultimately, to the Garden of Eden:

"And I will put enmity
between you and the woman,
And between your seed and her Seed;
He shall bruise your head,
And you shall bruise His heel."

—*Genesis 3:15*

It finds its crisis point in a picture in the Book of Revelation: "And the dragon stood before the woman who was ready to give birth, to devour her Child as soon as it was born. She bore a male Child who was to rule all nations with a rod of iron. And her Child was caught up to God and to His throne" (Rev. 12:4–5). Its final consummation—its ultimate fall and judgment—is described in Revelation 17—18.

Babylon and Jerusalem represent the two cities to which men and women belong. They symbolize the two loyalties of which Scripture speaks in many different word pictures: two gates, two ways, two masters. As such, Babylon and Jerusalem are permanently opposed to one another. That is a fundamental lesson of the Christian life: "You cannot serve God and mammon"; you will hate the one and love the other, or love the one and hate the other (Matt. 6:24). You must seek God's kingdom and His righteousness. That is always the case, but there are times when those perennial hostilities erupt violently and the poison that has been festering in the bloodstream of Babylon manifests itself publicly. Nebuchadnezzar's siege of Jerusalem was such a time.

The consequence of the Babylonian siege was evident. God was robbed of His possessions and blasphemies were committed against His name. The temple vessels were placed in the shrine of a pagan deity (v. 3). The city of this world always has such theft in view when it attacks the city of God. It was the object Satan had in view in the Garden of Eden—to rob God of His creation, His "child" (Luke 3:38), the "vessel" of His image in the world. Satan led Adam to share his blasphemy against God by making himself, rather than the Lord, the center of his universe.

We should never forget that this is the meaning of history on both the cosmic and personal scales. A spiritual conflict lies at the heart of every event, however great, however mundane. Our own contribution to history depends on our answer to this question: Am I living for the city of God and according to its code of conduct or am I living according to the by-laws of the city of destruction?

The immediate consequence of Nebuchadnezzar's siege was the defeat, if not the disappearance, of the city of God. He brought God's possessions and some of the citizens of God's kingdom into his own city. His victory could not have been more complete. From all outward appearances, the forces of hell had prevailed. What Nebuchadnezzar did not realize was that history can be read from two perspectives: our point of view and God's point of view. Indeed, God's viewpoint is transcending; His is the ultimate perspective. Could Nebuchadnezzar have stood on the vantage ground that Daniel later occupied, he would have seen another hand than his own governing and directing these affairs. God had not taken His hand off the rudder that guides the history of His creation.

The viewpoint of theology. Parallel to the description of the siege of Jerusalem and its sad aftermath in the exile of its inhabitants, we find a startling statement: *"And the Lord gave Jehoiakim king of Judah into his [Nebuchadnezzar's] hand"* (v. 2). The Lord Himself was involved in the defeat of His own people and the overthrow of His own city. No doubt, given the prevailing spirit in Jerusalem, that was not the majority viewpoint. By contrast their cry would have been: "Where is God in this catastrophe?" Had He forgotten His people? Had He forgotten His promises to them, deserting them in their hour of greatest need?

The perspective of our author is very different. He did not have access to information about the siege that was hidden from others. The facts for him were the same as those for all others. How then could he say with such confidence that even this tragedy was in the hands of his Lord? He believed God's prophetic word. In Scripture prophecy involves both foretelling and forth-telling. It speaks of the future but also of the covenant principles by which God works in both the present and the future. Both of these elements of prophecy are expressed in verse 2. Already in the reign of Hezekiah, the prophet Isaiah had declared, """Behold, the days are coming when all that *is* in your house, and what your fathers have accumulated until this day, shall be carried to Babylon; nothing shall be left," says the LORD. "And they shall take away *some* of your sons who will descend from you, whom you will beget; and they shall be eunuchs in the palace of the king of Babylon"'" (Is. 39:6–7). As the Lord of history, God had foretold through Isaiah what would take place. In this sense, His hand was present in the defeat of Jerusalem.

Scripture, however, contains more than predictive prophecy. It also gives us the prophetic principles by which God governs His people. Thus, in the Jewish canon of the Old Testament, The Prophets included various historical books as well as the books we normally describe as the prophets. Prophecy is the interpretation of history from the standpoint of God's covenant word and promise. That was the key to the prophets' ministries—they interpreted history on the basis of what God had said in His covenant. So when the reign of Jehoiakim is assessed from this prophetic standpoint, we are told "he did evil in the sight of the LORD his God" (2 Chr. 36:5), and the inevitable consequence was judgment. Thus the author of 2 Kings writes: "Surely at the commandment of the LORD *this* came upon Judah, to remove *them* from His sight because of the sins of Manasseh [the rot did not begin with Jehoiakim], according to all that he had done, and also because of the innocent blood that he had shed" (2 Kin. 24:3–4).

The downfall of Jerusalem was actually the fulfillment of the promise God made in His covenant with Moses (of which the prophets were interpreters and to which they summoned the people to return): "'Because you did not serve the LORD your God with joy and gladness of heart, for the abundance of everything, therefore you shall serve your enemies, whom the LORD will send against you. . . . The LORD will bring a nation against you from afar . . . They shall besiege you at all your gates until your high and fortified walls, in which you trust, come down. . . . If you do not carefully observe all the words of this law that are written in this book, that you may fear this glorious and awesome name, THE LORD YOUR GOD'" (Deut. 28:47, 49, 52, 58).

God is faithful to His word—always—no matter what the consequences for Himself or for His people. He is faithful in the blessings He sends, but He is no less faithful in chastisement and judgment. The siege of Jerusalem and its terrible consequences formed the most undeniable proofs that God does what He has promised.

Yet God's ultimate purpose here was not judgment but rather mercy. Babylon was to be the scene of Daniel's lifelong service in the kingdom of God and the sphere in which he would demonstrate what it means to "sing the LORD's song in a foreign land" (Ps. 137:4). In fact, the reason he was able to do that so well lies here in the opening words that set the scene of the entire book: He knew that if he was in a foreign land, it was because of the hand of the Lord. He knew that there was nothing either accidental or incidental in the life of the children of God. He would have been able to say in his day what Paul was later to enunciate as one of the great principles of his life: "I want you to know, brethren, that the things which happened to me have actually turned out for the furtherance of the gospel" (Phil. 1:12).

The same pattern employed by Nebuchadnezzar to draw Daniel away from the Lord is employed all around us today: isolation from God's influence to produce holiness in our lives; indoctrination with the worldly ways of thinking (of course, we do not share all of the world's conclusions, but too often we think about everything in the same way and operate with the same value system—how many of us would rather die for the glory of God than live halfheartedly for Him in a measure of comfort?); compromise with the riches of this world instead of commitment to what John Newton's hymn calls "solid joys and lasting treasures" that "none but Zion's children know"; confusion about our real identity and purpose in life.

BRAINWASHING

> ³ Then the king instructed Ashpenaz, the master of his eunuchs, to bring some of the children of Israel and some of the king's descendants and some of the nobles, ⁴ young men in whom there was no blemish, but good-looking, gifted in all wisdom, possessing knowledge and quick to understand, who had ability to serve in the king's palace, and whom they might teach the language and literature of the Chaldeans. ⁵ And the king appointed for them a daily provision of the king's delicacies and of the wine which he drank, and three years of training for them, so that at the end of that time they might serve before the king. ⁶ Now from among those of the sons of Judah were Daniel, Hananiah, Mishael, and Azariah. ⁷ To them the chief of the eunuchs gave names: he gave Daniel the name Belteshazzar; to Hananiah, Shadrach; to Mishael, Meshach; and to Azariah, Abed-Nego.
>
> —*Daniel 1:3–7*

Sin is not merely a matter of a lack of intelligence or education. Some of the most depraved people have been among the most intelligent. Intelligence coupled with evil purposes is a very formidable enemy. Such an enemy was Nebuchadnezzar to the people of God.

Nebuchadnezzar had a well-formulated plan. Not only would he make Jerusalem bow down before him, but he would employ its outstanding young people in his own service. This is why he *"instructed Ashpenaz, the master of his eunuchs, to bring . . . young men in whom there was no blemish, but good-looking, gifted in all wisdom, possessing knowledge and quick to understand, who had ability"* (vv. 3–4) in order to retrain them in the ways of Babylon.

What was in Nebuchadnezzar's mind? He was taking a long-term view of his defeat of Jerusalem. He knew that to overcome God's people by military force was not enough. If they continued to resist him, his endeavors to subjugate them would demand more and more of his resources. Instead of strengthening his position, he would have weakened it by creating additional demands on his own army. He must be able to employ Jewish resources for his own purposes if his victory was to prove worthwhile. So he weakened Jerusalem's prospects by exiling the cream of its youth, and he prepared for the future by giving them a thoroughly Babylonian education. What better agents could he use in his future dealings with Jerusalem than the sons of Jerusalem's nobility and intelligentsia? Nebuchadnezzar was not the last leader to see the value of infiltrating the colleges and universities to find candidates for his future service.

Perhaps there was another element in Nebuchadnezzar's thinking. Within the Book of Daniel we are given hints of Nebuchadnezzar's love for self-glorification. In his megalomania, he claimed, "Is not this great Babylon, that I have built for a royal dwelling by my mighty power and for the honor of my majesty"(Dan. 4:30). One of his aims seems to have been to surround himself with scholars and wise men of every variety (cf. 2:2, 4, 7). No doubt he hoped to augment his private university by adding the wisdom of these young Jews. His chief aim, however, was never in question. Nebuchadnezzar was determined that these citizens of Jerusalem should learn to live and think like citizens of Babylon. They, too, would in time *"serve in the king's palace"*(v. 4).

Nebuchadnezzar appears to have used several tactics in order to conform these citizens of God's kingdom to the ways of his own kingdom. They are worth noting because they are the strategies that operate in the spiritual warfare in which Christians continue to be involved (cf. Eph. 6:10–20).

(1) *Isolation.* In the first place, they were isolated from the influences that would mold their lives and characters in the ways of the Lord. In Babylon they were separated from the regular public worship of God, from the teaching of the Word of God, from the fellowship and wisdom of the people of God, and from the daily illustration of what it meant to be a citizen of Jerusalem. Separated from the furnace of godliness, the king anticipated that the last dying embers of true faithfulness to the Lord would die out.

(2) *Indoctrination.* They were taught *"the language and literature of the Chaldeans"* (v. 4). That might seem harmless enough. After all, there is surely nothing wrong with God's people studying foreign literature. The aim of this course in Chaldean language and literature, however, was not merely academic. It was to retrain their minds to think as Babylonians rather than Israelites.

In this, as in so many other things, our Lord's warning is profoundly true: The children of this world often have more "horse sense" than the children of God. We too often ask the more superficial questions, such as "Are there any embarrassing phrases used by this author?" The deeper issue we need to recognize is that the ungodly think differently from the godly. This is evident not simply in the language used, but in the whole way of looking at life. The ungodly view life without God. God is not in their thoughts, and there is no fear of God before their eyes. Their writing and teaching convey a completely different worldview from that of Scripture. It was this ungodly worldview with which the children of Jerusalem were being indoctrinated.

(3) *Compromise.* The Jewish youngsters enrolled in Nebuchadnezzar's school were given *"a daily provision of the king's delicacies and of the wine which he drank"* (v. 5). There is some disagreement among scholars as to the significance this would have had for Daniel and his companions (who refused it [v. 8]). It may be that they viewed eating it as a compromise of their commitment to the Lord, as food over which a pagan prayer of consecration had been offered. In reply to this view it may be asked whether the vegetables were separate from this. Perhaps what Daniel perceived (correctly) in this food allotment was an effort to seduce him into the lifestyle of a Babylonian through the enjoyment of pleasures he had never before known. High living very easily masters the senses and blunts the sharp-edged commitment of young Christians. The good life that Daniel was offered was intended by the king to wean him away from the hard life to which God had called him. It would encourage him to focus on himself and on a life of enjoyment. It would lead him to think of himself no longer as a servile Israelite but as a distinguished courtier. There is an echo here of the wilderness temptations of our Lord (cf. Luke 4:1ff.).

No mention is made of Daniel being confronted with an apologetic for Babylonian theology or with intellectual arguments against Old Testament faith. The attack was far more subtle than that, and therefore potentially far more lethal. Somebody in Nebuchadnezzar's palace knew enough about the human heart to see that most men have their price, and that good times, comfort, self-esteem, and a position in society are usually a sufficient bid for a soul.

(4) *Confusion.* The fourth element in the process of weaning these young men from the truth was the changing of their names. It is not always possible for us to be dogmatic about the precise nuance of many Old Testament names, and that may be true of

those listed in verses 6 and 7. What is certain is that anything that reminded them of their origin and destiny was removed in the change of names given to these four youths. Instead of incorporating the Hebrew words for God (El, Jah[iah]), these names incorporate the names of Babylonian deities (Bel, Nabu).

As they heard their names called day after day, it was an additional temptation for them to yield to the pressure to think of themselves as citizens of Babylon rather than of Jerusalem, to forget the rock from which they were hewn and the pit from which they were dug. The fact that in the royal court people could still remember that Daniel was Belteshazzar's real name is a testimony to the way in which he continued to sing the Lord's song in a foreign land (cf. Dan. 5:12–13).

This incident illustrates for us an important principle: The way we think—about God, ourselves, others, the world—determines the way we live. If Nebuchadnezzar could only change these men to *think* like Babylonians, then they would live like Babylonians. Conversely, so long as they thought of themselves as the Lord's, they would live as His servants—even in Babylon. That principle is still true. The secret of faithfully living for God today lies in the way we think. We are not to be conformed to the world, says Paul. Yet how can we avoid it? Christians have their lives transformed by the renewing of their minds (Rom. 12:1–2). This, Paul says, is where the true worship of God begins.

Few people who read these pages live in the kind of totalitarian state into which Daniel was brought. Totalitarianism, however, has many forms. Political or military figures are not its only symbol. In the Western world it may well be some far more sophisticated figure. Judging by the image-makers of our world, Western Christians are no less under pressure to conform to this world's thinking than Christians elsewhere. Perhaps there has never been an age when so many Christians have been so fashion-conscious and so few professing Christians have been willing to dare to be different, not for the sake of being different but for the sake of being a disciple of Christ.

The same pattern employed by Nebuchadnezzar to draw Daniel away from the Lord is employed all around us today: isolation from God's influence to produce holiness in our lives; indoctrination with the worldly ways of thinking (of course, we do not share all of the world's conclusions, but too often we think about everything in the same way and operate with the same value system—how many of us would rather die for the glory of God than live halfheartedly for Him in a measure of comfort?); compromise with the riches of this world instead of commitment to what John Newton's hymn calls "solid joys and lasting treasures" that "none but Zion's children know"; confusion about our real identity and purpose in life.

Yes, too many of us would have found quite excellent reasons for compromise in Nebuchadnezzar's court. After all, "How can we sing the Lord's song in a foreign land?"

A PURPOSE FIRM

⁸ But Daniel purposed in his heart that he would not defile himself with the portion of the king's delicacies, nor with the wine which he drank; therefore he requested of the chief of the eunuchs that he might not defile himself. ⁹ Now God had brought Daniel into the favor and goodwill of the chief of the eunuchs. ¹⁰ And the chief of the eunuchs said to Daniel, "I fear my lord the king, who has appointed your food and drink. For why should he see your faces looking worse than the young men who are your age? Then you would endanger my head before the king."

¹¹ So Daniel said to the steward whom the chief of the eunuchs had set over Daniel, Hananiah, Mishael, and Azariah, ¹² "Please test your servants for ten days, and let them give us vegetables to eat and water to drink. ¹³ Then let our appearance be examined before you, and the appearance of the young men who eat the portion of the king's delicacies; and as you see fit, so deal with your servants." ¹⁴ So he consented with them in this matter, and tested them ten days.

¹⁵ And at the end of ten days their features appeared better and fatter in flesh than all the young men who ate the portion of the king's delicacies. ¹⁶ Thus the steward took away their portion of delicacies and the wine that they were to drink, and gave them vegetables.

—*Daniel 1:8–16*

Some Christians are heroes in their daydreams only. The characteristic mark of such heroism is imagining ourselves as faithful on great and public occasions and in rarefied atmospheres when others will be impressed. In stark contrast, true faithfulness in Scripture is first exercised in small things and in private. If we fail there, any faithfulness we show in public will be hypocrisy, a performance for the crowd and not an expression of loyalty to our Lord.

Daniel and his three friends were under intense pressure. Their consciences (educated by God's Word and devoted to it) were under attack. The pressures to conform were intense. No doubt there were others, Jerusalem-born like themselves, who laughed at their sensitivities. What harm would good food do them, or new names? It is interesting and instructive to see their response.

What did Daniel do? He approached the senior official (*"the chief of the eunuchs"*) and asked to be excused from the king's provisions. Despite Daniel's good relationship with him, he was not prepared to take the risks that would be involved. So Daniel made a pact with the steward who was, presumably, directly responsible for their provisions. They would eat vegetables and drink only water for ten days. Then the steward was to compare them with the others. To his surprise they appeared to be much healthier specimens. Later, when Nebuchadnezzar examined them, he found their wisdom and understanding far more impressive than that of his other scholars. Daniel and his three companions were vindicated.

Several features of this incident stand out as Daniel is set before us as the model for the servants of God when they are under particular pressure and temptation.

(1) *Daniel's decisiveness. "Daniel purposed in his heart that he would not defile himself"* (v. 8). He realized that for the child of God some things cannot be negotiated or compromised. From the outset, therefore, he refused the court's delicacies. In many ways his usefulness in the kingdom of God throughout the rest of the book depends on this single decision. Had he not made it, or even left it until later while he maneuvered for a position of bargaining strength, he would not have found himself in the positions he later occupied nor would he have been faithful enough to cope with them as he did. Instead, from the beginning, in what to others seemed a trivial matter, he nailed his colors to the mast. In doing so, he gained a bridgehead into enemy-occupied territory and found himself increasingly strong in the Lord.

This is a great lesson for all Christians to learn, not least those who are younger and at the beginning of so many new experiences: relationships, occupations, and roles in life. Do not wait until you are in a position of social strength before you confess Christ and obey His commands. By the time you have gained that social position you may well have lost all moral strength to confess Christ openly and joyfully. For how can you confess Him later, as Savior and Lord, when the one thing you have failed to allow Him to be for you is Savior and Lord—saving you in your fears and ruling over your lips and your life? Always take the first opportunity to show yourself a decided Christian. It may not be easy, but the fact of the matter is that no easier opportunity will present itself. The second opportunity is always more difficult if the first has been refused.

Notice too that Daniel did not leave his actions to a spur-of-the-moment response. He *"purposed in his heart that he would not defile himself"* (v. 8). He had made a decision before God. He had found one of the great biblical secrets of spiritual success that was better known to our forefathers than it is to us: He entered into a solemn covenant in the presence of God that he would turn away from sinful behavior in whatever form it presented itself.

There is no finer example of such living in the presence of God than the eighteenth-century American preacher, theologian, and philosopher Jonathan Edwards, whose life and work have prompted so much interest in recent years. In his late teens, he began to write a series of resolutions, seventy of which were completed prior to his twentieth birthday. They include:

> Resolved, never to do any manner of thing, whether in
>   soul or body, less or more, but what tends to the
>   glory of God . . .
> Resolved, that I will live just so as I can think I shall
>   wish I had done, supposing I live to old age.
> Resolved, never to give over, nor in the least to slacken,
>   my fight with my corruptions, however unsuccess-
>   ful I may be.
> Resolved, never to do anything, which I should be
>   afraid to do, if I expected it would not be above
>   an hour before I should hear the last trump.[1]

It is not difficult to imagine the teenage Daniel writing words to the same effect and including:

> Resolved, that I shall never defile myself here in
>   Babylon, God helping me, whatever the conse-
>   quences may be.

Daniel had no taste for being a compromised believer.

(2) *Daniel's modesty.* If the strength of Daniel's stand is impressive, no less so is the manner in which he took it. We do not read

of any harsh words, proud bearing, or histrionics. Rather he responded to his situation in a spirit of humility and respect. He requested permission of the chief of the eunuchs (v. 8). His words to the steward were *"Please test . . ."* (v. 12). He did not go out of his way to embarrass either man on account of his own faithfulness. He allowed no harsh words about others to pass his lips. Indeed, at this stage he does not seem to have explained to either man that he had already resolved that, whatever their response, on no account would he defile himself. He seems rather to have patiently explained his situation, his desire to be faithful to his Lord, and his request that he might receive this dispensation.

There is something Christlike about such a spirit. We do not need to be either gauche or obnoxious to be faithful to God. Indeed, Daniel illustrates the principle that true faithfulness is seen not only in our determination to stand firm (that, after all, might simply be native stubbornness) but in the way we stand firm and the spirit in which we do so. Jesus is the illustration of this par excellence: "When He was reviled, [He] did not revile in return; when He suffered, He did not threaten, but committed Himself to Him who judges righteously" (1 Pet. 2:23). There lies the secret of both Jesus and Daniel: They knew they lived and spoke before the judgment of God. They had no need to judge those with whom they dealt; God Himself would be their judge.

To be able to stand firm and hold to biblical convictions modestly is a great grace that far too few of us attain. Why should that be? Is it because we are overconcerned about the fact that these convictions are our own and too little concerned for the glory of God in them? Daniel took his stand because he was impressed by the holiness of God. He did not want to offend that holy God. It was as simple as that. He was able, as a result, to be faithful to the Lord in a way that would show the Lord's glory, not in a way that would leave people staring at Daniel himself. There is a world of difference in these two reactions.

(3) *Daniel's expectation.* It is evident from Daniel's request to the steward that he believed God would honor his and his companions' desire to be faithful to Him. It was Daniel who suggested the ten-day trial in the expectation that his plain diet would produce a healthy complexion.

Of course it might not have been God's will (cf. Dan. 3:17–18). Daniel had good reason, however, to believe that the Lord would crown their faithfulness because the issue at stake was God's glory and kingdom. Living for God's glory produces a spirit of humble confidence that God will act. Such confidence marked the Old Testament heroes of the faith and marks men and women of faith in every age. Those whose hearts are set on self-glory rather than on God's can never have any confidence that their heart's desire will be granted. On the other hand, those who see their chief end as bringing glory to God know that they will never be disappointed.

We need such confidence not only for its own sake but because it is an accompaniment of faith in God's power. One of the many stories about Charles H. Spurgeon, the great Victorian preacher in London, illustrates this rather well. On one occasion a young preacher was lamenting to him about how few people seemed to be converted under his preaching. "What?" said Spurgeon, "You don't expect people to be converted every time you preach, do you?" Taken aback that he might have appeared presumptuous to the great Spurgeon, the young preacher replied, "No, of course not." To which Spurgeon responded, "Perhaps, then, that is the very reason you have seen so few converted."

It is possible to turn the idea of the confidence of faith into a kind of magic trick: If only you persuade yourself that something is going to happen, it will happen. That is far from the spirit that characterized either Daniel or Spurgeon. The confidence of faith is an assurance based on what God has the power to perform and what He has promised to do. If we know what He has promised and trust in His power, we will have every reason to live in a spirit of expectancy that He will hear and answer the prayers of our hearts.

GOD HONORS FAITHFULNESS

17 As for these four young men, God gave them knowledge and skill in all literature and wisdom; and Daniel had understanding in all visions and dreams.
18 Now at the end of the days, when the king had said that they should be brought in, the chief of the eunuchs brought them in before Nebuchadnezzar.
19 Then the king interviewed them, and among them all none was found like Daniel, Hananiah, Mishael, and Azariah; therefore they served before the king. 20 And in all matters of wisdom and understanding about which the king examined them, he found them ten times better than all the magicians and astrologers who were in all his

realm. [21] Thus Daniel continued until the first year of King Cyrus.

—Daniel 1:17–21

The faithful stand that Daniel and his companions took was not in vain. That was true in terms of their immediate situation. *"At the end of ten days their countenance appeared better and fatter in flesh than all the young men who ate the portion of the king's delicacies"* (v. 15). Why did Daniel anticipate that this would be the case? He recognized that the Lord alone blesses our food in order to nourish our bodies. Unless He does so, we may eat the fat of the land and be no stronger or healthier. That is why, even in the affluent West, there is still reason to pray that God will give us the food we need and bless it to us. In giving thanks for our meals, we acknowledge that we are constantly dependent on the Lord's strengthening and keeping of our lives. Recognizing this, Daniel and his companions knew that the Lord could easily strengthen them through their vegetarian diet and also easily withdraw His blessing from the diet set by Nebuchadnezzar. That is a principle that has application to home and marriage, to children and family life, to work and play.

There was a long-term repercussion from the early stand of these young men. This first test (and their success in it) prepared them for the temptations and trials that lay ahead. Had they failed here, they would certainly have failed when the greater tests came. By standing firm on this occasion, they were gaining equipment that would aid them in the future.

For example, they were learning the nature of temptation and perhaps also their own points of personal weakness; they were learning the faithfulness of God and His ability to keep them in trials. Of course they knew that God had promised in His Word to keep His people. Perhaps they remembered the prophecy that Isaiah had brought to the people as he foresaw the Exile in Babylon:

> Fear not, for I have redeemed you;
> I have called you by your name;
> You are Mine.
> When you pass through the waters, I will be with you;
> And through the rivers, they shall not overflow you.
> When you walk through the fire, you shall not be
>   burned,

Nor shall the flame scorch you.
For I am the Lord your God,
The Holy One of Israel, your Savior.

—Isaiah 43:1–3

Little did Shadrach, Meshach, and Abed-Nego realize how literally these words would soon be fulfilled. In the meantime they had committed themselves to the promise of God, and there is no other way to discover whether or not He keeps His promises to us. The service of God and convictions about the reliability of His Word are not theoretical matters. We grow in both through obedience.

All too frequently we take a different view of our trials and temptations. We tend to see them as isolated nightmares. God, however, sees them from a different perspective. They are important and connected punctuation marks in the biography of grace He is writing in our lives. They give formation, direction, and character to our lives. They are all part of the tapestry He is weaving in history. He uses them to build up our strength and to prepare us to surmount greater obstacles, perhaps fiercer temptations.

Jesus Himself is the great illustration of this principle. His whole life was a period of testing and temptation (Luke 4:13, 22, 28). As He continued to withstand pressures, His human character was developed so that He might be the kind of Savior we need (Heb. 2:17–18, 4:15–16). In the same way, God invests in our lives in order to make us strong and useful. No piece of equipment is fit for use unless it has been tested. The same is true of the citizens of the kingdom of God.

There is, however, a further sense in which the stand that Daniel and his companions took seems to have borne fruit. Centuries after their witness among the wise men of Babylon, we are told of certain wise men from the East who came seeking the One who had been born as king of the Jews (Matt. 2:1–2). They did not have crystal clear ideas about Him, but they had seen His star and had come to worship Him. How did they know anything about the promised Messiah? We do not know for certain, but if we possessed a detailed knowledge of history, could we perhaps trace their search back to Daniel and the faithful witness he bore in the court of Nebuchadnezzar? It is certainly not impossible. Unborn generations would feel the impact of his faithful testimony.

The history of the Christian church abounds in illustrations of men and women whose lives have had an effect on the advance of the kingdom of God because of their faithfulness to Christ. Many of them have lived far away from the Jerusalems of this world, in hard and unromantic places. There was nothing romantic for Daniel about Babylon; his heart was in Jerusalem (Dan. 6:10). Yet his witness there had a lasting impact on the lives of others.

It is not who you are or where you are that ultimately matters in the kingdom of God. It is what you are. Faithfulness, not reputation or situation, is what counts in God's kingdom.

NOTE

1. Jonathan Edwards, *The Works of Jonathan Edwards*, 2 vols. (London: Westley, 1834), 1:xx—xxii.

CHAPTER TWO—BAD DREAMS
DANIEL 2:1–49

Scripture Outline

Humanity's Basic Insecurity (2:1–13)

Knocking at Heaven's Door (2:14–30)

A Kingdom that Cannot Be Shaken (2:31–49)

Although lengthy, the second chapter of Daniel forms a unity and should be read as a whole. It is set "in the second year of Nebuchadnezzar's reign" (2:1).

It is not clear how this statement should be reconciled with the suggestion in Daniel 1:18 that Daniel and his friends had completed three years of training (1:5) beginning in the year Nebuchadnezzar had besieged Jerusalem (1:1). Some scholars have suggested that the period covers three different calendar years rather than three periods each of twelve months. That would adequately explain the time frame involved, and there is evidence elsewhere in the Old Testament that the Hebrews dated events in this inclusive way.

By this time, Daniel and his companions had graduated *summa cum laude* from the Babylonian college (1:19–20). Their faithfulness there, as we have seen, was remarkable. While admirable in itself, faithfulness to the Lord as a student is only the beginning. It is important to persevere and to complete the course. Perhaps in Daniel's day, as in our own, there were many who did not survive the pace and in whose lives the good seed of the Word of God was ultimately choked (Mark 4:18–19).

The most arresting feature of this section is signaled to the English reader by the words in verse 4, "The Chaldeans spoke to the king in Aramaic." From 2:4b to 7:28 the Book of Daniel is written in Aramaic. While not the only section of the Old Testament in Aramaic (other examples can be found in Ezra 4:8—6:18;

7:12–26; and Jer. 10:11), it is the longest section and requires some examination.

There is no simple explanation for this phenomenon. It has been strongly argued by some interpreters that this extensive use of Aramaic dates Daniel in the third or second century B.C. (thus confirming the fictitious nature of its contents). This view, however, has been ably and convincingly contested. Aramaic was an international language in the time of Daniel. Perhaps the explanation of this unusual phenomenon lies in the content of these chapters. Daniel 2—7 deals with the purposes of God in history. The figures and symbols point us to the rise, decline, and fall of the great empires of the ancient world. History is viewed on a cosmic scale. So also is the foundation and development of the kingdom of God. Chapters 1 and 8—12, by comparison, reflect God's special interest and concern for His chosen people, the Hebrew nation. This is the view adopted by E. J. Young:

> All in all, the solution which seems to be most free from difficulty is that Aramaic, being the language of the world, is used in those portions of the book which outline the future history of worldly empires and their relation to the people of God, and Hebrew is used in those portions which interpret for the Hebrews the meaning of the visions of the world empires. The present writer is fully aware of the difficulties which are entailed in this position, and hence, has no desire to be dogmatic upon the point.[1]

This approach in itself teaches us an important lesson about interpreting the Book of Daniel (or any biblical book for that matter). We are not required to have all the answers to all the questions people may ask about the Bible. The fact that we cannot yet answer all questions is no reason for ceasing to believe it is God's word any more than our imperfect knowledge of the working of the human body is a reason for ceasing to breathe.

If the cosmic scale of their contents is the primary reason for the use of Aramaic in Daniel 2:4b—7:28, it underscores a point that is made repeatedly in those chapters: God fulfills His purposes in the world in space and time. His kingdom is not established in an otherworldly, mystical way but through the lives of men and women in flesh and blood, here and now. It comes into being in the world, in the context of the rise and fall of empires, in the midst of good days and bad, good rulers and evil kings. Furthermore, the great and thrilling message of Daniel 2 is that in this context the kingdom of God will be established, grow, and ultimately triumph throughout the whole earth.

How Godlike (as our eighteenth-century evangelical forefathers would have said) that God should reveal His glorious purpose through the forgotten dream of Nebuchadnezzar. All of our instincts would tend to insist that God should give such revelation only through the most holy of men. He demonstrates, however, His ability to establish His purposes in the world by whatever means He pleases. That was why Daniel was able to say with such joy that it is the Lord who "changes the times and the seasons . . . removes kings and raises up kings" (2:21).

HUMANITY'S BASIC INSECURITY

2:1 Now in the second year of Nebuchadnezzar's reign, Nebuchadnezzar had dreams; and his spirit was so troubled that his sleep left him. [2] Then the king gave the command to call the magicians, the astrologers, the sorcerers, and the Chaldeans to tell the king his dreams. So they came and stood before the king. [3] And the king said to them, "I have had a dream, and my spirit is anxious to know the dream."

[4] Then the Chaldeans spoke to the king in Aramaic, "O king, live forever! Tell your servants the dream, and we will give the interpretation."

[5] The king answered and said to the Chaldeans, "My decision is firm: if you do not make known the dream to me, and its interpretation, you shall be cut in pieces, and your houses shall be made an ash heap. [6] However, if you tell the dream and its interpretation, you shall receive from me gifts, rewards, and great honor. Therefore tell me the dream and its interpretation."

[7] They answered again and said, "Let the king tell his servants the dream, and we will give its interpretation."

[8] The king answered and said, "I know for certain that you would gain time, because you see that my decision is firm: [9] if you do not make known the dream to me, there is only one decree for you! For you have agreed to speak lying and corrupt words before me till the time has changed. Therefore tell me the dream, and I shall know that you can give me its interpretation."

¹⁰ The Chaldeans answered the king, and said, "There is not a man on earth who can tell the king's matter; therefore no king, lord, or ruler has ever asked such things of any magician, astrologer, or Chaldean. ¹¹ It is a difficult thing that the king requests, and there is no other who can tell it to the king except the gods, whose dwelling is not with flesh."

¹² For this reason the king was angry and very furious, and gave the command to destroy all the wise men of Babylon. ¹³ So the decree went out, and they began killing the wise men; and they sought Daniel and his companions, to kill them.

—Daniel 2:1–13

Already in the second year of his reign, Nebuchadnezzar was having divinely prompted nightmares. We know from other historical sources that his expansionist policy met with some fierce resistance during the early years of his reign. We know, too, perhaps from our own experience, that the problems of the day often appear in different guise in the dreams of the night. The anxieties of daylight can become the monsters of the darkness.

Dreams often have these effects on all of us, even in our supposed twenty-first century sophistication. They force us to face up to the fact that we are "fearfully and wonderfully made" (Ps. 139:14), that there are deep-seated mysteries, fears, ambitions, and passions in our being that normally lie dormant. It is not surprising that the ancients saw special significance in dreams, for they certainly do have significance, even if not always the significance some schools of psychology have suggested. Nor is it difficult to see the wisdom of God in using dreams as a means of special revelation throughout Scripture. They provide a mode of revelation in which God's authorship can be clearly seen. When God gave Nebuchadnezzar his dream, it left him with a restless spirit. He was *"troubled"* (v. 1) and his spirit became *"anxious"* (v. 3), such was the sense of foreboding that he experienced. His anxiety was exacerbated by the fact that he apparently could not remember the content of the dream. That is a common enough experience. Coupled with the uneasy spirit in which he had wakened, it prompted his unreasonable demand that his advisers (*"the magicians, the astrologers, the sorcerers, and the Chaldeans"* [v. 2]) should tell him both the content and the meaning of his dream.

It is possible, of course, that Nebuchadnezzar could remember his dream; nothing in the text itself forbids that interpretation. It may be that his mistrust of his personal cabinet was profound. Perhaps he wanted to make sure they would not pull their intellectual wool over his eyes by providing whatever interpretation of the dream they thought would most appropriately meet the king's mood and receive his approval.

In either case we learn the same fact about this ruler. Despite his power and position as king of Babylon, in his heart of hearts he was like a lost child in the darkness. His panic is displayed in the way in which he dealt with his advisers. Not only did he insist that they tell him the meaning of his dream, but despite their understandable protests, he demanded that they tell him its content as well (v. 5). Quite reasonably they responded that *"There is not a man on earth who can tell the king's matter; therefore no king, lord, or ruler has ever asked such things of any magician, astrologer, or Chaldean"* (v. 10). In effect they were saying to Nebuchadnezzar: "You are asking us to tell you what God alone can tell you. We are men, not God."

Two features of this description of Nebuchadnezzar call for comment because they so graphically illustrate the truth about those who live their lives apart from God. The one is insecurity, and the other is hostility.

(1) *Human insecurity.* Nebuchadnezzar had everything a person could dream of possessing: power, fame, influence. Not only so, but he was in the process of creating an empire that would memorialize him for posterity and a city whose gardens would be known as one of the wonders of the ancient world. Why, then, should a mere dream fill him with such anxiety?

The answer is that Nebuchadnezzar was a man whose heart was set on goals that would in the long run prove to be mirages in the desert. He lived exclusively for this world; thus the horizons of his ambition always moved with the change and decay of this world.

God made humanity for Himself. The human heart, in Augustine's memorable words, "is restless until it finds its rest in God." It matters not whether we are rich or poor, among the haves or the have-nots. In either case "the cares of this world, the deceitfulness of riches, and the desires for other things" (Mark 4:19) destroy our peace. Those of us who have plenty are anxious because we want to guarantee that there will always be plenty; those of us who lack what others have are anxious until we have it too. So long as we think of life on the horizontal plane alone, we can never be delivered from the deep-seated insecurity, the profound sense of *Angst* that haunts our lives.

As long as Nebuchadnezzar sought security and rest in possessions or power or future reputation, he could never be content. Nebuchadnezzar, like so many people, had everything except the one thing he most needed: peace.

(2) *Human hostility.* As the narrative in verses 1–13 unfolds, Nebuchadnezzar's true character is unveiled in his reactions to his situation. It is worth noting in the cameos of this king's life in Daniel that we learn as much about Nebuchadnezzar from his reactions as from his actions. This is true of all of us. His reactions are consistently characterized by a spirit of hostility as well as a sense of insecurity.

These two reactions are intimately connected. Nebuchadnezzar is not at peace with the world because he is not at peace in himself. Because this sense of personal peace is absent, he cannot be at peace with or ultimately trust others, not even his closest advisers. This emerges when his counselors ask him to tell them the content of the dream so that they can interpret it. Nebuchadnezzar immediately accuses them of having formed a cabal in the hope of outlasting his death threat: *"If you do not make known the dream to me, there is only one decree for you! For you have agreed to speak lying and corrupt words before me till the time has changed"* (v. 9).

We often allow such reactions to slide by without further analysis. What is their ultimate cause? They are symptoms of a basic conflict. The strife and conflict in his heart—which show him how little he can trust his own integrity—teach him enough to induce a fear that others similarly live for themselves and therefore cannot be fully trusted. Nebuchadnezzar's further reaction unveils a yet more sinister element. He knows that he is asking the impossible of his counselors. No one on earth could tell him both the dream and its interpretation (v. 10). His cabinet went further, perhaps not realizing that they were about to scratch him where he really itched: *"There is no other who can tell it to the king except the gods, whose dwelling is not with flesh"* (v. 11). It was a simple statement, and given the pagan religion of these men, it made some sense. "You are asking us to do what only divine beings can do. You are forgetting, Nebuchadnezzar, we are mortal men, not Almighty God." Verse 12 carefully chronicles the king's response: *"For this reason the king was angry and very furious."*

As we noted earlier, Nebuchadnezzar's hostility toward others was based on his not having a sense of peace with himself. The reason for that absence was his deep-rooted hostility toward God. When these pagan intellectuals casually reminded him that they and he were human and not gods, he flew into a rage and reacted in a way that is reminiscent of the words of the nineteenth-century German philosopher Friedrich Nietzsche: "If there is a God, how can I bear not to be that God?" Nebuchadnezzar's conflict was the conflict of everyone. He was ill-prepared to allow God to show Himself to be God and Lord of all history; he was unwilling for God to be the God and Lord of his life either as a king or as a human. What haunted him about his dream was that (as we shall see) God was saying in it: "Nebuchadnezzar, your kingdom may be great, but it will fade and decay. Only the kingdom that I build will stand and last forever." It will "break in pieces and consume all these kingdoms, and it shall stand forever" (v. 44).

No wonder Nebuchadnezzar's spirit grew anxious in reaction to his dream. In some hazy sense he may have realized what it meant: The ambitions of his heart were not hidden from God. God, not Nebuchadnezzar, was and is God. Nebuchadnezzar was one of those who "exchanged the truth about God for the lie, and worshiped and served the creature rather than the Creator . . . [they are] . . . backbiters, haters of God, violent, proud" (Rom. 1:25, 30).

The rest of chapter 2 relates how Daniel, similarly exposed to the king's wrath against the entire faculty of scholars, was preserved and indeed promoted (v. 48) because God revealed both the king's dream and its interpretation to him. It is a striking illustration of the psalm: "Surely the wrath of man shall praise You; with the remainder of wrath You shall gird Yourself" (Ps. 76:10). The psalmist Asaph presents a picture of God as a warrior defeating His enemy and then, as a sign of conquest, girding His enemy's belt on Himself. God takes the garment worn by His enemy and turns it into a sign of His own majesty and victory. He uses Nebuchadnezzar's wrath against his wise men (which, as we have seen, has its ultimate roots in his wrath against God) and employs it as the instrument by which Daniel will be promoted and his testimony will reach the throne room of Babylon. How Godlike indeed.

KNOCKING AT HEAVEN'S DOOR

14 Then with counsel and wisdom Daniel answered
Arioch, the captain of the king's guard, who had gone out
to kill the wise men of Babylon; 15 he answered and said
to Arioch the king's captain, "Why is the decree from the

47

king so urgent?" Then Arioch made the decision known to Daniel.

16 So Daniel went in and asked the king to give him time, that he might tell the king the interpretation. 17 Then Daniel went to his house, and made the decision known to Hananiah, Mishael, and Azariah, his companions, 18 that they might seek mercies from the God of heaven concerning this secret, so that Daniel and his companions might not perish with the rest of the wise men of Babylon. 19 Then the secret was revealed to Daniel in a night vision. So Daniel blessed the God of heaven. 20 Daniel answered and said:

"Blessed be the name of God forever and ever,
For wisdom and might are His.
21 And He changes the times and the seasons;
He removes kings and raises up kings;
He gives wisdom to the wise
And knowledge to those who have understanding.
22 He reveals deep and secret things;
He knows what is in the darkness,
And light dwells with Him.
23 "I thank You and praise You,
O God of my fathers;
You have given me wisdom and might,
And have now made known to me what we asked of
You,
For You have made known to us the king's demand."
24 Therefore Daniel went to Arioch, whom the king had appointed to destroy the wise men of Babylon. He went and said thus to him: "Do not destroy the wise men of Babylon; take me before the king, and I will tell the king the interpretation."
25 Then Arioch quickly brought Daniel before the king, and said thus to him, "I have found a man of the captives of Judah, who will make known to the king the interpretation."
26 The king answered and said to Daniel, whose name was Belteshazzar, "Are you able to make known to me the dream which I have seen, and its interpretation?"
27 Daniel answered in the presence of the king, and said, "The secret which the king has demanded, the wise men, the astrologers, the magicians, and the soothsayers cannot declare to the king. 28 But there is a God in heaven

who reveals secrets, and He has made known to King
Nebuchadnezzar what will be in the latter days. Your dream,
and the visions of your head upon your bed, were these:
[29] As for you, O king, thoughts came to your mind while on
your bed, about what would come to pass after this; and He
who reveals secrets has made known to you what will be.
[30] But as for me, this secret has not been revealed to me
because I have more wisdom than anyone living, but for
our sakes who make known the interpretation to the king,
and that you may know the thoughts of your heart.

—Daniel 2:14–30

The picture of the servant of God standing before the lords of
the earth to bear witness to God's truth is one that occurs regularly
in Scripture; consider, for example, the stories of Joseph, Moses,
Elijah, Isaiah, Jeremiah, John the Baptist, Jesus, Peter, John, and
Paul. Daniel's life is similarly set in contrast with the ungodly. This
contrast between God's servants and worldly rulers reveals a pattern in the lives and testimonies of faithful men. Although Joseph,
John the Baptist, Isaiah, and Peter were very different personalities, we find some characteristics emerging repeatedly in their stories. The reason is simple enough: They were men whose lives
were filled and controlled by the Spirit of Christ both before and
after the Incarnation.

It is possible to observe the same principle in the church
today. Since we are members of the same family, the same features
of Christian character will appear in our lives. After all, God's eternal plan is that we should all ultimately be "conformed to
the image of His Son" (Rom. 8:29). What are these features that
the Spirit of God produced in Christ and reproduced, or copied, in
the lives of His servants? Part of the answer lies in the description
of the Messiah in Isaiah:

> The Spirit of the LORD shall rest upon Him,
> The Spirit of wisdom and understanding,
> The Spirit of counsel and might,
> The Spirit of knowledge and of the fear of the LORD
> His delight is in the fear of the LORD,
> And He shall not judge by the sight of His eyes,
> Nor decide by the hearing of His ears.

—Isaiah 11:2–3

As a servant of the Lord, Daniel had received the Lord's Spirit. Even Nebuchadnezzar understood this ("In him is the Spirit of the Holy God," he later confessed [Dan. 4:8–9]). In this section Daniel displays several of the Spirit's graces.

(1) *Daniel's speech was marked by wisdom.* When Arioch, the head of Nebuchadnezzar's secret police, came to Daniel and his friends in fulfillment of the king's decree, Daniel asked why the king's decree was so urgent (v. 15). Apparently Daniel was already well known to the high officials of the court; not only did Arioch restrain his hand, but Daniel himself was able to take the matter directly to the king and ask for time in order to discover the meaning of the dream.

Verse 14 describes Daniel's approach here as one of *"counsel and wisdom."* There was discretion in Daniel's behavior, not only in what he said but in the way he said what he said. The word translated "wisdom" is variously rendered in the Old Testament. It is related to the Hebrew verb meaning "to taste" (*taam*). Here it conveys those spiritual instincts of judgment, discernment, and what we might call a sense of the realities of the situation. Daniel's wisdom was a well-developed sense of spiritual "taste."

We speak about people having a highly developed taste in many spheres. What we mean is that they are able to tell the difference between foods or drinks or even clothes that seem to the rest of us virtually indistinguishable. Taste is a mysterious sense and one which experience can develop to a very high degree. There are people who can tell the year of a certain wine or the origin of the leaves for a cup of tea. In some ways, spiritual wisdom is just like that. It is a highly developed sense of God's ways, learned through obedience to God's Word. It is a sensitive awareness of the kind of behavior that is appropriate to the child of God in different circumstances. It does not necessarily come with age but with understanding of the Lord's Word and ways. It is not the same thing as zeal. Christians, too, can have a zeal that is not according to knowledge (Rom. 10:2) and obscure the glory of God by their insensitive behavior. Some live long and lack it; others, like Daniel, develop it when they are young. This taste (or wisdom) should to some degree characterize all those who are leaders of God's people. It certainly featured prominently in Daniel's dealings with his fellowmen. It was one reason that he, like all leaders, had "a good testimony among those who are outside" (1 Tim. 3:7).

(2) *Daniel's life was marked by prayer.* When Daniel returned home, the first thing he did was to contact his three companions

(v. 17) and arrange for a special season of prayer. As we learn later, Daniel's life was centered on a prayerful relationship with God ("he knelt down on his knees three times that day, and prayed and gave thanks before his God, as was his custom since early days" [Dan. 6:10]). Notice how the burden of the time of prayer is described. We might expect that they would focus on the need of a special revelation from God. Indeed that was the answer they received when *"the secret was revealed to Daniel in a night vision"* (v. 19). In fact the focus of their prayer was for *"mercies from the God of heaven concerning the secret"* (v. 18). Why this concentration on mercies? Were they concerned primarily for their own skins? Were they self-centered in asking God to see them in their plight and come to their aid? On the contrary, they sought mercy from God because they recognized that they (and perhaps they alone) were His appointed servants. They were men of destiny who had been placed in Babylon for His glory to make His name known. It was because their lives were so intimately intertwined with God's glory that they sought His mercy in order that His glory might be displayed in Babylon. In revealing the dream and its meaning, Daniel explains that God had a purpose in Nebuchadnezzar's life as well. Even there he stresses that the mystery had been revealed *"for our sakes"* (v. 30).

Rather than being a self-centered prayer, there is something Christlike about it. Jesus' great High Priestly Prayer in John 17 breathes this same spirit in which the glory of His Father is intertwined with His own life and experience. Only those whose lives are devoted to God's glory can ever pray in this way.

(3) *Daniel was filled with a spirit of worship.* When God showed Daniel the secret of the dream in a night vision, his immediate response was not to rush to his friends or Nebuchadnezzar but to God in worship and thankfulness. That tells us a great deal about his spirit. Earlier we noted that Nebuchadnezzar's character was revealed by his reactions as well as by his actions, by how he responds as much as by what he initiates. Now we see how true this is of Daniel also. His God-centered reaction to the impending catastrophe is matched by his God-centered response when the catastrophe is averted. It is not always so. The test of our spirituality does not lie only in the fervency of our prayers in times of crisis, but in the wholeheartedness of our worship when God acts in grace. Relief unaccompanied by worship is never an adequate response to the mercies of God.

For what does Daniel praise his God? He sees this special revelation as a cause to worship God in several ways: (1) for His eternal wisdom and power (v. 20); (2) for His governing of history (v. 21), (3) for His fellowship with His people, making His ways and His will known to them. We have no less reason to worship Him as He makes His purposes known to us. In a sense, the test of our spirituality comes after our intercession, not just before it.

These characteristics combined to make Daniel the kind of man who was faithful to God over the long term and in the presence of both the lowly and the mighty. The one who recognizes that it is the Lord (and not someone else) who *"removes kings and raises up kings"* (v. 21) is able to speak the truth to every situation.

In verses 24–30, Daniel speaks with great grace and boldness. He has a sense of taste, but he also has a sense of righteousness. He is not afraid to use the kind of language that previously enraged Nebuchadnezzar. Humans are dust, Daniel says; it is beyond their natural powers to do what the king has demanded. In contrast, *"there is a God in heaven who reveals secrets"* (v. 28). Furthermore, God has revealed the secret, partly to honor His own name in His servants' lives but also to show that He is the knower and judge of Nebuchadnezzar's heart. He knows Nebuchadnezzar better than the king knows himself. He reveals the dream so *"that you [Nebuchadnezzar] may know the thoughts of your heart"* (v. 30). All through Daniel's address we see the same God-centeredness that we noted earlier: God is in heaven, God gave Nebuchadnezzar his dream, God reveals secrets for His own glorious purposes.

This is the spirit of Jesus before the high priests and Pilate; it is the spirit of Elijah before Jezebel; it is the spirit of John the Baptist before Herod. Daniel is full of the spirit of truth. Even Nebuchadnezzar can recognize that, unlike his other courtiers, Daniel can be trusted implicitly since all his investments (and therefore his vested interests) are in God alone. It was once said of Thomas Hooker, the New England Puritan, that when he preached he seemed to grow in size until "you would have thought he could have picked up a king and put him in his pocket." True spiritual stature like that can never be hidden, as Nebuchadnezzar knew when he listened to Daniel.

We need men and women with that spirit today. We do not need more pomp or noise or triumphalism. In the last analysis, we do not need money in order to establish a witness to God in the highest reaches of our society. We need Christians of complete integrity who know that God's eye is on them. With that we need people who pray. Perhaps more than anything else we need Daniel's spirit of prayer.

As we stand back from this display of Daniel's spiritual wisdom (v. 14), we should notice that God reveals His multifaceted wisdom (Eph. 3:13). See what He is doing in this one event. He is testing the faith of Daniel and his companions, and in doing so He is strengthening them for the great trials of faith that lie ahead in the burning furnace (ch. 3) and in the lions' den (ch. 6). At the same time and through the same events, He is dealing with Nebuchadnezzar. He brings circumstances to bear on his life that are calculated to show him his smallness, to reveal his sinful heart, and to humble him before the Lord. Then, as we shall see in the next section, He is revealing His purposes to His people through this pagan monarch. Truly *"wisdom and might are His"* (v. 20). Daniel and his friends might well sing:

> When all thy mercies, O my God,
> My rising soul surveys,
> Transported with the view,
> I'm lost in wonder, love and praise.
>
> —*Joseph Addison*

A KINGDOM THAT CANNOT BE SHAKEN

31 "You, O king, were watching; and behold, a great image! This great image, whose splendor was excellent, stood before you; and its form was awesome. 32 This image's head was of fine gold, its chest and arms of silver, its belly and thighs of bronze, 33 its legs of iron, its feet partly of iron and partly of clay. 34 You watched while a stone was cut out without hands, which struck the image on its feet of iron and clay, and broke them in pieces. 35 Then the iron, the clay, the bronze, the silver, and the gold were crushed together, and became like chaff from the summer threshing floors; the wind carried them away so that no trace of them was found. And the stone that struck the image became a great mountain and filled the whole earth.

36 "This is the dream. Now we will tell the interpretation of it before the king. 37 You, O king, are a king of kings. For the God of heaven has given you a kingdom, power, strength, and glory; 38 and wherever the children of men dwell, or the beasts of the field and the birds of the heaven, He has given them into your hand, and has

made you ruler over them all—you are this head of gold. [39] But after you shall arise another kingdom inferior to yours; then another, a third kingdom of bronze, which shall rule over all the earth. [40] And the fourth kingdom shall be as strong as iron, inasmuch as iron breaks in pieces and shatters everything; and like iron that crushes, that kingdom will break in pieces and crush all the others. [41] Whereas you saw the feet and toes, partly of potter's clay and partly of iron, the kingdom shall be divided; yet the strength of the iron shall be in it, just as you saw the iron mixed with ceramic clay. [42] And as the toes of the feet were partly of iron and partly of clay, so the kingdom shall be partly strong and partly fragile. [43] As you saw iron mixed with ceramic clay, they will mingle with the seed of men; but they will not adhere to one another, just as iron does not mix with clay. [44] And in the days of these kings the God of heaven will set up a kingdom which shall never be destroyed; and the kingdom shall not be left to other people; it shall break in pieces and consume all these kingdoms, and it shall stand forever. [45] Inasmuch as you saw that the stone was cut out of the mountain without hands, and that it broke in pieces the iron, the bronze, the clay, the silver, and the gold—the great God has made known to the king what will come to pass after this. The dream is certain, and its interpretation is sure."

[46] Then King Nebuchadnezzar fell on his face, prostrate before Daniel, and commanded that they should present an offering and incense to him. [47] The king answered Daniel, and said, "Truly your God is the God of gods, the Lord of kings, and a revealer of secrets, since you could reveal this secret." [48] Then the king promoted Daniel and gave him many great gifts; and he made him ruler over the whole province of Babylon, and chief administrator over all the wise men of Babylon. [49] Also Daniel petitioned the king, and he set Shadrach, Meshach, and Abed-Nego over the affairs of the province of Babylon; but Daniel sat in the gate of the king.

—Daniel 2:31–49

In this final section of the chapter, Daniel describes Nebuchadnezzar's dream and shares with him its significance. His opening words set the tone: *"You, O king, were watching . . ."* (v. 31). Nebuchadnezzar was a despot and a megalomaniac seeking world domination. With a word he could take the life of virtually anyone he chose, such was his power. On the stage of history he was the great figure of his day, not only in his own eyes but in the view of others. Left to himself he might well have prided himself on his position in history. Even Daniel said of him, *"You, O king, are a king of kings . . . you are this head of gold"* (vv. 37–38). From the standpoint of the divine purpose, however, Nebuchadnezzar was reduced to the level of a spectator. Do what he will to build his kingdom, he will never rise higher than being a spectator of the building of the kingdom of God. That is Daniel's message. The *"kingdom, power, strength, and glory"* (v. 37) that are Nebuchadnezzar's are his only because God has given them to him in His sovereign providence. If he is a world ruler, it is because God rules the world (v. 38). What Daniel knew in secret prayer and praise to be true, he was not ashamed to say to the face of the king: "God removes kings and raises up kings" (v. 21).

We must examine the vision in more detail. Nebuchadnezzar had dreamed of a huge statue, magnificent in its design and awe-inspiring in its size. It had a head of gold, chest and arms of silver, belly and thighs of bronze, legs of iron, and feet of a mixture of iron and clay. As the king watched, a strange stone struck the image on its feet, breaking them into pieces and crushing the entire statue. Rather than break into pieces itself, however, the stone mysteriously grew and became a huge mountain, growing all the time until it filled the whole earth.

The historical significance of this vision has long been debated. Certain features of it are clear enough from the passage itself. Daniel indicates that these different parts of the statue's body represent successive kingdoms or empires. Of these, the Babylonian Empire is the first, *"you are this head of gold"* (v. 38). Three empires follow. If Babylon is the first, then the second (chest and arms of silver) represents the Medo-Persian Empire. The *"kingdom of bronze"* represents the Greek Empire. It was to *"rule over all the earth"* (v. 39). Here we instinctively think of the remarkable rise to power of Alexander the Great, who is said to have wept while still in his twenties because there were no more lands for him to conquer.

Daniel describes the fourth kingdom in greater detail because it marks the era in which especially significant events occur. It is strong as iron and shatters everything in its path: *"that kingdom will break in pieces and crush all the others"* (v. 40). Again almost instinctively we may think of the Roman Empire—of which it was said, "they make a desert and call it peace." Inherent in the development of this empire— "in its feet"—would lie the seeds of its own decay. Although the Roman Empire possessed a longevity surpassing those empires immediately preceding it, according to Edward Gibbon's famous thesis, it was subject to a decline and fall in its moral and spiritual corruption. Historians tell us that Paul's description of the Roman world (Rom. 1:18ff.) is no exaggeration. Notice, however, none of these great empires takes center stage in Nebuchadnezzar's dream. Thus not only he but all the emperors are relegated to the role of spectators (v. 31). The centerpiece of the vision is the kingdom that God establishes. There are two elements to this description. The first is the establishing of this fifth kingdom and the second is its character.

Daniel says that God's kingdom will be established *"in the days of these kings"* (v. 44), that is, during the period of the four empires previously described. The time frame is not given in detail. Indeed the suggestion seems to be that the work of establishing the kingdom of God will run parallel with, and even unnoticed, by the great leaders of history. Ultimately, however, all the kingdoms of the world will be shattered against the kingdom that God establishes.

What more can we say about this kingdom on the basis of these verses? We should notice two allusions to the first and second psalms. In verse 35, the destruction of these empires is described: *"Then the iron, the clay, the bronze, the silver, and the gold were crushed together, and became like chaff from the summer threshing floors; the wind carried them away so that no trace of them was found."* This is a direct and deliberate echo of Psalm 1 in which a stark contrast is drawn between the destiny of the righteous and that of the wicked. In contrast with the righteous,

> The ungodly are not so,
> But are like the chaff which the wind drives away.
> Therefore the ungodly shall not stand in the judgment,
> Nor sinners in the congregation of the righteous.
>
> —*Psalm 1:4–5*

Here the divine message emphasizes that the key to understanding the rise and fall of empires and emperors is not military or financial, but rather moral and spiritual. The destruction of these great kingdoms is not an accident of history, but instead the outworking of the judgment of God on kingdoms that have turned from His laws and forsaken His Word.

Later in the passage we are told of the stone that shall *"break in pieces"* all other dominions (v. 44, cf. v. 45). Here the echo is of the promise given to the Messiah:

Ask of Me, and I will give You
The nations for Your inheritance,
And the ends of the earth for Your possession.
You shall break them with a rod of iron;
You shall dash them to pieces like a potter's vessel.

—*Psalm 2:8–9*

There can be no doubt that the kingdom represented by this stone is the messianic kingdom of God.

This kingdom has several features. It is God's creation, His kingdom: *"And in the days of these kings the God of heaven will set up a kingdom"* (v. 44). It is an indestructible and infallible kingdom *"which shall never be destroyed; and the kingdom shall not be left to other people"* (v. 44). It is an all-victorious kingdom, eternal in its duration: *"it shall break in pieces and consume all these kingdoms, and it shall stand forever"* (v. 44). Furthermore, it will be a universal kingdom: *"And the stone that struck the image became a great mountain and filled the whole earth"* (v. 35). All this will occur despite the obscurity and apparent weakness of its origin; it is represented by a mere stone, *"cut out without hands"* (v. 34).

The stone of course represents Christ. He is the stone that crushes the kingdoms of this world because He is the one into whose hands the Father has committed all judgment (John 5:22). He is the stone that the builders rejected which became the chief cornerstone (Acts 4:11).

Few subjects evoke more discussion and controversy among scholars than the topic of the kingdom of God. It is relatively common at this point in the text of Daniel to look from verses 44–45 (*"in the days of these kings"*) to some future period of history when ten kings will reign over the earth (the ten toes of the feet of the great statue). There are, however, several elements in the text that suggest a different interpretation.

(1) No mention is made in the dream or its interpretation of toes or the number ten. The words "these kings" in verse 44 refer to the great emperors and empires of Babylon, Medo-Persia, Greece, and Rome, not to some far-distant period of history. That

is certainly the most natural way to read verse 44. The most obvious antecedent of *"these kings'* is undoubtedly the great empires.

(2) The coming of the kingdom of God takes place in such a way that all empires collapse before it (v. 35). It will *"break in pieces and consume all these kingdoms"* (v. 44). The establishing of this kingdom therefore in some way runs parallel to the rise and fall of the kingdoms of the world. The fifth kingdom, the kingdom of God, the stone that becomes a mountain and fills the whole earth, must appear in stages and develop through history. It must have been present when Babylon, Medo-Persia, Greece, and Rome all fell. It must be present now. It must be present in the future. This certainly harmonizes with the apparently unpretentious beginnings and mysterious origins of the kingdom that God Himself would establish.

(3) The decisive moment for the kingdom of God is seen as taking shape in the days of the fourth empire. It was during the period of the Roman Empire, when Palestine was an occupied country, that Jesus came in Galilee, preaching that the kingdom of God had drawn near in His ministry (Mark 1:15). It is clear from His teaching (in which other imagery than that of the stone was usually employed) that He too saw the kingdom growing from unrecognized beginnings until it filled the whole earth. The kingdom had come; its powers were already released in the world, but in a full and final sense it was still coming, all that it promised would be fulfilled.

If we understand these verses against that background, Daniel and his friends were receiving a message that would give them strength, hope, and confidence in the dark days that were still to come; a message that has had the same effect on God's children in every age. This message has two elements: (1) The people of God already belong to the kingdom of God. They have come to Him and sought entrance by faith into His kingdom. He has received them, and they are His. The people of God live in a world that is dominated by other kingdoms. Totalitarian rulers and systems arise, demanding loyalty and persecuting the kingdom of God. We find ourselves living in a constant tension that at times and in various contexts erupts painfully. When it does, however, our pathway is clear. There is no doubt as to where our loyalties lie. We must obey God rather than rulers.

This was the principle immortalized in the speech of Andrew Melville. Believing that his king (James VI of Scotland [James I of England]) was seeking to usurp the authority of God, he said to him:

Sir, we will always humbly reverence your majesty in public; but since we have this occasion to be with your Majesty in private . . . we must discharge our duty, or else be traitors both to Christ and you. Therefore, Sir, at diverse times I have told you, so now again I must tell you. There are two kings and two kingdoms in Scotland. There is King James, the Lord of the Commonwealth, and there is Christ Jesus, the King of the Church, whose subject James the Sixth is, and of whose kingdom he is not a king, nor a lord, nor a head. . . . We will yield to you your place, and give you all due obedience, but again I say, You are not the head of the church; you cannot give us that eternal life that we seek for even in this world, and you cannot deprive us of it.[2]

(2) The people of God have the assurance from God's Word of the ultimate triumph of the kingdom of God. In both the dream and the interpretation, this is the central fact. Whatever other elements of this chapter might fascinate us, we must allow nothing to obscure this: God's kingdom will triumph. He must reign (1 Cor. 15:25), and "The kingdoms of this world have become *the kingdoms* of our Lord and of His Christ, and He shall reign forever and ever" (Rev. 11:15). We have received a kingdom that cannot be shaken (Heb. 12:28).

This has often been the great hope that has encouraged the people of God in times of physical trials and in spiritual darkness. It was one of the great prospects that gripped the hearts and prayers of the leaders of the missionary revival of the eighteenth century. It gave courage to Daniel and has given hope and energy to many Daniels since.

No wonder Nebuchadnezzar fell prostrate before Daniel when his dream was revealed and interpreted. In his insecurity and instability it was all he could do as he confessed the greatness of Daniel's God. No wonder he made Daniel and his companions rulers of his people (vv. 48–49). Yet it is significant, as the rest of his biography confirms, that, unlike Daniel, he did not "seek mercies from the God of heaven" (v. 18). He was awed, but he was not converted. Nonetheless, God transformed the king's wrath into His praise, and the chapter that began with Daniel under sentence of death (v. 14) ends with him sitting in the king's court (v. 49).

Does this chapter not give heightened meaning to our prayer:

> Our Father in heaven
> Hallowed be Your name.
> *Your kingdom come . . .*

NOTES

1. E. J. Young, *A Commentary on Daniel* (London: Banner of Truth Trust, 1978), 22.

2. James Melville, *The Autobiography and Diary of Mr. James Melvill[e]*, ed. Robert Pitcairn (Edinburgh: Wodrow Society, 1842), xx.

CHAPTER THREE—THE INQUISITION
DANIEL 3:1–30

Scripture Outline
  Totalitarianism (3:1–7)
  Obeying God Rather than Men (3:8–18)
  Through Fiery Trials (3:19–25)
  Impressed Once More (3:26–30)

The third chapter of Daniel continues the conflict motif that we have already noted runs throughout the book. From one point of view (and one of which the teacher or preacher needs to be aware in the study of Daniel) there is a certain monotony about the underlying structure and theme of the succeeding chapters of this book. The scenario changes, but the plot remains the same. Yet even this feature of Daniel teaches us valuable lessons. Later, in Daniel's visions in chapter 7, we will read of the activity of a beast that will "persecute the saints of the Most High" (7:25). "Persecute," here, is literally "to wear out." Both Scripture and personal experience teach us that the dogged persistence of the kingdom of darkness may wear down the resistance of God's people. Isolated trials may be withstood, but only by wearing "the whole armor of God" (Eph. 6:10) can we stand in the face of continuing onslaughts. This is why the New Testament places such emphasis on watching, praying, and persevering in obedience to the Lord.

Here in chapter 3 the conflict is focused on the image that Nebuchadnezzar erects. It is a symbolic representation of Babylon and the kingdom of this world. In contrast to it, Shadrach, Meshach, and Abed-Nego are those in whom the image of God is being re-created (cf. Eph. 4:24; Col. 3:10). In that sense they are God's representatives. The issue therefore is this: Will the image of God that He has made (cf. Gen. 1:26–27) bow to the image which man has made? This is resolved by the faith of the three friends. It was through faith that they "quenched the violence of fire" (Heb. 11:34).

We should not be so impressed by the persistence of the kingdom of darkness in its conflict with the city of God that we fail to notice a second underlying pattern. The three friends are promoted at the end of the crisis. They were graduated with highest honors in chapter 1; they were promoted following the crisis in chapter 2; and now they attain higher rank in chapter 3 (v. 30). God can also be monotonous in His commitment to honor His people. In fact, trials and tribulations are the pruning knife He uses to produce yet more lavish and significant fruit in our lives (John 15:2). This chapter well illustrates the maxim of John Calvin (many of whose students quite literally faced the same trial of faith as Daniel's friends and, having been well schooled under Calvin's ministry, yielded their bodies to the flames for Christ's sake): "The church of Christ has been so constituted from the beginning that death has been the way to life and the cross the path to victory."

TOTALITARIANISM

3:1 Nebuchadnezzar the king made an image of gold, whose height was sixty cubits and its width six cubits. He set it up in the plain of Dura, in the province of Babylon. ² And King Nebuchadnezzar sent word to gather together the satraps, the administrators, the governors, the counselors, the treasurers, the judges, the magistrates, and all the officials of the provinces, to come to the dedication of the image which King Nebuchadnezzar had set up. ³ So the satraps, the administrators, the governors, the counselors, the treasurers, the judges, the magistrates, and all the officials of the provinces gathered together for the dedication of the image that King Nebuchadnezzar had set up; and they stood before the image that Nebuchadnezzar had set up. ⁴ Then a herald cried aloud: "To you it is commanded, O peoples, nations, and languages, ⁵ *that* at the time you hear the sound of the horn, flute, harp, lyre, and psaltery, in symphony with all kinds of music, you shall fall down and worship the gold image that King Nebuchadnezzar has set up; ⁶ and whoever does not fall down and worship shall be cast immediately into the midst of a burning fiery furnace."

⁷ So at that time, when all the people heard the sound of the horn, flute, harp, and lyre, in symphony with all kinds of music, all the people, nations, and languages fell down and worshiped the gold image which King Nebuchadnezzar had set up.

—Daniel 3:1–7

The previous chapter recorded Nebuchadnezzar's dream. There can be little doubt that the building of the image of gold expressed Nebuchadnezzar's desire to see that dream not only fulfilled, but surpassed. Daniel had said to him, "You, O king, *are* a king of kings . . . you *are* this head of gold" (2:37, 38). The image Nebuchadnezzar had seen was composed of various metals, which indicated that inferior empires would arise in the course of history. What seems to have stung Nebuchadnezzar was the underlying assumption that Daniel had dared to make explicit: "But after you shall arise another kingdom" (2:39). Nebuchadnezzar's "little kingdom" would have its day, but it would perish and the glory he had created would be destroyed.

Had Nebuchadnezzar wanted to memorialize the revelation God had given him—namely, to point out that only the kingdom God builds cannot be shaken—he would have built an image with a head of gold, chest and arms of silver, belly and thighs of bronze, legs of iron, and feet of iron and clay. Beside it he would have placed a large stone. Apparently Nebuchadnezzar resisted God's revelation. The image he commissioned symbolized his desire that no kingdom should destroy his—not even the kingdom of God. So the opening seven verses of chapter 3 state no less than six times that Nebuchadnezzar set up on the plain of Dura a massive statue entirely of gold. Nebuchadnezzar's own name appears seven times. We are left in no doubt that Nebuchadnezzar foreshadowed Nietzsche's sentiment quoted earlier, "If there is a God, how can I bear not to be that God?"

As the king in the city of this world, several features of Nebuchadnezzar's character surface in this passage. They are recurring aspects of the manifestation of ultimate ungodliness. (1) *Nebuchadnezzar possessed immense power but misused it.* He was given "power, strength, and glory" (2:37). Instead of showing "mercy to the poor" (4:27), he misused his wealth, spending it on his own inflated ego. History celebrates him as a builder rather than as a warrior, a planner rather than a hero, but egomaniacs can further expand their egos in any area in which they have an ability.

There is something megalomaniacal about Nebuchadnezzar's statue, notably its size—sixty cubits by six (the cubit varied from nation to nation but was approximately twenty inches, making this statue ninety feet tall [probably including the base] and nine feet wide). Even if we assume that the statue was gold-plated rather than of solid gold, the message he was sending was all too clear for others to read. He thought he was worth every ounce. At the appropriate moment (although he may well have spoken to Nebuchadnezzar about it on several occasions), Daniel later indicated that Nebuchadnezzar squandered the riches God had providentially bestowed upon him as a stewardship. Instead of nourishing his people, Nebuchadnezzar had fed his pride and vainglory (4:27). As king of Babylon, he shared in the hubris of the people of Babel when their motivation in building the tower was to "make a name for [them]selves" (Gen. 11:4).

An intriguing feature of the arrangements made for the statue's unveiling is that they were shrouded in a religious atmosphere. There was a dedication (v. 2); the occasion was enhanced by the finest orchestral accompaniment (even if "bagpipes," or rather "dulcimer" [v. 5 (KJV)] is to be given the unlikely rendering *"in symphony"*). Indeed the entire ceremony was imbued with a spirit of worship (v. 5). All this, however, simply provided a veneer for the deepest blasphemy: This worship was man-centered, not God-honoring. Nebuchadnezzar, not God, was the object of worship. The lie was substituted for the truth of God; the "creature rather than the Creator" (Rom. 1:25) was to be adored.

Two warning lights are illuminated by this description. The first is that blasphemy can be disguised by the trappings of religion. Could that even be true of evangelical religion? After all, why would Satan waste his energy on an all-too-obvious counterfeit? The clearest indication of this is when individuals, not God, are at the center of worship. Whenever much is made of a person, less is made of the Lord. It is a great mistake to think that blasphemy needs to be carefully planned and thought out. Blasphemy is natural to the human heart; it will therefore manifest itself in our religious activities unless it is deliberately rejected. Nebuchadnezzar would have been horrified if anyone had accused him of blasphemy. Could it be that much that passes for religion and worship in our own day, because it is so centered on ourselves, is also a form of blasphemy?

The second warning light illuminated by this event is the danger of assuming that the really important thing about worship is its aesthetic effect. There was aesthetic effect in abundance on the plain of Dura. A person would have had to have been extremely narrow-minded not to share in the sheer magnificence of the occasion and the splendor of the music. The sad reality is that "all that glitters is not gold." The important thing about our worship is its object. Do we worship God or ourselves? The test of whether worship is God-centered or centered on ourselves will be found in the question: Do we worship God according to His revelation or according to our own disposition? In worship, the statement "How I like to worship is . . ." is irrelevant. All that matters is how God chooses to be worshiped: "True worshipers will worship the Father in spirit and truth; for the Father is seeking such to worship him" (John 4:23). The worship on the plain of Dura was not inspired by the Spirit nor was it in accordance with the truth. Instead it "changed the glory of the incorruptible God into an image made like corruptible man [and] exchanged the truth of God for the lie, and worshiped and served the creature rather than the Creator, who is blessed forever" (Rom. 1:23, 25).

Nebuchadnezzar gathered the richest, most influential, most educated people of his day on the plain of Dura (vv. 2–3). Surely some of them must have realized what they were being asked to do? If they did, they could not cast a stone of condemnation at Nebuchadnezzar, for they themselves were willing to blaspheme God. The saying is that everyone has a price, and these men had theirs. If Henry IV of France thought that "Paris is worth a mass," these people believed that the king's favor (and their positions of power) were worth a moment of blasphemy.

They could not have been more mistaken, as they were later to discover in the three companions whose testimony was stronger than either Nebuchadnezzar's threats or his fire (v. 27).

(2) *Nebuchadnezzar had experienced religious conviction without spiritual conversion.* When Daniel explained his dream to him, he had prostrated himself. He knew he was in the presence of a greater wisdom than his own. Daniel's God he confessed to be "God of gods, the Lord of kings" (2:47). We might be forgiven for thinking that Nebuchadnezzar was a changed man, that he had been truly converted. In fact he had experienced only a superficial and temporary setback to his self-glorification. His sinful heart had been shaken, not renewed. The truth was that instead of having a new heart, he had the same old heart, now a little more hardened, as his blatant blasphemy on the plain of Dura demonstrated. Like a fire that momentarily

seems under control but suddenly explodes, Nebuchadnezzar seemed to have undergone a major change, but in fact was none the better. Indeed the next stage of his sin was to be worse than the first. Before he had been prepared to put to death those whom he did not trust (2:8); now he was prepared to execute the only people in his realm he could trust, those who were under an oath to their God to be loyal in all human relations. Sometimes the worst and most cynical persecutors of God's people are those who themselves have had some kind of religious experience in earlier life.

Nebuchadnezzar vividly illustrates the difference between temporary spiritual diversion and true conversion. This condition is well described by the eminent Puritan, John Owen:

> As a traveler, in his way meeting with a violent storm of thunder and rain, immediately turns out of his way to some house or tree for his shelter, but yet this causeth him not to give over his journey—so soon as the storm is over he returns to his way and progress again: so it is with man in bondage to sin. They are in a course of pursuing their lusts; the law meets with them in a storm of thunder and lightning from heaven, terrifies and hinders them in their way. This turns them for a season out of their course; they will run to prayer or amendment of life, for some shelter from the storm of wrath which is feared coming upon their consciences. But is their course stopped? are their principles altered? Not at all; so soon as the storm is over, [so] that they begin to wear out that sense and the terror that was upon them, they return to their former course in the service of sin again.[1]

Our forefathers would have said that Nebuchadnezzar experienced divine impressions and convictions but was actually a stranger to true conversion. The events that followed demonstrated this to be so. Unlike the Thessalonians, he did not turn from idols to serve the living and true God (1 Thess. 1:9). Perhaps the fact that Nebuchadnezzar's response in chapter 2 is described in terms of how he responded to Daniel rather than to the Lord indicates that his heart was as human-centered as ever it had been despite the revelation of the Lord.

OBEYING GOD RATHER THAN MEN

[8] Therefore at that time certain Chaldeans came forward and accused the Jews. [9] They spoke and said to King

Nebuchadnezzar, "O king, live forever! [10] You, O king, have made a decree that everyone who hears the sound of the horn, flute, harp, lyre, and psaltery, in symphony with all kinds of music, shall fall down and worship the gold image; [11] and whoever does not fall down and worship shall be cast into the midst of a burning fiery furnace. [12] There are certain Jews whom you have set over the affairs of the province of Babylon: Shadrach, Meshach, and Abed-Nego; these men, O king, have not paid due regard to you. They do not serve your gods or worship the gold image which you have set up."

[13] Then Nebuchadnezzar, in rage and fury, gave the command to bring Shadrach, Meshach, and Abed-Nego. So they brought these men before the king. [14] Nebuchadnezzar spoke, saying to them, "Is it true, Shadrach, Meshach, and Abed-Nego, that you do not serve my gods or worship the gold image which I have set up? [15] Now if you are ready at the time you hear the sound of the horn, flute, harp, lyre, and psaltery, in symphony with all kinds of music, and you fall down and worship the image which I have made, good! But if you do not worship, you shall be cast immediately into the midst of a burning fiery furnace. And who is the god who will deliver you from my hands?"

[16] Shadrach, Meshach, and Abed-Nego answered and said to the king, "O Nebuchadnezzar, we have no need to answer you in this matter. [17] If that is the case, our God whom we serve is able to deliver us from the burning fiery furnace, and He will deliver us from your hand, O king. [18] But if not, let it be known to you, O king, that we do not serve your gods, nor will we worship the gold image which you have set up."

—Daniel 3:8–18

No incident in the Bible more clearly illustrates the affirmation of the early apostles that "We ought to obey God rather than men" (Acts 5:29). Down through the ages this section of Daniel has proved to be a constant encouragement to God's people. Two things about it are noteworthy: (1) the accusation brought against the three friends, and (2) the response of faith they made to it.

Verses 9–12 record the accusation brought by a number of Chaldeans. The very form of chapter 3 heightens the drama because no mention had yet been made of Shadrach, Meshach, and Abed–Nego. The royal decree had been proclaimed (v. 4); the music had begun (v. 7); the people had bowed down. Naturally we are left wondering what response was made by the children of God. The very style of narration underlines a principle that was also evident in chapter 1: The people of faith do not have a psychological need to make a "big deal" out of their acts of heroism. They do not need always to be drawing attention to the fact that they are different from others. They simply act according to the Lord's Word and allow their actions to speak without unnecessary histrionics.

In fact, it was the Chaldeans who drew Nebuchadnezzar's attention to what happened. The wording of verse 1 suggests that they did so as the result of a well-prepared strategy. They accused the Jews (literally, "ate their pieces," or as we might say, "got their teeth into them"). Perhaps jealousy was their main motivation. Their words, *There are certain Jews whom you have set over the affairs of the province of Babylon"* (v. 12), express a sense of glee that they have an opportunity to destroy the influence of these people and also, perhaps, a sense of vindication (since Nebuchadnezzar had not granted them such favor). Notice that their statement is utterly without compassion. Rather than plead for mercy on the grounds that these Jews were servants of the Most High God whose kingdom can never be destroyed—and doubtless were of all people the most faithful to Nebuchadnezzar in the administration of his affairs—they accuse them of not paying *"due regard"* (v. 12) to the king. Rather than throw oil on troubled waters (which the three companions evidently did by their low-key approach), these men were out to destroy the influence of God's kingdom under the guise of their own faithfulness to Nebuchadnezzar.

The children of this world have a wisdom of their own. The Chaldeans had a firm grasp of human psychology; they knew their man. If they had a price so that Nebuchadnezzar could buy them (they chose to worship his idol rather than lose their lives), they likewise knew he had a price. They bought his anger against the three Jews by their plot to betray their faithfulness to their God. They knew that whatever religious impressions Nebuchadnezzar recently experienced, he was no true convert to the God of Daniel. All they needed to mention was the failure of the Hebrews to pay respect to his wishes (v. 12) and his rage was guaranteed. They knew his arrogance would erupt in a clear expression of the conflict between the kingdom of this world and the kingdom of God: *"Who is the God who will deliver you from my hands?"* (v. 15).

What was the response of the Hebrew believers to this undisguised challenge to the majesty of God? It was a part of their earlier simple obedience to God. It brings to light even more clearly the leading characteristics of that faith that quenches the violence of fire (Heb. 11:34).

(1) They had confidence in the power of God: *"Our God whom we serve is able to deliver us from the burning fiery furnace, and He will deliver us from your hand, O king"* (v. 17). Trust in God implies the recognition of His power, of His omnipotence. It is one thing to have a general conviction about God's omnipotence; it is quite another to believe that He can do what seems to be completely contrary to nature, namely, deliver men from fire. On what did these confessors base their confidence that God could and might preserve them? It may have been the revelation God had given through Nebuchadnezzar (ostensibly for his benefit, but now it becomes apparent that it is for the encouragement of His own people). God had promised to establish a kingdom that could never be destroyed. If He meant to do that in the future, then (these men may have reasoned) we are part of His preparation for that great day. God plans to preserve and keep His people—and if need be He will do that even contrary to all expectation.

Yet as with all true faith, their confidence was not blind to the realities of the situation nor to the fact that God works out His purposes in the way He chooses, not in the way we would choose. So there was a second element to their faith.

(2) They were completely submissive to God's will, whatever that might be: *"But if not, let it be known to you, O king, that we do not serve your gods, nor will we worship the gold image which you have set up"* (v. 18). If there is any true faith in our own hearts, we will want to stand up and cheer as we read these words. In the last analysis, the friends' faith was not in their deliverance but in their God. It was of the same order as Job's: "Though He slay me, yet will I trust Him" (Job 13:15). With Paul, they wanted to glorify God in their body either by life or by death. In a sense it was all one to them, as long as God's name could be exalted (cf. Phil. 1:20). They knew that should God deliver them, His name would be vindicated. They also knew that should they die, their faithful testimony would display the worthiness of their God and the unworthiness of Nebuchadnezzar's self-created idol. By the manifestation of the truth they would commend themselves to everyone's conscience in the sight of God. Death would work in them, but life would surely spring forth in others through their witness (cf. 2 Cor. 4:2, 12).

Notice that these men of faith would not have regarded their deaths in the flames to be a failure of faith but rather an indication of God's will. By faith the flames may be quenched, but in that same faith "others were tortured, not accepting deliverance, that they might obtain a better resurrection. . . . They were stoned, they were sawn in two, were tempted, were slain with the sword" (Heb. 11:35, 37). Faith means trusting in God and His Word. Faith does not mean that we either know or understand what His specific purpose in our lives may be. It means a ready willingness to follow Him whatever His purpose.

No one can make the sacrifices of faith without grasping these principles. What was true of Christ—the seed who fell into the ground to die in order to produce much grain (John 12:24)—is perennially true of God's people, both before and since His coming. We see it demonstrated throughout church history, from Stephen (whose death so clearly affected the young Saul) to Patrick Hamilton (the young reformation martyr [the smell of whose burning corpse blew over the town of Saint Andrews in Scotland and (as was said) "infected as many as it blew upon"]) and beyond.

This was the finest hour of these three confessors. Their faith did not hold fast simply by accident or by the decision of the moment. It had grown strong because in previous tests they had grown strong in faith as they had given glory to God (cf. Rom. 4:20). As they looked back on the crisis of the fiery trial, they must have seen the previous tests in a new light. Their significance was to prepare them for this monumental crisis so that through their faithfulness glory would redound to God throughout the generations.

One of Oliver Cromwell's contemporaries once commented on the remarkable fact that before his first battle Cromwell had no real experience in warfare and yet he appeared to be a skilled general as he directed his troops. What was his secret? Long before the day of his first public battle, Cromwell had won victory after victory in the inner battle for holiness and obedience in his own life. He therefore took the field as a mature and experienced soldier. The same was true of these three Hebrews.

> Each victory will help you
> some other to win.

THROUGH FIERY TRIALS

19 Then Nebuchadnezzar was full of fury, and the expression on his face changed toward Shadrach,

Meshach, and Abed-Nego. He spoke and commanded that they heat the furnace seven times more than it was usually heated. ²⁰ And he commanded certain mighty men of valor who were in his army to bind Shadrach, Meshach, and Abed-Nego, and cast them into the burning fiery furnace. ²¹ Then these men were bound in their coats, their trousers, their turbans, and their other garments, and were cast into the midst of the burning fiery furnace. ²² Therefore, because the king's command was urgent, and the furnace exceedingly hot, the flame of the fire killed those men who took up Shadrach, Meshach, and Abed-Nego. ²³ And these three men, Shadrach, Meshach, and Abed-Nego, fell down bound into the midst of the burning fiery furnace.

²⁴ Then King Nebuchadnezzar was astonished; and he rose in haste and spoke, saying to his counselors, "Did we not cast three men bound into the midst of the fire?"

They answered and said to the king, "True, O king."

²⁵ "Look!" he answered, "I see four men loose, walking in the midst of the fire; and they are not hurt, and the form of the fourth is like the Son of God."

—Daniel 3:19–25

The response of Nebuchadnezzar to the faithfulness of the three witnesses is what we would expect of an ancient Near Eastern despot. It is also characteristic of our natural disposition. He has been crossed and he therefore seeks revenge. Irrationally he commands the furnace (already burning as a symbolic threat to anyone who would disobey him) to be heated *"seven times more than it was usually heated"* (v. 19).

The three friends, apparently clad in their festal clothing, were thrown into the furnace (execution by cremation was not unknown in Old Testament times, see Jer. 29:22). Those whose task it was to thrust them into the flames were burnt alive by the excessive heat. The lives of others were cheap as far as Nebuchadnezzar was concerned—well worth the price of having the last laugh. His behavior makes it all the more obvious that he had never really experienced the grace of God in his heart. He was a living illustration of the proverb that "a dog returns to his own vomit" (Prov. 26:11; 2 Pet. 2:22).

The entire scene underlines the helplessness and apparent hopelessness of the situation in which the kingdom of God is often placed. However, the three friends had committed themselves to God's providence. "Providence," wrote the seraphic Samuel Rutherford, "hath a thousand keys to open a thousand sundry doors for the deliverance of his own, when it is even come to a *conclamatum est* ["when it is all over with us"]. Let us be faithful, and care for our own part, which is to do and suffer for Him, and lay Christ's part on Himself, and leave it there. Duties are ours, events are the Lord's."[2] The Lord will establish His kingdom in His own time and in His own way. Our task is that of obedience to His revealed Word and will.

In a miraculous way Shadrach, Meshach, and Abed-Nego were delivered from the flames, or more accurately in the flames. The significance of the event is highlighted when we remember that there is a remarkable economy of the miraculous in the Bible. Outbreaks of extraordinary phenomena are limited to several relatively brief periods in biblical history: Moses and the days of the Exodus; Elijah and Elisha and the period when the prophetic ministry was established; Daniel and the time of the Exile; and Jesus and the days of the apostles. The miraculous interventions of God are largely absent from vast tracts of biblical history. These periods of the miraculous all seem to have several features in common. They were days of special crisis for the kingdom of God and special pressure on the people of God. In each period the miraculous was an in-breaking of the future kingdom of God to vindicate God's servants and their message.

The paradigm miracle was Christ's resurrection. There the kingdom of darkness seemed to have overcome the kingdom of God, but God raised His Son from the dead in power and glory. His kingdom was protected and His servant vindicated. In the same way, when all seemed to be lost for Shadrach, Meshach, and Abed-Nego, God vindicated them and their message, giving them new life in the face of certain death.

In Isaiah the Lord had given a special promise to His people who were destined for exile:

> When you walk through the fire, you shall not be
> burned,
> Nor shall the flame scorch you.
> For I am the LORD your God,
> The Holy One of Israel, your Savior;
> I gave Egypt for your ransom, . . .
> Since you were precious in My sight,

You have been honored,
And I have loved you;
Therefore I will give men for you,
And people for your life.
Fear not, for I am with you;
I will bring your descendants. . . from the ends of the
     earth—
Everyone who is called by My name,
Whom I have created for My glory;
I have formed him, yes, I have made him.

—Isaiah 43:2–5

In a remarkable way this promise was given fulfillment in the trial by fire. The reason for the deliverance was the love of the Lord for His people and especially the fact that they were created for His glory—and what glory God gained through their faithfulness to Him and their deliverance.

These men held on to the assurance that in either life or death, the Lord Himself would be with them: "Fear not, for I *am* with you" (Is. 43:5). This was what took Nebuchadnezzar's breath away as he watched: *"'Look!' he answered, 'I see four men loose, walking in the midst of the fire; and they are not hurt, and the form of the fourth is like the Son of God'"* (v. 25). Later in the passage Nebuchadnezzar refers to this fourth figure as an angel sent by God.

Much ink has been spilt in the history of the church debating the identity of this figure. Was it the Son of God in a preincarnate epiphany? Was it an angelic figure? Scripture itself does not shed any direct light on what this pagan king witnessed. The vital thing is that God fulfilled His promise. The fire did not harm the three confessors, and the Lord was with them. In the last analysis this was and is the only thing that really matters because it is the fulfillment of the promise of God's covenant of grace: "I will be your God," "I will be with you." It was the promise given to Moses in the days of the Sinaitic covenant: "'I am the God of your father—the God of Abraham, the God of Isaac, and the God of Jacob. . . . I will certainly be with you'" (Ex. 3:6, 12). It is the same promise that our Lord gave to His disciples when He had forged the new covenant in His death and resurrection: "All authority has been given to Me in heaven and on earth . . . and lo, I am with you always, even to the end of the age" (Matt. 28:18, 20).

The only explicit New Testament reference to this incident is in the Book of Hebrews (11:34), but it may also lie behind the references that Peter made to the fiery trials of our Christian experience. The three Hebrew witnesses experienced the prototype; as Christians we experience similar—if not always such extreme—trials. What is Peter's counsel? He assures us: (1) such trials purify and strengthen true faith; (2) in them we will be kept by God's power through faith just as Shadrach, Meshach, and Abed-Nego were in their day (1 Pet. 1:5–7). Peter later adds something else, again echoing the experience of the three Hebrews—(3) we should not be taken by surprise when we encounter such trials as though something strange and unexpected were happening. On the contrary, since we belong to Christ and are citizens in His kingdom, we should expect them. We should rejoice that, because we are the Lord's, those who oppose His kingdom want to oppose us, too. He will be with us, and His Spirit will rest upon us (1 Pet. 4:12–14).

What then was the secret of the faith of these three men in the face of Nebuchadnezzar? They trusted God's promise never to leave or forsake them. They feared Him with the reverent fear of loving sons. They would rather die than offend the One who had meant everything to them in the past. It could be said of them, as was said at the grave of the Reformer John Knox, that they feared the face of no man, because they had learned to live in the fear of the Lord.

IMPRESSED ONCE MORE

26 Then Nebuchadnezzar went near the mouth of the burning fiery furnace and spoke, saying, "Shadrach, Meshach, and Abed-Nego, servants of the Most High God, come out, and come here." Then Shadrach, Meshach, and Abed-Nego came from the midst of the fire. 27 And the satraps, administrators, governors, and the king's counselors gathered together, and they saw these men on whose bodies the fire had no power; the hair of their head was not singed nor were their garments affected, and the smell of fire was not on them.

28 Nebuchadnezzar spoke, saying, "Blessed be the God of Shadrach, Meshach, and Abed-Nego, who sent His Angel and delivered His servants who trusted in Him, and they have frustrated the king's word, and yielded their bodies, that they should not serve nor worship any god except their own God! 29 Therefore I make a decree that any people, nation, or language which speaks anything amiss against the God of Shadrach, Meshach, and Abed-

74

Nego shall be cut in pieces, and their houses shall be made an ash heap; because there is no other God who can deliver like this."

[30] Then the king promoted Shadrach, Meshach, and Abed-Nego in the province of Babylon.

—Daniel 3:26–30

This chapter, which began with Nebuchadnezzar's decree threatening to destroy Shadrach, Meshach, and Abed-Nego for worshiping their God, ends with a second decree in which the same king threatens to destroy anyone who spoke a word against the God of these same men. The words "the same king" are used advisedly. Nebuchadnezzar was unchanged. He breathed the same spirit now as he did at the beginning of this remarkable event. Admittedly he gave protection to God's people; admittedly he promoted the three heroes of the faith; but his decree and his concession (such as it was) show that there was no deep spiritual change in him—as the next chapter will make clear. Yet a superficial reading of his words might lead to the conclusion that Nebuchadnezzar did have a new heart. He certainly had been impressed. What are the indications that these impressions were superficial and would prove to be temporal?

The first is that Nebuchadnezzar was impressed purely by the miraculous. It astonished him (v. 24). It was evident to all that these men had not only been rescued; they had been divinely protected—their hair had not been singed, their garments were unscorched, they did not even smell of smoke. No wonder he was impressed and confessed that God had delivered them (vv. 27, 29). Dedicated to increasing his own power, however, it was the sheer power of God that had impressed him rather than the fact that His power had been exercised in the fulfillment of His promise of grace to His children. He was impressed by the fact that the Hebrews had frustrated his word (v. 28), but he showed little or no interest in the Word of God in which they trusted.

Nebuchadnezzar would not have been impressed by the weakness and foolishness of the cross by which God would bring final salvation to His people. It was the show of strength that had delivered the witnesses, the demonstration of wisdom that had frustrated his own that impressed him. He still did not think in terms of his pride being humbled or of his need of grace.

Nebuchadnezzar was impressed, secondly, by the faithfulness of the Hebrew witnesses. They had yielded their bodies to the flames rather than worship another god (v. 28). Notice his response: He proclaimed their God to be unique, and he promoted them to positions of considerable authority and influence. The God of Nebuchadnezzar's decree was still *"the God of Shadrach, Meshach, and Abed-Nego."* There was no hint that Nebuchadnezzar himself had trusted Him and would serve Him. The Lord was not "the God of Nebuchadnezzar."

What was true in Nebuchadnezzar's life is repeated time and again in our contemporary world. The modern version occurs when someone impressed by the faith of a Christian under trial comments, "What wonderful faith you have," without having any desire or intention to seek and find (or better, be found by) God in His saving grace. Such people are impressed, but the impressions are skin deep. They mask a heart that remains hardened.

One cannot help wondering if Nebuchadnezzar left the idol standing on the plain of Dura for the rest of his reign. Better by far to have destroyed it as a token of true repentance than to have promoted the three faithful witnesses. Did he do that to secure their trustworthiness in his own service and perhaps to quell whatever protests his conscience made against his ungodly behavior and superficial response to all that God had done before his eyes? Nothing is more common—and foolish—in the unregenerate heart than to assume that God is satisfied with a life in which we compensate for our sin by deeds that we wrongly assume cancel it out. Poor Nebuchadnezzar made that elementary mistake. He did not really know the first thing about true religion.

In addition to the particular lessons that arise from a study of the sections of this chapter, there are also two significant general lessons for Christians in the chapter as a whole. The first is that "all things work together for good to those who love God, to those who are called according to His purpose" (Rom. 8:28). In Psalm 148, the psalmist calls on the whole creation and everything in it to praise the Lord. He includes "fire" (v. 8). Daniel 3 illustrates how God uses even fire as part of His purpose, to work everything together for the good of His children and for His own greater glory.

When we see this, we begin to recognize that ultimately Christians do not live in an alien environment. In fact they alone can know that everything in the universe is caught up into the eternal plan of God and is used to further His purposes in our lives. The story of the Hebrew confessors unfolds the purpose of God—that the fire intended by Nebuchadnezzar for persecution should serve the glory of its maker.

The second lesson is an extension of the first. God has promised to give us grace in our time of need (Heb. 4:16). He will always give it in time. The three friends were already committed to the flames before they knew precisely what form that grace would take. Would it be the grace of deliverance or the grace to die well for God's glory? Only in the moment of trial did it become clear exactly how God would show His faithfulness. So it is with us:

> For You, O God, have tested us;
> You have refined us as silver is refined.
> You brought us into the net;
> You laid affliction on our backs.
> You have caused men to ride over our heads;
> We went through fire and through water;
> But You brought us out to rich fulfillment.
>
> —*Psalm 66:10–12*

NOTES

1. John Owen, *The Works of John Owen*, ed. William H. Goold, 16 vols. (1850–53; London: Banner of Truth Trust, 1965–68), 6:317–18.

2. Samuel Rutherford, *The Letters of Samuel Rutherford*, ed. Andrew A. Bonar (Edinburgh: Oliphant, Anderson & Ferrier, 1891), 238.

CHAPTER FOUR—SIGNS AND WONDERS
DANIEL 4:1–37

Scripture Outline
> Night Visions (4:1–18)
> Warnings from God (4:19–27)
> The Kingdom Departs (4:28–33)
> Reason Restored (4:34–37)

Chapter 4 is the last of the cycle of events in which God is dealing with Nebuchadnezzar. It is similar to chapter 2 in the sense that it has a dream as its centerpiece, but it stands in contrast to both chapters 2 and 3 because there is no hint that Daniel or his companions are in personal danger. The focus of attention here is on the way in which God deals with Nebuchadnezzar. Consequently the chapter opens and closes with a declaration about the sovereign power of God (vv. 1–3, 34–37).

The sovereignty of God over nations and individuals has already been stressed in the way that God gave wisdom to His faithful servants (ch. 1), in the interpretation of Nebuchadnezzar's dream (ch. 2), and in the preservation of the three witnesses in the fiery furnace (ch. 3). Chapter 4 is distinct because it contains a confession of that sovereignty on the part of the heathen king.

The possibility that this may be an accurate reflection of an event in history has frequently been minimized by some scholars. No record is said to exist of such a change of heart in the Babylonian king. Yet beyond the pages of Scripture some secondhand evidence exists that a strange event did occur in Nebuchadnezzar's life. In any case, the events recorded in this chapter and the recognition of the Lord with which it begins and ends were not likely to be recorded in the chronicles of Babylon—especially when it is remembered that the Babylonian monarch was thought of in terms tantamount to deity. The possibility (suggested by some scholars) that Nebuchadnezzar's "Open Letter to the Nations" (cf. v. 1) was composed by Daniel himself, or at least under his influence, may explain why this chapter's proclamation of God's kingdom has such a rich biblical ring to it.

NIGHT VISIONS

4:1 Nebuchadnezzar the king,
To all peoples, nations, and languages that dwell in all the earth:
Peace be multiplied to you.
² I thought it good to declare the signs and wonders that the Most High God has worked for me.
³ How great are His signs,
And how mighty His wonders!
His kingdom is an everlasting kingdom,
And His dominion is from generation to generation.
⁴ I, Nebuchadnezzar, was at rest in my house, and flourishing in my palace. ⁵ I saw a dream which made me afraid, and the thoughts on my bed and the visions of my head troubled me. ⁶ Therefore I issued a decree to bring in all the wise men of Babylon before me, that they might make known to me the interpretation of the dream.
⁷ Then the magicians, the astrologers, the Chaldeans, and the soothsayers came in, and I told them the dream; but they did not make known to me its interpretation. ⁸ But at last Daniel came before me (his name is Belteshazzar, according to the name of my god; in him is the Spirit of the Holy God), and I told the dream before him, saying:
⁹ "Belteshazzar, chief of the magicians, because I know that the Spirit of the Holy God is in you, and no secret troubles you, explain to me the visions of my dream that I have seen, and its interpretation.
¹⁰ These were the visions of my head while on my bed:
I was looking, and behold,
A tree in the midst of the earth,
And its height was great.
¹¹ The tree grew and became strong;
Its height reached to the heavens,
And it could be seen to the ends of all the earth.

¹² Its leaves were lovely,
Its fruit abundant,
And in it was food for all.
The beasts of the field found shade under it,
The birds of the heavens dwelt in its branches,
And all flesh was fed from it.
¹³ "I saw in the visions of my head while on my bed,
and there was a watcher, a holy one, coming down from
heaven. ¹⁴ He cried aloud and said thus:
'Chop down the tree and cut off its branches,
Strip off its leaves and scatter its fruit.
Let the beasts get out from under it,
And the birds from its branches.
¹⁵ Nevertheless leave the stump and roots in the
earth,
Bound with a band of iron and bronze,
In the tender grass of the field.
Let it be wet with the dew of heaven,
And let him graze with the beasts
On the grass of the earth.
¹⁶ Let his heart be changed from that of a man,
Let him be given the heart of a beast,
And let seven times pass over him.
¹⁷ 'This decision is by the decree of the watchers,
And the sentence by the word of the holy ones,
In order that the living may know
That the Most High rules in the kingdom of men,
Gives it to whomever He will,
And sets over it the lowest of men.'
¹⁸ "This dream I, King Nebuchadnezzar, have seen.
Now you, Belteshazzar, declare its interpretation, since all
the wise men of my kingdom are not able to make known
to me the interpretation; but you are able, for the Spirit of
the Holy God is in you."

—*Daniel 4:1–18*

Like many of the Psalms that record God's dealings with an
individual's deep spiritual needs, this chapter begins with a summary of the revelation God has given of Himself. God has shown
"signs and wonders" (vv. 2, 3). Like every sign or wonder in
Scripture, these have been revelations of His divine power and, in
particular, intimations of His own coming kingdom. They are the

clues God gives in an apparently chaotic world that He is the one who rules over all things and will establish His kingdom. Their message is ultimately the same as Nebuchadnezzar's earlier dream (cf. 2:44 and 4:3).

God spoke to Nebuchadnezzar when he least expected it. He was *"at rest . . . and flourishing."* He was apparently in the golden years of his reign; he felt his program had been highly successful. It is not difficult to imagine him relaxing in the Hanging Gardens, enjoying the luxuries he must have felt he well deserved. He thought himself successful and secure on his throne. He was master of all he surveyed.

Yet this is the man who earlier in his reign had been so disturbed by dreams about the end of his kingdom. This was the king who more recently had been stunned by a remarkable display of God's power. On two previous occasions his conscience had been awakened and his heart stirred to consider spiritual realities. Is it not inconceivable that he should have now developed such apparent spiritual lethargy?

We would reach that conclusion only if we were ignorant of our own hearts and the way in which we despise or treat lightly the disciplines God exercises in our lives (cf. Prov. 3:11–12; Heb. 12:5). John Calvin rightly comments on Nebuchadnezzar: "When God, therefore, wishes to lead us to repentance, he is compelled to repeat his blows continually, either because we are not moved when he chastises us with his hand, or we seem roused for the time, and then we return again to our former torpor. He is therefore compelled to redouble his blows."[1]

God broke in upon the spiritual lethargy of Nebuchadnezzar and sent him a nightmare that both frightened and troubled him (v. 5). The calloused spirit Nebuchadnezzar had developed is revealed in his response. In his agitation he turned once again to his magicians and astrologers, his Chaldeans and soothsayers. They had failed him before; the Chaldeans had been responsible for turning him against the wisest counselors in his realm (see 3:8). Despite all that God had so clearly spoken to him, he fell back onto the mind-set of unregenerates. The carnal mind experiences enmity against God and cannot ever truly submit itself to God's law. Nebuchadnezzar had set his mind on the flesh, and the wisdom and guidance he sought were of the flesh (cf. Rom. 8:5–8). He was a practical atheist. He knew of the wisdom of Daniel and his three friends, but he sought counsel elsewhere. Those who could tell him his horoscope or perform some magic were more attractive avenues of wisdom to him than the four men who could explain to him what God was saying.

Why did he not call Daniel or the three witnesses first? Perhaps the answer lies in his sense of guilt. Satan has an uncanny ability to blackmail us on account of our sin. We will not confess it openly. He blackmails us into leaving our sin unconfessed. So it was with Nebuchadnezzar. He knew he had abandoned the conscience that on several occasions had been sensitized to God by these men who had commended themselves to his conscience in the sight of God (cf. 2 Cor. 4:2).

Yet the magicians and astrologers again failed him. At last Daniel appears. Two things are obvious: (1) Nebuchadnezzar knew that Daniel could be trusted implicitly to tell him the truth. He knew Daniel was a man full of *"the Spirit of the Holy God"* (v. 8). He knew too that Daniel was a man of a different quality from himself; *"no secret troubles you"* (v. 9). He knew why that was so. He had seen in Daniel's words and in his friends' actions that their trust was in their Lord. As Daniel stood before him, Nebuchadnezzar knew that this man was all he himself should have been as a king but had failed to be.

Daniel was not troubled by any secret because he lived in the presence of the one from whom no secrets could be hidden. He did not need to be afraid of strange and mysterious events since every event of history was under the control of his God. In this respect, Daniel is a beautiful example of what every child of God is called to be in the world. He was quite simply qualitatively different from others. The song he sang in this strange land was the Lord's song.

(2) Although Nebuchadnezzar trusted Daniel, knowing that he alone would tell him the truth, he appears to have been afraid of the influence that Daniel might have upon him. Is this the significance of the parenthesis in verse 8: *"(his name is Belteshazzar, according to the name of my god . . .)"*? From one viewpoint the words appear to be complimentary. Daniel is honored with the name of Nebuchadnezzar's god, but from Daniel's point of view this name is a constant reminder of the exile God's people suffer and an insult to his own God.

Notice how the king calls Daniel *"chief of the magicians."* Did he know no better than that? Or was he repressing the voice of his own conscience by putting Daniel in the same category as the other religious men in his court? If so, it was simply another defense mechanism against the power of God's word. Despite all that God had done, Nebuchadnezzar persisted in interpreting the events of his life in human terms. He petitioned Daniel, but he had not yet learned to petition God.

Nebuchadnezzar's dream was a disturbing one. It is not difficult to sense why it would haunt him, even though he did not fully understand its significance. He had seen a cosmic tree reaching into the heavens and visible throughout the earth. It was not only beautiful, but it was also fruitful and provided protection and nourishment for the birds and beasts. Suddenly a heavenly creature—"a *watcher, a holy one*" (v. 13)—commanded the tree to be chopped down to the stump and the roots. Clearly the tree represented someone, for the watcher commanded that it should be bound with a band, exposed to life among the wild beasts, and its heart *"changed from that of a man"* into *"the heart of an animal"* (v. 16). *"Seven times"* were to *"pass over him."* The same heavenly creature that Nebuchadnezzar heard pronounce this word of doom also explained in verse 17 why it was happening:

> *"In order that the living may know*
> *That the Most High rules in the kingdom of men,*
> *Gives it to whomever He will,*
> *And sets over it the lowest of men."*

It is difficult to believe that either Nebuchadnezzar or his counselors were lacking in clues as to what this dream meant. For one thing, the symbol of a cosmic tree was not unique; for another, Nebuchadnezzar himself clearly recognized that his dream was a sobering one, the import of which filled him with a sense of foreboding. Whatever the interpretation might be, the general message was of doom and destruction. A superhuman empire would be reduced to subhuman proportions. There were, however, important details that required interpretation. Who was the cosmic tree in the dream? What were these watchers? What would be the meaning of the stump grazing with the beasts and receiving the heart of an animal? What would happen when the seven times had passed over?

The purpose of this decree was not left to Nebuchadnezzar's imagination: It was to teach men that God reigns, that He sets up and pulls down kingdoms, that His actions in history focus on the work of humbling men in order that they may dispense with their foolish pride and acknowledge Him as their God. It is the same truth as that in which Mary rejoiced:

> "He has scattered the proud in the imagination of their
> hearts.

He has put down the mighty from their thrones,
And exalted the lowly."

—*Luke 1:51–52*

Nebuchadnezzar doubtless needed Daniel for the skilled interpretation of what God was saying. He surely did not need him in order to understand the basic message and apply it to himself. The watcher in the dream had already done that. Nebuchadnezzar's trouble was that he did not like what he already understood of God's Word.

There is a modern ring to this part of the narrative. We live in an age of specialized knowledge. That is true of the knowledge of the Bible also. Entire dissertations have been written on the use of a single pronoun in the New Testament. It would be very wrongheaded to be cynical about the value of such careful and precise study, but it is all too easy for us to hide our disobedience to what God has made abundantly clear in Scripture behind our lack of expert knowledge. All God's revelation is adequate to show His majesty and power and to evoke in us a consciousness of our need to turn to Him (cf. Acts 17:26ff.; Rom. 1:20ff.). Those who do not seek him or submit to Him are without excuse. That was true of Nebuchadnezzar; it is no less true today.

WARNINGS FROM GOD

19 Then Daniel, whose name was Belteshazzar, was astonished for a time, and his thoughts troubled him. So the king spoke, and said, "Belteshazzar, do not let the dream or its interpretation trouble you."
Belteshazzar answered and said, "My lord, may the dream concern those who hate you, and its interpretation concern your enemies!
20 "The tree that you saw, which grew and became strong, whose height reached to the heavens and which could be seen by all the earth, 21 whose leaves were lovely and its fruit abundant, in which was food for all, under which the beasts of the field dwelt, and in whose branches the birds of the heaven had their home— 22 it is you, O king, who have grown and become strong; for your greatness has grown and reaches to the heavens, and your dominion to the end of the earth.
23 "And inasmuch as the king saw a watcher, a holy one, coming down from heaven and saying, 'Chop down

the tree and destroy it, but leave its stump and roots in the earth, bound with a band of iron and bronze in the tender grass of the field; let it be wet with the dew of heaven, and let him graze with the beasts of the field, till seven times pass over him'; 24 this is the interpretation, O king, and this is the decree of the Most High, which has come upon my lord the king: 25 They shall drive you from men, your dwelling shall be with the beasts of the field, and they shall make you eat grass like oxen. They shall wet you with the dew of heaven, and seven times shall pass over you, till you know that the Most High rules in the kingdom of men, and gives it to whomever He chooses.

26 "And inasmuch as they gave the command to leave the stump and roots of the tree, your kingdom shall be assured to you, after you come to know that Heaven rules. 27 Therefore, O king, let my advice be acceptable to you; break off your sins by being righteous, and your iniquities by showing mercy to the poor. Perhaps there may be a lengthening of your prosperity."

—Daniel 4:19–27

This section in Daniel is one of the classic confrontations in the whole of Scripture and ranks with those between Moses and Pharaoh, Elijah and Ahab, John the Baptist and Herod, Jesus and Pilate, and Paul and Agrippa. A common theme runs through them all: God's person, not the person of the world, is truly free and grows to full stature while the person of the world shrinks. This is brought out here by a series of illuminating contrasts.

(1) *The contrast between Nebuchadnezzar's insensitivity and Daniel's sensitivity.* Contrary to what Nebuchadnezzar had earlier said to Daniel ("no secret troubles you"), he was profoundly disturbed when he heard the contents of the dream—he *"was astonished for a time, and his thoughts troubled him"* (v. 19). In a reversal of roles, the king sought to encourage Daniel, but his encouragement was superficial and altogether inappropriate. Daniel was right to be troubled. He believed the revelation God gave, and he cared enough for his sinful monarch to have compassion on him and to fear for his future. The Lord would have said to Nebuchadnezzar about Daniel what Paul wrote of Timothy: "I have no one like-minded, who will sincerely care for your state. For all seek their own, not the things which are of Christ Jesus" (Phil. 2:20–21).

This spirit was conceived in Daniel's life of prayer, which is a marked feature of this book. We know he spent regular periods in prayer each day (Dan. 6:10). It is certain Nebuchadnezzar's spiritual condition figured regularly in his petitions. That is why Daniel could address him both caringly and appropriately. It is noteworthy that Daniel was observing the social customs of the Babylonian court by wishing that the contents of the dream were intended for the king's enemies. Even when he speaks directly to Nebuchadnezzar in God's name, there is nothing vulgar about his address: *"Therefore, O king, let my advice be acceptable to you"* (v. 27). Daniel was completely faithful to his God and at the same time completely faithful to his king. How rare that was and is.

Faithfulness compelled him to speak the truth. Nebuchadnezzar was the cosmic tree (v. 22), and he was the one whom God would humble. He would—in some way as yet unexplained—be driven from human society and live like an animal. He would be soaked with the dew of heaven until seven times had passed. (Daniel's courage is noteworthy considering the glimpses of Nebuchadnezzar's anger contained in earlier chapters.)

(2) *The contrast between the decree of Nebuchadnezzar and the decree of God.* In verse 6, Nebuchadnezzar had made his own royal decree. It was obvious that his dream illustrated significant historical developments. The intention of his decree was that the meaning of history would be revealed to him by men like himself. No doubt his intention was that knowing what might take place, he would be able to alter the course of events by taking appropriate action. He did not seem to appreciate that:

"This decision is by the decree of the watchers,
And the sentence by the word of the holy ones" (v. 17).

Daniel indicated that this decree was *"the decree of the Most High, which has come upon my lord the king"* (v. 24). Nebuchadnezzar must willingly or painfully learn that ultimate power did not rest in Babylon or in his own hands but in heaven—in God's hands. So he would be humbled *"till you know that the Most High rules in the kingdom of men, and gives it to whomever He chooses. . . . [Y]our kingdom shall be assured to you, after you come to know that Heaven rules"* (vv. 25–26).

It is instructive for our generation to hear the tone of Daniel's preaching to Nebuchadnezzar here and elsewhere. It is not just because Nebuchadnezzar was king that the theme of the divine kingship and kingdom was Daniel's central message, although that fact made the message all the more striking. The theme of the kingdom (or kingship or sovereignty) of God is central to the entire Bible. All men (not only Nebuchadnezzar and other political leaders) must come to know that "Heaven rules" and that it is God who decrees what comes to pass (Eph. 1:11).

Today a minority would lay the same emphasis as Daniel on the absolute sovereignty of God, but that is to our spiritual detriment. For it is this strand of biblical teaching (as Daniel clearly understood) that humbles the pride of man. Few things are more necessary in our own day or indeed in any day. Jonathan Edwards bears eloquent testimony. In the days of the eighteenth-century Great Awakening, he came to see how conversion was prefaced by a "humiliation before the Sovereign Disposer of life and death, whereby God is wont to prepare them for his consolations." In one of the most illuminating paragraphs from his writings, he adds "I think I have found that no discourses have been more remarkably blessed, than those . . . [on] the doctrine of God's *absolute sovereignty* with regard to the salvation of sinners."[2] Edwards, following Daniel, saw this to be vital. He realized that by declaring God's sovereignty over everyone, one simply emphasized that God really is God. Consequently no truth about God is more likely to evoke either humility or rebellion. In many ways, as Daniel had come to see in his dealings with Nebuchadnezzar, this is the litmus test that indisputably indicates an individual's true spiritual condition.

(3) *The contrast between who Nebuchadnezzar was in his own eyes and who he would be under God's judgment.* This dream was given by direct divine revelation. It was prophetic in nature (and thus provides a striking illustration of the fact that phenomena produced by God's Spirit in an individual's life are not necessarily indications of the presence of God's grace [cf. Matt. 7:22–23]). Yet it also bears an intensely human quality. God regularly works in accordance with our personalities in order to reveal Himself; thus, Scripture (to give one example) bears the stamp of its human authors' personalities.

Here the central element in the dream—the cosmic tree—is obviously a reflection of Nebuchadnezzar's self-image. His sense of his own worth was made plain in chapter 3; it has not diminished in the events of chapter 4. He sees himself as lord of the universe, as a beneficent despot providing for the nations in his empire.

The essence of sin, as William Temple vividly expressed it, is that "I make myself, in a host of ways, the center of the universe." Nebuchadnezzar had done this on a large scale. He apparently had no one, except Daniel, who would whisper in his ear (as a Roman slave was appointed to do when a victorious general returned to Rome with the honor of triumph) *Homo es* ("You are only a man").

What Nebuchadnezzar was oblivious to was that *"the Most High rules in the kingdom of men, and gives it to whomever He chooses"* (vv. 17, 25). His heart was not submitted to the truth that caused Daniel's heart to sing, "He changes the times and the seasons; He removes kings and sets up kings" (2:21). God would therefore deal in new severity with him to rid him of his fatal spiritual blindness. In a moment of time He would divest him of all his regal glory and reduce him to a beast. According to the dream, "the beasts of the field [had] found shade" under Nebuchadnezzar, the cosmic tree (v. 12); now God would reduce him to being one of those beasts who needed shelter and provision.

Nebuchadnezzar is simply a macrocosmic version of the kind of situation every pastor encounters from time to time. Individuals who have lived for themselves, built their own kingdoms, and (from a human vantage point) have "made it" will boast that they have accomplished so much because they did it "their" way. Yet in one terrible moment—a phone call, a letter, some words spoken by a physician—the foundations may begin to tremble and the former securities begin to crumble.

I have never forgotten one of my earliest experiences in pastoral ministry. I was twenty-three years old, recently married, and recently ordained to the gospel ministry. I had been appointed assistant pastor to an inner-city church where each weekday morning we had a short service prior to the beginning of the working day. As I gathered my belongings in the office at the end of the service, someone knocked on my door. A man in his early thirties entered, and he was in great distress. He told me of the extraordinary success story his life had been, of how financially secure he and his wife had become. He had reached that category of lifestyle in which a surprise birthday gift might be a new car (paid for with cash). He had just received news that his wife had only a few months to live. The axe had been laid to the tree of life for him. I had never before shared with someone so relatively young such a moment of utter despair. A moment can be the turning point for a whole life. So it was with Nebuchadnezzar. In a moment God would show how fragile the great king really was.

(4) *The contrast between the mercy of God, on the one hand, and the mercilessness of Nebuchadnezzar, on the other.* Daniel's message was full of solemnity and judgment. The divine decree, however, was not arbitrary. Daniel's application of the dream-vision counseled the king *"break off your sins by being righteous, and your iniquities by showing mercy to the poor"* (v. 27). Like so many other despots, whatever independence Nebuchadnezzar believed he had autonomously exercised, in actual fact he was a slave to his sinful passions. That was the yoke he had to break (Gen. 27:40). Whatever benevolence he seemed to himself to have demonstrated, the reality of the situation was that he had trampled on the poor in order to complete a building program that was to memorialize his own glory.

God's true king "will bring justice to the poor of the people; He will save the children of the needy, and will break in pieces the oppressor" (Ps. 72:4). That was God's model for kingship. Nebuchadnezzar had manifestly failed to illustrate it. He had apparently shown little or no mercy to the poor. In chapters 2 and 3 we have already noted how little mercy he was prepared to show to his own closest advisers. He richly deserved the full force of divine judgment.

Remarkably, however, Nebuchadnezzar was offered a ray of hope. There was a divine "perhaps" in Daniel's message (v. 27). There was also an assurance that the Lord's purpose in His judgment was to bring Nebuchadnezzar into a proper spiritual relationship: *"Your kingdom shall be assured to you, after you come to know that Heaven rules"* (v. 26). This was not yet the final judgment; there was still time and opportunity to repent. The revelation of the divine decree was not given to promote a spirit of fatalism in the king but to encourage him to change.

THE KINGDOM DEPARTS

28 All this came upon King Nebuchadnezzar. 29 At the end of the twelve months he was walking about the royal palace of Babylon. 30 The king spoke, saying, "Is not this great Babylon, that I have built for a royal dwelling by my mighty power and for the honor of my majesty?"

31 While the word was still in the king's mouth, a voice fell from heaven: "King Nebuchadnezzar, to you it is spoken: the kingdom has departed from you! 32 And they shall drive you from men, and your dwelling shall be with the beasts of the field. They shall make you eat grass

like oxen; and seven times shall pass over you, until you know that the Most High rules in the kingdom of men, and gives it to whomever He chooses."

33 That very hour the word was fulfilled concerning Nebuchadnezzar; he was driven from men and ate grass like oxen; his body was wet with the dew of heaven till his hair had grown like eagles' feathers and his nails like birds' claws.

—Daniel 4:28–33

Sadly, the words most appropriate for Nebuchadnezzar are found in Paul's devastating denunciation: "Do you despise the riches of His goodness, forbearance, and longsuffering, not knowing that the goodness of God leads you to repentance? But in accordance with your hardness and your impenitent heart you are treasuring up for yourself wrath in the day of wrath and revelation of the righteous judgment of God, who *'will render to each one according to his deeds'*" (Rom. 2:4–5).

God appears to have given Nebuchadnezzar an extended opportunity to repent of his hardness of heart and to make amends for his life of arrogant empire-building. Not only did He send him dreams to disturb him and a Daniel to instruct and warn him, but He also gave him an extended period of months during which he could have turned from his sin. The evidence is that, like others, Nebuchadnezzar presumed on the patience of God. As the weeks passed and the promised terrible judgment did not eventuate, perhaps he assumed that the experience had been simply a "bad dream." There was no sign of the chastisement of God. Relieved, he continued in his old ways.

Nebuchadnezzar made the most fatal mistake an individual can make. He assumed that he would interpret God's activity by his own plumb line. It is the same attitude that Peter rebuked when he said,

[S]coffers will come in the last days, walking according to their own lusts, and saying, "Where is the promise of His coming? For since the fathers fell asleep, all things continue as they were from the beginning of creation." For this they willfully forget: that by the word of God the heavens were of old, and the earth standing out of water and in the water, by which the world that then existed perished, being flooded with water. But the heavens and earth which which are now preserved by the same word, are reserved for fire until the day of judgment and perdition of ungodly men. But, beloved, do not forget this one thing, that with the Lord one day is as a thousand years, and a thousand years as one day. The Lord is not slack concerning His promise, as some count slackness, but is longsuffering toward us, not willing that any should perish but that all should come to repentance. But the day of the Lord will come as a thief in the night.

—*2 Peter 3:3–10*

Nebuchadnezzar scoffed at the warnings that had been planted in his conscience—and the day of the Lord did come.

John Elias, an eighteenth-century Welsh evangelist, once used a vivid illustration of the conscience-silencing that took place in Nebuchadnezzar's life. He recalled the time when the local blacksmith had bought a new dog. Shortly afterward, when Elias visited the blacksmith's shop, the dog could be heard barking fiercely as the blacksmith's hammer beat rhythmically on the metal of the horseshoes. As time went on, however, the barking became quieter and less frequent until one day Elias looked into the smithy to catch the blacksmith hammering away at the anvil and saw the dog, asleep by the fire, silent at last.

Nebuchadnezzar had grown similarly accustomed to the hammering of the Word of God. Ignoring it had rendered his conscience increasingly immune to its impact on his life. As though God had never spoken to him, he walked around the Hanging Gardens and boasted of his achievements: *"Is not this great Babylon, that I have built for a royal dwelling by my mighty power and for the honor of my majesty?'"* (v. 30). Even as his thoughts were forming words for his lips, *"a voice fell from heaven: 'King Nebuchadnezzar, to you it is spoken: the kingdom has departed from you'"* (v. 31).

Why did the voice speak at this particular juncture? Was Nebuchadnezzar afflicted for lying? The historical evidence suggests that his claims were to all intents and purposes justified. He had renovated or restored over a dozen temples, completed the great city wall of Babylon, and built a new palace with which the famous Hanging Gardens were connected. So from one point of view he was simply cataloging what he had achieved. He was, however, flying in the face of all the divine warnings he had received by his continuing fascination with his own glory and the way in which he was utterly absorbed in his personal achievements. All this he had done *"for a royal dwelling by [his] mighty power and for the honor of [his] majesty"* (v. 30). He had resisted the burden of Daniel's ministry which is so well expressed in the Psalms:

> Unless the LORD builds the house,
> They labor in vain who build it;
> Unless the LORD guards the city,
> The watchman stays awake in vain.
>
> —*Psalm 127:1*

All things are in God's hands. The very breath we breathe we owe moment by moment to Him. No one achieves anything by his unaided strength. Nothing exists for anyone's exclusive glory.

God's judgment struck suddenly— "the master of that servant will come on a day when he is not looking for him, and at an hour when he is not aware" (Luke 12:46). Nebuchadnezzar was smitten with the symptoms of what is known as lycanthropy (from the Greek, *lukos*, meaning "a wolf," and *anthropos*, meaning "man"). With what can only be described as suitable restraint, we are told that Nebuchadnezzar began to act like a beast: *"he was driven from men and ate grass like oxen; his body was wet with the dew of heaven till his hair had grown like eagles' feathers and his nails like birds' claws"* (v. 33).

It is a tragic and pathetic scene; Superman has become Subman. The one who refused to honor God's glory loses his own glory. Refusing to share what he has with the poor, he becomes poorer than the poor. He becomes outwardly what his heart had been spiritually and inwardly—bestial. Disorders of the mind are surely one of the saddest of all maladies in human experience. Sometimes these disorders appear to have a significant physical factor in their cause, and consequently physical means may be employed as part of the restorative process. Clearly there was a deep moral and spiritual significance in Nebuchadnezzar's experience. His delusion that he was an animal is significant—the prophecy of his dream was thus fulfilled.

We have already hinted that although his dream was a divine revelation, it was mediated through Nebuchadnezzar's own thought processes and subconscious realm. Bizarre though his dream must have seemed (whose dreams are not bizarre?), he was aware in the depths of his being that he had been bestial in his lifestyle. We can only imagine that he knew from God's Word through the Hebrew witnesses that he merited the judgment of God. Perhaps through the mechanism of the dream God had shown him what he knew to be true but had consistently repressed from his thoughts. If so, this would be entirely in harmony with Paul's later teaching that individuals do not reject God in ignorance nor are they unaware of the judgment they deserve (Rom. 1:18ff.). In this case, the voice of God acted like a trigger in Nebuchadnezzar's mind. He could no longer resist the pent-up pressure of his conscience; his guilt burst forth in this powerful psychosomatic manner. He became externally what he knew himself to be internally—bestial. All restraints on his subconscious mind were lifted; in some mysterious way (paralleled elsewhere in human experience) the only escape valve his personality could discover, the only relief mechanism available for him, was to act as an animal. Nothing is hidden that will not ultimately be brought to light. God is not mocked; all of us reap what we have sown.

REASON RESTORED

34 And at the end of the time I, Nebuchadnezzar,
lifted my eyes to heaven, and my understanding returned
to me; and I blessed the Most High and praised and honored Him who lives forever:
For His dominion is an everlasting dominion,
And His kingdom is from generation to generation.
35 All the inhabitants of the earth are reputed as
nothing;
He does according to His will in the army of heaven
And among the inhabitants of the earth.
No one can restrain His hand
Or say to Him, "What have You done?"
36 At the same time my reason returned to me, and
for the glory of my kingdom, my honor and splendor
returned to me. My counselors and nobles resorted to me,
I was restored to my kingdom, and excellent majesty was
added to me. 37 Now I, Nebuchadnezzar, praise and extol
and honor the King of heaven, all of whose works are
truth, and His ways justice. And those who walk in pride
He is able to put down.

—Daniel 4:34–37

God's word of judgment was fulfilled on Nebuchadnezzar; however, it was tempered with a promise of mercy: "seven times shall pass over you, until you know that the Most High rules in the kingdom of men, and gives it to whomever He chooses" (v. 32). The single word "until" was a glimmer of light in an otherwise dark tunnel of chastisement. The narrative is vague, perhaps deliberately, about any details of Nebuchadnezzar's condition. We do not know how long these lycanthropic symptoms lasted. "Seven times" (vv. 16, 23, 25, 32) may refer to months, years, or (most probably) the complete period fixed by God's decree (seven being taken as the number representing perfection or completeness in Scripture).

Nebuchadnezzar did not experience spontaneous remission; no one does. The term is a convenient description of a cause-and-effect sequence for which there is no explanation in terms of our ordinary expectations. In Nebuchadnezzar's case, the narrative underlines the fact that the remission was as attributable to God as was the affliction. The chain of cause and effect is clearly delineated in a series of well-marked steps: He lifted his eyes to heaven, his reason returned to him, and he praised God (v. 34). His repentance involved a retracing of the steps taken in his rebellion. Once he had looked at Babylon as his own creation in a spirit of pride and self-worship; now he lifted his eyes to heaven in recognition of the sovereign reign of God. In his sin he lost his perspective on life and his reasoning became twisted. (Sin is always ultimately irrational since it is against God, the author of rational thinking and living.) Now his reason returned to him. Whereas before he had usurped the Lord, now he bowed before Him and honored Him. The devastating course of sin's dominion in his heart had been stopped and now gave every appearance of being reversed. Additionally, God showed mercy on him: *"And for the glory of my kingdom, my honor and splendor returned to me. My counselors and nobles resorted to me, I was restored to my kingdom, and excellent majesty was added to me"* (v. 36). Sin had brought him to shame; repentance marked the beginnings of the restoration of his former glory.

Nebuchadnezzar's sin is, of course, a life-size model of all sin, and the consequence of his guilt is equally a case study in the havoc sin wreaks in our lives—we are cast down from the glory for which we were created; we distort the image of the glory of God. Thus Nebuchadnezzar's repentance and his ensuing restoration to former glory is a vivid illustration of the benefits God bestows. He begins to restore His image to us; touches of His glory appear again; we begin to function again as the royal children of God.

Repentance, as Calvin says, "is the true-turning of our life to God, a turning that arises from a pure and earnest fear of him; and it consists in the mortification of our flesh and of the old man, and in the vivification of the Spirit . . . in a word, I interpret repentance as regeneration, *whose sole end is to restore to us the image of God that has been disfigured and all but obliterated.*"[3]

What was it that lay at the heart of Nebuchadnezzar's confession? There are four elements in what he says in verses 34–35. (1) He confesses the sovereignty of God. He establishes a kingdom that is without end. God does according to His will in the army of heaven and among the inhabitants of earth. No one can restrain His hand or say to Him, "'What *have You done?*'" (v. 35). There is a hint of something else in Nebuchadnezzar's words; he states, *"His kingdom is from generation to generation"* (v. 34). That phrase or its equivalent is frequently associated with God's covenant relationship with His people (cf. Ex. 20:5–6; Ps. 103:17–18). God's reign is not only sovereign, it is expressed in His covenant faithfulness to His people. Despite the hesitance of some commentators to see a true conversion occurring in Nebuchadnezzar, this covenantal element provides a hint that he learned more from his experience than that God is sovereign.

(2) He confesses also the creatureliness of humankind: *"All the inhabitants of the earth are reputed as nothing"* (v. 35). The king no longer recognizes divine power at a merely theoretical level. He confesses that even the greatest of men (and he had been in his own eyes the greatest) are nothing before the majestic Lord. This is always a mark of the subdued heart; the creatureliness and dependence of individuals on God is seen. He is not autonomous; he is dependent and creaturely. His true joy is found only when he has come to recognize that this is the case.

(3) Nebuchadnezzar confesses the truthfulness and righteousness of God, *"all of whose works are truth, and His ways justice"* (v. 37). He has been dealt with severely by God, but he acknowledges how true and righteous God's judgments have been. They have been true in the sense that God's dealings with him were appropriate to his sins. They have been just in the sense that in His righteousness God has kept His promise to deliver him and restore him. "If we confess our sins, He is faithful and just to forgive us our sins and to cleanse us from all unrighteousness" (1 John 1:9).

(4) Finally, he came to recognize that God resists the proud and gives grace to the humble (cf. Prov. 3:34). His life was a portrayal of

the application Peter made of this principle: "Therefore humble yourselves under the mighty hand of God, that He may exalt you in due time" (1 Pet. 5:6). That is always the pattern of His saving grace.

> With the merciful You will show Yourself merciful;
> With a blameless man You will show Yourself blame-
>   less;
> With the pure You will show Yourself pure;
> And with the devious You will show Yourself shrewd.
> For You will save the humble people,
> But will bring down haughty looks. . . .
> You have also given me the shield of Your salvation;
> Your right hand has held me up,
> Your gentleness has made me great. . . .
> The LORD lives!
> Blessed be my Rock!
> Let the God of my salvation be exalted. . . .
> Great deliverance He gives to His king.
>
> —*Psalm 18:25–27, 35, 46, 50*

NOTES

1. John Calvin, *Commentaries on the Book of the Prophet Daniel,* tr. Thomas Myers, 2 vols. (Edinburgh: Calvin Translation Society, 1852–53), 1:245.

2. Jonathan Edwards, *Jonathan Edwards on Revival* (Edinburgh: Banner of Truth Trust, 1984), 31.

3. John Calvin, *Institutes of the Christian Religion,* ed. John T. McNeill, tr. Ford L. Battles, Library of Christian Classics, vols. 20–21 (Philadelphia: Westminster Press, 1960), 3.3.5, 9.

CHAPTER FIVE—THE WRITING ON THE WALL
DANIEL 5:1–31

Scripture Outline
   The Moving Finger Writes (5:1–9)
   Weighed in the Balances of God (5:10–31)

The Book of Daniel is not merely a record of the history of God's people in exile in Babylon. In fact, the author shows relatively little interest in chronology in the historical section of the book. We must look elsewhere if we want to understand the events of Jewish or world history in the period covered by Daniel. Instead, as we have seen, the book is concerned with the spiritual conflict that underlies history and comes to the surface in dramatic form in particular events of crucial significance to the kingdom of God. What is at stake in the Exile is the threat posed by the kingdom of this world against the kingdom of God.

This perspective helps to explain the abrupt way in which Belshazzar appears in chapter 5 without introduction, biographical information, or explanation of his place in the line of succession to the throne of Babylon. He is to serve as a further illustration of the sovereignty of God and His ability to pull down kings from their thrones (Luke 1:52). For that reason, the drama of God's dealings with Belshazzar is heightened by the fact that he appears and disappears in the space of a single chapter.

This element is one that has made little sense to scholars who have engaged the historical critical method in their examination of the Book of Daniel. It has presented something of a puzzle to orthodox scholarship in the past since no Belshazzar appears in the sequence of Babylonian kings. Some identified him with Evil-Merodach (2 Kin. 25:27; Jer. 52:31) who was slain in a coup led by his brother-in-law Nergal Sharezer in August 560 B.C.

There was, however, a Belshazzar who—certainly from the point of the Jewish exiles—was king (v. 1). Bel-sar-usur (Belshazzar) was the eldest son of Nabonidus, the last king of Babylon. Nabonidus (556–539) sought to exalt the moon god, Sin, as the chief deity among the Babylonian pantheon, replacing Marduk. Perhaps in part due to the local reaction to his attempts to redefine the hierarchy of the gods, Nabonidus set up his royal residence in Teiman, southeast of Edom, and for a decade left his son, Belshazzar, serving as regent. So unpopular does Nabonidus—and perhaps Belshazzar—seem to have been that when the city was later captured, the event was welcomed by the people of Babylon. Belshazzar therefore seems to have been virtually co-opted as monarch for practical purposes. A significant clue that the writer understood this situation may be found in verses 7, 16, and 29. Belshazzar offers not the second but the third place in the realm to anyone who can interpret the writing he has seen on the palace wall (contrast Gen. 41:40 where Joseph was exalted to the second place in the realm).

Nebuchadnezzar is, however, called the "father" of Belshazzar (vv. 2, 11, 13, 18, 22). It is widely recognized that in Scripture, and in the ancient Near East generally, "father" denotes a variety of relationships—from natural fatherhood to simple ancestry (cf. the way in which the Jews appealed to Abraham as their father in their conflict with Jesus [John 8:39]). This was readily understood by the earlier commentators. For example, Calvin wrote: "The Prophet calls Nebuchadnezzar the father of Belshazzar, since it is usual in all languages to speak of ancestors as fathers."[1] In any case, the Old Testament employs no separate terms to designate more remote ancestry. "Grandfather" and "great-grandfather" are unknown terms in the Old Testament.

What then is the thrust of the narrative of Belshazzar? What particular nuance does it contribute to the unfolding of God's sovereign dealings with us? Clearly Belshazzar's experience stands in marked contrast to that of Nebuchadnezzar (to whom God displayed such remarkable patience). Belshazzar was suddenly and speedily cut off; the kingdom was dramatically taken from him. The Book of Proverbs speaks about such sudden judgment coming on the wicked: "His calamity shall come suddenly; suddenly he shall be broken without remedy" (Prov. 6:15). It is a reminder that we dare not presume upon the grace that God has shown to others. To know that God is gracious and yet not turn from sin in the light of that grace is to fall under His righteous judgment. Such was the experience of Belshazzar.

THE MOVING FINGER WRITES

5:1 Belshazzar the king made a great feast for a thousand of his lords, and drank wine in the presence of the thousand. 2 While he tasted the wine, Belshazzar gave the command to bring the gold and silver vessels which his father Nebuchadnezzar had taken from the temple which had been in Jerusalem, that the king and his lords, his wives, and his concubines might drink from them. 3 Then they brought the gold vessels that had been taken from the temple of the house of God which had been in Jerusalem; and the king and his lords, his wives, and his concubines drank from them. 4 They drank wine, and praised the gods of gold and silver, bronze and iron, wood and stone.

5 In the same hour the fingers of a man's hand appeared and wrote opposite the lampstand on the plaster of the wall of the king's palace; and the king saw the part of the hand that wrote. 6 Then the king's countenance changed, and his thoughts troubled him, so that the joints of his hips were loosened and his knees knocked against each other. 7 The king cried aloud to bring in the astrologers, the Chaldeans, and the soothsayers. The king spoke, saying to the wise men of Babylon, "Whoever reads this writing, and tells me its interpretation, shall be clothed with purple and have a chain of gold around his neck; and he shall be the third ruler in the kingdom."
8 Now all the king's wise men came, but they could not read the writing, or make known to the king its interpretation. 9 Then King Belshazzar was greatly troubled, his countenance was changed, and his lords were astonished.

—Daniel 5:1–9

The nineteenth-century philosopher G. W. F. Hegel once said that the only thing we learn from history is that we have learned nothing from history. Despite its cynicism, that was the fundamental truth about Belshazzar. He displayed one of the ugliest of sinful traits; he was unteachable.

With dramatic artistry, this record of Belshazzar's last hours reserves to the very end of the chapter the information that his city must already have been under siege when he threw *"a great feast for a thousand of his lords, and drank wine in the presence of the thousand"*

(v. 1). The ancient author Xenophon, who records the taking of Babylon, suggests that the city was magnificently well protected against a siege and had stores of food that would last for years. Belshazzar felt he could take pride in his security. He was doubtless ignorant of Isaiah's words concerning the ultimate humiliation of Babylon. Had he known, there is little likelihood that he would have tempered his arrogance.

> For you have trusted in your wickedness;
> You have said, "No one sees me";
> Your wisdom and your knowledge have warped you;
> And you have said in your heart,
> "I am, and there is no one else besides me."
> Therefore evil shall come upon you;
> You shall not know from where it arises.
> And trouble shall fall upon you;
> You will not be able to put it off.
> And desolation shall come upon you suddenly,
> Which you shall not know.
>
> —*Isaiah 47:10–11*

Belshazzar is perhaps the supreme Old Testament parallel to the rich fool in Jesus' parable. Having already given expression to their lust for more (in the case of the rich fool his lust for more money), they would never be satisfied without more. Blinded by the pursuit of that lust, they were oblivious to the possibility that "'This night your soul will be required of you; then whose will those things be which you have provided?'" (Luke 12:20).

What was the nature of Belshazzar's sin that evoked this shift and final judgment of God? Daniel himself later analyzed it, but already in these opening verses we see its major ingredients. (1) It was a blatant transgression of his responsibilities as a monarch whom God had privileged with high rank in life. This emerges not so much in the size of the feast as in the motive for it and in the manner of his behavior. It was a display of Belshazzar's own inflated ego. He *"drank wine in the presence of the thousand"* (v. 1) seems to mean more than the face value of the words used. It conveys a sense of the theatrical. All eyes are on Belshazzar (which is what he wants), and before the gaze of a thousand pairs of eyes he begins to drink himself under the table as a demonstration of his bravado. He has a pride in the fact that he is a hard drinker, which is as sad to see in an ancient king as it is in any of our contemporaries. In his pathetic display of manliness, Belshazzar has crossed the line of proper restraint in God's world. What follows confirms and develops his sinfulness.

(2) Belshazzar expressed his transgression in specific blasphemy. As he drank, the alcohol began to depress the restraining element in his mental powers. The caged monster of his heart was released. We can almost hear his boastful spirit calling out to some of the servants, doubtless to the horror of some present at the table, "Get those Jewish holy cups here, and we'll drink a toast to those parasites too."

What explanation is there for his action? After all, the Jews posed no threat to him or his empire. There is only one proper explanation. The Jews and their sacred vessels symbolized the presence and power of God. Belshazzar's heart was a factory of rebellion against God. Now he cast off restraint and showed it. What Nebuchadnezzar had not dared to contemplate even in his worst moments, Belshazzar did with apparent equanimity. He knew exactly what these vessels were and from where they had come. He did not sin in ignorance but with knowledge. Paul's words provide the true analysis: "And even as they did not like to retain God in *their* knowledge, God gave them over to a debased mind, to do those things which are not fitting; . . . who, knowing the righteous judgment of God, that those who practice such things are worthy of death, not only do the same but also approve of those who practice them" (Rom. 1:28, 32). Belshazzar sought to mock God, but the lesson of this chapter is "Do not be deceived, God is not mocked; for whatever a man sows, that he will also reap. For he who sows to his flesh will of the flesh reap corruption" (Gal. 6:7–8).

(3) Belshazzar's sinful heart caused spiritual blindness, spiritual deafness, and a pervasive sense of unreality. It was not his drunken state that caused him to lose sight of ultimate reality; he had already done so. Rich as he was and secure in his well-fortified city, he said to his soul, "'Soul, you have many goods laid up for many years; take your ease; eat, drink, *and* be merry'" (Luke 12:19). Suddenly his blindness would be banished by the appearance of writing where he least expected it; his deafness would be dissipated by the voice of God's prophet telling him that on that very night his soul would be required of him. Yet he anticipated neither the judgment of God nor the judgment of others, both of which waited in the wings of the stage on which he now enjoyed the spotlight. "Before destruction the heart of a man is haughty" (Prov. 18:12).

Belshazzar led his company in honoring his idols, *"the gods of gold and silver, bronze and iron, wood and stone"* (v. 4). His revelries, however, were suddenly arrested. On the plaster wall opposite where he sat, he saw the fingers of a man's hand write a series of words that filled him with a deep sense of foreboding.

Palace walls often speak with mute eloquence, covered as they often are with paintings and artifacts of an entire lineage of rulers and their achievements. Such walls characteristically display the royal family's estimation of itself and its judgment of its dynasty. Here, however, an artist who neither possessed nor required any royal patronage depicted His estimation of the king's rule. The melancholy words of Edward Fitzgerald's *The Rubiyat of Omar Khayyam* describe Belshazzar's reign:

Ah, fill the Cup—what boots it to repeat
How time is slipping underneath our Feet:
Unborn To-morrow, and dead Yesterday,
Why fret about them if To-Day be sweet!

The Moving Finger writes; and having writ,
Moves on: nor all thy Piety nor Wit
Shall lure it back to cancel half a Line,
Nor all thy tears wash out a Word of it.

I have never forgotten casually tuning in to a radio program while driving to an out-of-town engagement in Scotland. To my great interest I had happened upon a series of interviews with a number of well-known people, all of them virtually household names. The thrust of the interviews was to discover how they thought of the world to come. I listened mesmerized as each one described what she or he imagined life after death to be like. Almost without exception their view of the world to come was a reflection of their own strongest desires for comfort and pleasure. Without exception as I recall, not one of them even mentioned the presence of God. They wanted a heaven that was Godless. That was the ultimate evidence of their present godlessness. If even only a fraction of the teaching of Scripture is true, they are in for the rudest of awakenings, similar to that which Belshazzar experienced: *"The king's countenance changed, and his thoughts troubled him, so that the joints of his hips were loosened and his knees knocked against each other. The king cried aloud . . ."* (v. 6–7).

What had happened? Belshazzar had been made conscious of the reality of the judgment of God. He may not have fully understood the significance of the words written on the wall, but not even a fool would fail to recognize how ominous they were. He was thrown into a state of apoplexy; the foundations of his life were being shaken; the presence of God brought a state of shock to his whole being.

Were we completely unfamiliar with the sequel to this experience, we might (in the light of the patient dealings of God with Nebuchadnezzar) anticipate that Belshazzar was on the verge of being converted, but that would be a great misunderstanding. Indeed it is always mistaken to imagine that a sense of mental anxiety, accompanied by physical manifestations, is a mark of a true conversion. We do well to remember the wise words of Jonathan Edwards in this connection:

> A work [of God's grace] is not to be judged by any effects on the bodies of men; such as tears, trembling, groans, loud outcries, agonies of body, or the failing of bodily strength. The influence persons are under is not to be judged of one way or other by such effects on the body; and the reason is because the Scripture nowhere gives us any such rule. We cannot conclude that persons are under the influence of the true Spirit because we see such effects upon their bodies, because this is not given as a mark of the true Spirit. . . . It is easily accounted for from the consideration of the nature of divine and eternal things, and the nature of man, and the laws of the union between soul and body, how a right influence, a true and proper sense of things should have such effects on the body . . . such as taking away the bodily strength, or throwing the body into great agonies, and extorting loud outcries. . . . No wonder that the wrath of God, when manifested but a little to the soul, overbears human strength.[2]

The reason we know that Belshazzar's response was natural, indeed carnal, appears in verse 7. In the face of this harbinger of the judgment of God and in view of the circumstances, it is hard to believe that Belshazzar did not realize that it was connected with his blasphemy against the sacred vessels of the God of the Jews. He summoned his pagan counselors, *"the astrologers, the Chaldeans, and the soothsayers."* In desperation he promised them everything he was able to give. He was prepared to offer them anything in exchange for his soul (Mark 8:37). In his own spiritual bankruptcy he turned to the bankrupt wisdom of the world and found it to be empty too: *"All the wise men came, but they could not read the writing, or make known to the king its interpretation"* (v. 8).

We can only speculate why it was that these pagan counselors could not read the writing. It may be that they quite simply could not make sense of what they read and therefore they could not interpret it. Since only the consonants could be written, this is certainly possible. Alternatively, the writing may have taken the form of some kind of ideogram. It is clear that all human resources failed the king. At the end of verse 9 we see him slumped in despair: *"Belshazzar was greatly troubled, his countenance was changed, and his lords were astonished"* (v. 9).

Belshazzar had been found eating and drinking judgment on himself from the sacred vessels of God (1 Cor. 11:29). He was about to hear the first strains of the death march of Babylon that would eventually erupt in the closing chapters of the Bible:

> "Her sins have reached to heaven, and God has remembered her iniquities. Render to her just as she rendered to you, and repay her double according to her works; in the cup which she has mixed, mix double for her. In the measure that she glorified herself and lived luxuriously, in the same measure give her torment and sorrow. . . . For strong is the Lord God who judges her. . . . The fruit that your soul longed for has gone from you, and all the things which are rich and splendid have gone from you, and you shall find them no more at all."
>
> —*Revelation 18:5–7, 8, 14*

"The city of God remains" (Luther). Daniel, the keeper of the city of God, emerges from obscurity and becomes once again the symbol of God's sovereign providence.

WEIGHED IN THE BALANCES OF GOD

10 The queen, because of the words of the king and his lords, came to the banquet hall. The queen spoke, saying, "O king, live forever! Do not let your thoughts trouble you, nor let your countenance change. 11 There is a man in your kingdom in whom is the Spirit of the Holy God. And in the days of your father, light and understanding and wisdom, like the wisdom of the gods, were found in him; and King Nebuchadnezzar your father— your father the king—made him chief of the magicians,

astrologers, Chaldeans, and soothsayers. [12] Inasmuch as an excellent spirit, knowledge, understanding, interpreting dreams, solving riddles, and explaining enigmas were found in this Daniel, whom the king named Belteshazzar, now let Daniel be called, and he will give the interpretation."

[13] Then Daniel was brought in before the king. The king spoke, and said to Daniel, "Are you that Daniel who is one of the captives from Judah, whom my father the king brought from Judah? [14] I have heard of you, that the Spirit of God is in you, and that light and understanding and excellent wisdom are found in you. [15] Now the wise men, the astrologers, have been brought in before me, that they should read this writing and make known to me its interpretation, but they could not give the interpretation of the thing. [16] And I have heard of you, that you can give interpretations and explain enigmas. Now if you can read the writing and make known to me its interpretation, you shall be clothed with purple and have a chain of gold around your neck, and shall be the third ruler in the kingdom."

[17] Then Daniel answered, and said before the king, "Let your gifts be for yourself, and give your rewards to another; yet I will read the writing to the king, and make known to him the interpretation. [18] O king, the Most High God gave Nebuchadnezzar your father a kingdom and majesty, glory and honor. [19] And because of the majesty that He gave him, all peoples, nations, and languages trembled and feared before him. Whomever he wished, he executed; whomever he wished, he kept alive; whomever he wished, he set up; and whomever he wished, he put down. [20] But when his heart was lifted up, and his spirit was hardened in pride, he was deposed from his kingly throne, and they took his glory from him. [21] Then he was driven from the sons of men, his heart was made like the beasts, and his dwelling was with the wild donkeys. They fed him with grass like oxen, and his body was wet with the dew of heaven, till he knew that the Most High God rules in the kingdom of men, and appoints over it whomever He chooses. [22] "But you his son, Belshazzar, have not humbled your heart, although you knew all this. [23] And you have

lifted yourself up against the Lord of heaven. They have brought the vessels of His house before you, and you and your lords, your wives and your concubines, have drunk wine from them. And you have praised the gods of silver and gold, bronze and iron, wood and stone, which do not see or hear or know; and the God who holds your breath in His hand and owns all your ways, you have not glorified. 24 Then the fingers of the hand were sent from Him, and this writing was written.

25 "And this is the inscription that was written:
MENE, MENE, TEKEL, UPHARSIN.

26 This is the interpretation of each word. MENE: God has numbered your kingdom, and finished it; 27 TEKEL: You have been weighed in the balances, and found wanting; 28 PERES: Your kingdom has been divided, and given to the Medes and Persians." 29 Then Belshazzar gave the command, and they clothed Daniel with purple and put a chain of gold around his neck, and made a proclamation concerning him that he should be the third ruler in the kingdom.

30 That very night Belshazzar, king of the Chaldeans, was slain. 31 And Darius the Mede received the kingdom, being about sixty-two years old.

—Daniel 5:10–31

Attracted by the confusion that must have reigned in the palace, and having already heard what had caused it, *"The queen . . . came to the banquet hall"* (v. 10). The eloquent speech she made leads us to believe that it was her good sense that had kept her from the revelries of the evening (which women also attended [vv. 2–3]). Belshazzar might have forgotten Daniel, but the queen had certainly not.

There is some question about the queen's identity. Since we regard Daniel 5 as an authentic prophetic record of the fall of Babylon under Belshazzar, it is probable that we should understand her to be the queen mother. She may even have been the grandmother of Belshazzar. Such members of a royal family often wield great influence simply because of the long-term view they are able to take. Whoever she was, this queen was very familiar with Daniel.

Perhaps we can suggest one possible explanation of this scenario. It seems clear from the sequence of events that Daniel would not have come to the king unless he had been summoned and brought (vv. 12–13). This suggests that whatever continuing role he played, it was acted out in relative obscurity. Perhaps the queen was the only one who continued to trust him as Nebuchadnezzar had.

From all we know of Belshazzar, he had fallen into the sin of Rehoboam. He once sought the advice of his elder statesmen and was counseled: "If you will be a servant to these people today, and serve them, and answer them, and speak good words to them, then they will be your servants forever." Rehoboam rejected this counsel, however, and consulted those who had grown up with him (1 Kin. 12:7–8); the result was the division of the tribes into two camps, Israel to the north and Judah to the south. Similarly, Daniel's counsel appears to have gone unheeded and eventually unsought. Finally, however, he was brought into Belshazzar's presence.

The queen had not forgotten Daniel, nor did she spare Belshazzar the embarrassment of a none-too-hidden tone of disapproval. In verse 11 she hints at the contrast between the behavior of Nebuchadnezzar and that of Belshazzar as though to stress the point that he had failed to learn the family history just as he failed to learn the lessons of history: *"In the days of your father, . . . Nebuchadnezzar your father—your father the king—made [Daniel] chief of the magicians, astrologers, Chaldeans, and soothsayers"* (v. 11). Doubtless the queen feared for the consequences of Belshazzar's open blasphemy; she sensed that this was no time for her to mince words. What is equally striking is that such is her respect for the man of God that she refers to him as *"this Daniel, whom the king named Belteshazzar"* (v. 12). Here clearly was an indication that through long years of faithful witness, Daniel's true identity—determined by God, not by kings—was still known. He possessed that quality and qualification required for all leaders among God's people. He had a "good testimony among those who are outside" (1 Tim. 3:7).

What did this woman observe in Daniel's life that made him distinct from his contemporaries? He had *"an excellent spirit"* (v. 12). She recognized this because he was possessed *by "the Spirit of the Holy God"* (v. 11). In this respect there is a clear parallel between Daniel and Joseph (cf. Gen. 41:38). What is this "excellent spirit"? The word *ruah* is used in various ways in the Old Testament: for wind, for the spirit of life, or for the Spirit of God. Its basic connotation seems to be the idea of wind in motion. It conveys a sense of power. To have a certain kind of spirit implies having a distinctly dominant disposition to one's personality, what we might call a driving force. This was what had undoubtedly impressed the queen about Daniel—there was a distinctive energy or driving force in his life that made him stand out from all others. This force gave a direction and quality to his life energy that she did not detect in others.

This energy is the secret of all spiritual work and the hallmark of all those whom God has used in special ways. It is not a physical energy, although it often manifests itself in the sheer tireless patience and determination God's people have to finish their tasks (cf. Paul's language in Phil. 3:12–14; Col. 1:29). It is not merely outstanding intellectual ability, although it is invariably accompanied by minds that have definite drive.

I have never met or read of a Christian leader of true quality who was not marked in one way or another by this excellent spirit that characterized Daniel. One extraordinary example may readily be encountered in Arnold Dallimore's two-volume biography of eighteenth-century evangelist George Whitefield. One is left breathless just reviewing his schedule. Additionally, he preached constantly while in a physical condition that today would see him regularly hospitalized. Although instrumental in drawing thousands of people to faith in Christ, energized to the end of his days by his desire to serve Christ, he spoke in his later years about the possibility that, at last, he might "begin to be" a Christian.

Daniel was such a man and recognizably so. As we noted, the queen also had some sense that his energy was not natural, but entirely supernatural: *"'There is a man in your kingdom in whom is the Spirit of the Holy God'"* (v. 11).

A glance at the various translations indicates the uncertainty scholars have over the nuance of the queen's affirmation. Rendered as it is by NKJV it might appear to suggest that the queen was a monotheist unlike her fellow subjects (v. 4). No more need be understood, however, than her recognition (and did she not have the evidence to underline it?) that the God whom Daniel worshiped was the Holy God. How did she know this? Nebuchadnezzar had confessed it (cf. 4:8, 9, 18). There was yet a further reason: Daniel's own holiness, so evidently the driving force in his life from his first days in Babylon (cf. 1:8). He was a wonderful illustration of the principle that our God's character is known by others through our own character and lifestyle.

Notice how this Spirit-inspired energy had manifested itself in Daniel's service in Babylon. A lengthy catalog of Daniel's credentials is provided by the queen, perhaps indicating that what is recorded in the Nebuchadnezzar cycle in chapters 1—4 was but part of his great usefulness. He had *"light and understanding and wisdom"* and *"an excellent spirit, knowledge, understanding, [and abilities to interpret] dreams, solv[e] riddles, and explain enigmas"* (vv. 11–12). This description is reminiscent of the prophetic description Isaiah gave of the Messiah:

> The Spirit of the LORD shall rest upon him.
> The Spirit of wisdom and understanding,
> The Spirit of counsel and might,
> The Spirit of knowledge and of the fear of the LORD.
> His delight is in the fear of the LORD,
> And He shall not judge by the sight of His eyes,
> Nor decide by the hearing of His ears.
> —Isaiah 11:2–3

Daniel had a share in the Spirit of the Messiah just as surely as what Christians now experience is a share in the Spirit of the Messiah and a taste of the powers of the age to come (cf. Heb. 6:5). No wonder there were so many ways that Daniel resembled Christ. This was what the queen tried to express. Daniel was in fellowship with another world; he knew God. All this we learn before Daniel appears in this chapter. His reputation goes before him. When he appears in verse 13 our expectations are not disappointed. That in itself presents us with a challenge. Are we all that we are reputed to be?

There may well be a touch of drunken cynicism in Belshazzar's address to Daniel, especially his emphasis on Daniel's origin. He stresses that Daniel is an alien captive, little better than a slave (*"one of the captives"*), and alludes to his old age (*"whom my father the king brought from Judah"*). Nevertheless, Daniel is presented in marked contrast to the men who represent the wisdom of the world: *"they could not . . . I have heard of you, that you can"* (vv. 15–16). This seems to be emphasized by the apparently sharp answer that Daniel gives, refusing the proffered reward yet agreeing to read the writing on the wall and interpret it. Daniel's refusal here is reminiscent of Elisha's response to Naaman, the Syrian leper-general (2 Kin. 5:1–19). It places him in the line of true prophets who are motivated by faithfulness to God and His word and not by the pursuit of material and financial gain. The principle Daniel embraces is of tremendous relevance to the life of the church and especially to those whose calling is to communicate God's Word.

Why did Daniel refuse the king's offer? Probably there were two reasons for his refusal. (1) It was important for him to make plain that spiritual gifts cannot be bought. Instinctively we are reminded of Simon Magus. When he saw "that through the laying on of the apostles' hands the Holy Spirit was given, he offered them money, saying, 'Give me this power also, that anyone on whom I lay hands may receive the Holy Spirit.' But Peter said to him, 'Your money perish with you, because you thought that the gift of God could be purchased with money!'" (Acts 8:18–20). (2) It was important for him to make plain that God's servants cannot be bought. They do not work harder, speak better, or give more pleasing messages for a price. "As we have been approved by God to be entrusted with the gospel, even so we speak, not as pleasing men, but God who tests our hearts. For neither at any time did we use flattering words, as you know, nor a cloak for covetousness—God *is* witness" (1 Thess. 2:4–5).

We need to recover something of that spirit in the Western church today. It is appropriate that those who preach the gospel should live by the gospel; that is a command of the Lord Jesus to the church (1 Cor. 9:11, 14). A congregation is under an obligation to provide for those who labor in God's Word (1 Tim. 5:17–18). It is, however, alarming when either a church believes it can "buy" the blessing of God's Word by the salary it offers or when preachers or teachers believe their ministry of God's Word is unavailable below a certain fixed honorarium (or, for that matter, unless a certain size audience can be guaranteed). Daniel resisted the temptation to "run greedily in the error of Balaam for profit" (Jude 11). It is interesting, in the light of all this, that in the end Daniel did receive the honors that he told Belshazzar to keep for himself or give to another. Perhaps only those who have genuinely refused material gain (not simply because it seems to be the spiritual thing to say) are fit to receive it.

Daniel's address to Belshazzar has a distinct and recognizable form. It resembles the lawsuit (Hebrew, *rib*) or covenant controversy that is elsewhere illustrated in the preaching of the prophets (for example, Hos. 4:1; 12:2; Mic. 6:1–8). In such lawsuits, the people were arraigned before God's judgment for their breach of the covenant. Commentators point out that there is no reference here to the covenant. Daniel, however, addresses Belshazzar as a covenant-breaker. For all people were originally created in a covenant relationship with God; it was first established and broken in Adam (cf. Rom. 5:12–21). All people are covenant-breakers (Rom. 1:31 [KJV]).

Daniel therefore sees Belshazzar's sin as a serious failure to live in the light of the privileges God has given.

First, the historical background to Belshazzar's sin is outlined (vv. 18–21). God had given Nebuchadnezzar his rule and his glory. This had been emphasized to him in different ways during his reign. Moreover, Nebuchadnezzar was Belshazzar's father (that is, not merely a predecessor but a relative). Within his own recent family history God had revealed Himself. Furthermore, God had demonstrated His moral government in Nebuchadnezzar's life. When the king had exalted himself, God had humbled him. His period of lycanthropy (about which Belshazzar must surely have known) had been a divine judgment on *him*—"*till he knew that the Most High God rules in the kingdom of men, and appoints over it whomever He chooses*" (v. 21). Again we may note the parallel with Rehoboam mentioned earlier. The wisdom of Solomon had been his inheritance, and yet he had chosen the folly of his contemporaries. Belshazzar similarly had turned away from the lessons he should have taken to heart. He had been what the Old Testament calls a "fool."

In verses 23–24 Daniel applied to Belshazzar the divine accusation. In these two verses the words "you" and "your" are used fourteen times in a machine-gun-like application of Belshazzar's foolishness. In the light of all he had known, the king had exalted himself against God. He had committed blasphemy; he had been guilty of idolatry. Refusing to worship the *"Most High God"* (v. 21) and the *"Lord of Heaven"* (v. 23), he had shown devotion to man-made gods that were only shaped metal, wood, and stone. He had worshiped powerless idols instead of the true and living God without whose help he could not breathe even breath enough to sin against Him (v. 23).

The third part of the covenant controversy contains the judgment against Belshazzar. In his case it has not been written by human hands, not even by a prophet. God Himself had already delivered His judgment in the writing on the wall. The fingers Belshazzar had seen had been *"sent from Him"* (v. 24), that is, from God Himself. He had been weighed in the balances of God's judgment and found wanting.

The words on the wall appear to represent three different weights. Daniel's interpretation seems to be based on the related verbs: *mene* from the verb "to number," *tekel* from the verb "to weigh or assess," and *peres* (*upharsin* is "and" with the plural form *parsin*) meaning "to part or divide." Daniel realized that God had weighed the kingdom's moral and spiritual levity and had determined that it would be given to the Medes and the Persians.

Belshazzar kept his word. Daniel was indeed *"clothed . . . with purple"* (v. 29). He was exalted to *"be the third ruler in the kingdom"*(v. 29). It may have been a last act of bravado on Belshazzar's part in the face of such sudden judgment. In any event, the party was over. God had spoken the last word on the Babylonian empire. Now Belshazzar too learned *"that the Most High God rules in the kingdom of men, and appoints over it whomever He chooses"* (v. 21). There is no word of the king even seeking an opportunity for repentance. It was too late. Xenophon records that the city was taken during a night festival and that the king was slain.

Daniel expresses it even more strikingly. *"That very night Belshazzar, king of the Chaldeans, was slain"* (v. 30).

> He who is often rebuked, and hardens his neck,
> Will suddenly be destroyed, and that without remedy
> . . . . Scorners delight in their scorning,
> And fools hate knowledge.
> Turn at my rebuke;
> Surely I will pour out my spirit on you;
> I will make my words known to you.
> Because I have called and you refused,
> I have stretched out my hand and no one regarded,
> Because you disdained all my counsel,
> And would have none of my rebuke,
> I also will laugh at your calamity;
> I will mock you when your terror comes.
> —*Proverbs 29:1; 1:22–26*

So it was with Belshazzar. He learned the hard way that God is the Most High. He is sovereign. He rules. The lesson is clear. Lest we "finish our years like a sigh" (Ps. 90:9) as Belshazzar did, let us pray: "So teach us to number our days, that we may gain a heart of wisdom" (Ps. 90:12).

NOTES

1. John Calvin, *Commentaries on the Book of the Prophet Daniel*, tr. Thomas Myers, 2 vols. (Edinburgh: Calvin Translation Society, 1852–53), 1:311.

2. Jonathan Edwards, *Jonathan Edwards on Revival* (Edinburgh: Banner of Truth Trust, 1984), 91.

CHAPTER SIX—IN THE LIONS' DEN
DANIEL 6:1–28

Scripture Outline
Kingdom Against Kingdom (6:1–9)
Faithful Unto Death (6:10–17)
Shut Your Mouth! (6:18–28)

If the name "Daniel" appeared in a word association test, the most common association would probably be "lions' den." Undoubtedly this is the best-known incident in Daniel's life. The way in which the lions' mouths were shut evokes from Darius the final confession of the first half of the book: Daniel's God is the living God whose kingdom will never be destroyed (v. 26). Only by faith in such a God could any man have "stopped the mouths of lions" (Heb. 11:33).

This event took place in the days of "Darius the Mede" (5:31). This in itself is intended to be an indication of the message of the chapter and indeed of the entire book. Another king comes with another kingdom; kingdoms rise and fall but Daniel, the symbol of the kingdom of God, remains. He has seen Nebuchadnezzar and Belshazzar come and go. Now Darius the Mede has arrived, and Daniel is still serving the King of kings.

Darius the Mede has presented major problems to students of the biblical text. Elsewhere in the Old Testament we are given the impression that it was Cyrus the Persian who was the great instrument in God's hand who liberated His people from their Babylonian captivity (Is. 45:1). Additionally, no record of Darius occurs in the historical records of that time. For some scholars, this—coupled with the sheer unbelievability of such a miracle as this chapter describes—is sufficient indication that what we have here is a fictitious narrative intended to bring encouragement to a much later period of Jewish history. This view supposes that two texts have been combined which merge some events of Daniel's days with segments of Darius's later reign (521–486 B.C.). The most obvious problem with this view is that Daniel 5:31ff. and 9:1 give us some detailed information about Darius, but it is not the kind of information one would include were the account wholly fictitious.

At least three alternative views have been offered by recent scholars. One is that we simply do not know who Darius the Mede was, but that should not cause us any anxiety about the reliability of the biblical witness since there are many gaps in our knowledge of ancient history. Darius may have been a regent who ruled Babylon for a short time, but his name did not find its way into the extant records. Another view, held by some scholars following D. J. Wiseman, is that Darius the Mede was Cyrus. We do know that Cyrus was approximately sixty years old at this time, and he was related to the Medes. Furthermore, Darius II is referred to explicitly in Nehemiah 12:22 as "the Persian," and it is argued that this epithet may intentionally distinguish him from Cyrus (also known as Darius the Mede). If this is the case, verse 28 would read (taking exception to "and" as it appears in the NKJV): "So this Daniel prospered in the reign of Darius [that is,] in the reign of Cyrus the Persian." A similar grammatical construction appears at 1 Chronicles 5:26. Another view that has appealed to other scholars is that Darius the Mede is the person known in the historical sources as Gubaru, the son of Ahasuerus. He was appointed governor (that is, "king" in a limited sense) of Babylon by Cyrus and is known to have installed undergovernors in Babylon following its fall (cf. 6:1) and to have exercised virtual regal authority in the absence of Cyrus.

These are, of course, only guesses; Scripture gives us no further information that would enable us to identify Darius with absolute certainty. These other possibilities, however, provide adequate alternatives to the mistaken assumption that Daniel is a compilation of fictional tales. It is a sad reflection on the biblical scholarship of the last century that in matters such as these the Bible has been treated as guilty until proved innocent. This attitude stands in marked contrast to the credibility given to other nonbiblical texts of the same period. We need constantly to remind ourselves that no one comes to Scripture with a mind free from a faith commitment; one will either have faith in Scripture as God's Word or one's attitude will be one of unbelief, rejecting Scripture's testimony to its own reliability. God's Word, like God's kingdom, will remain when all the theories that propose its inaccuracy have crumbled into dust. One is reminded of how a nineteenth-century book that attacked the reliability of Scripture was later pulped and the recycled paper used to print Bibles.

KINGDOM AGAINST KINGDOM

6:1 It pleased Darius to set over the kingdom one hundred and twenty satraps, to be over the whole kingdom; [2] and over these, three governors, of whom Daniel was one, that the satraps might give account to them, so that the king would suffer no loss. [3] Then this Daniel distinguished himself above the governors and satraps, because an excellent spirit was in him; and the king gave thought to setting him over the whole realm. [4] So the governors and satraps sought to find some charge against Daniel concerning the kingdom; but they could find no charge or fault, because he was faithful; nor was there any error or fault found in him. [5] Then these men said, "We shall not find any charge against this Daniel unless we find it against him concerning the law of his God."

[6] So these governors and satraps thronged before the king, and said thus to him: "King Darius, live forever! [7] All the governors of the kingdom, the administrators and satraps, the counselors and advisors, have consulted together to establish a royal statute and to make a firm decree, that whoever petitions any god or man for thirty days, except you, O king, shall be cast into the den of lions. [8] Now, O king, establish the decree and sign the writing, so that it cannot be changed, according to the law of the Medes and Persians, which does not alter." [9] Therefore King Darius signed the written decree.

—*Daniel 6:1–9*

Daniel was one of only three governors promoted over the one hundred twenty satraps appointed by Darius. Two recurring themes now surface in the text. The first of the twin themes is the insecurity of all monarchy. The reason for the appointment of the governors appears to have been a royal concern over deceit and graft: *"So that the king would suffer no loss"* (v. 2). Then as now the trust of public office was used to advance personal interests and to injure the interests of those being "served." From such office holders, *"Daniel distinguished himself"* (v. 3). He was different not only from the satraps but also from the other governors *"because an excellent spirit was in him"* (v. 3). Yet another ruler discovered that the one man he could trust implicitly was the man who served the God of the Jews. Even when others implied that Daniel was not to be trusted because he was "one of the captives of Judah" (v. 13) and therefore liable to lead an insurrection, it was plain to Darius that he could trust Daniel and his judgment more readily than he could trust his own (cf. v. 14). In the midst of graft and corruption on every hand, Daniel stood out as a man governed by a sense of loyalty and integrity that stemmed from his right relationship with God.

The second theme is that of the perpetual conflict of the kingdom of darkness against the kingdom of light, the kingdom of God. On this occasion it has its focus on the laws of these two kingdoms. The unchangeable law of the Medes and the Persians was used by devious men to attempt to overcome the laws of God's kingdom by which the righteous are ultimately vindicated: "'My God sent His angel and shut the lions' mouths . . . because I was found innocent before Him; and also, O king, I have done no wrong before you'" (v. 22).

What are the impressive things noted here about Daniel that mark him as a man of such *"excellent spirit"* (v. 3)? We cannot fail to be impressed that Daniel must now have been somewhere between seventy and eighty years old. His strength and integrity stand in contrast to Darius, a man of roughly the same generation ("about sixty-two years old" [5:31]). For all his considerable worldly wisdom, he was insecure in his exercise of authority and easily duped by the scheming governors and satraps (vv. 4–9).

It has been said that few great men finish well. That was certainly not so in Daniel's case. He epitomizes the words of the psalmist:

> The righteous shall flourish like a palm tree,
>> He shall grow like a cedar in Lebanon.
> Those who are planted in the house of the LORD
> Shall flourish in the courts of our God.
> They shall still bear fruit in old age;
> They shall be fresh and flourishing,
> To declare that the LORD is upright;
> He is my rock, and there is no unrighteousness in
>> Him.
>
> —*Psalm 92:12–15*

Later in the vision in chapter 7 Daniel was to learn of a figure who would "persecute" or literally "wear out" the saints of the Most High (7:25). Certainly the powers of darkness had endeavored to wear out Daniel since the beginning of his captivity by wave upon wave of attacks on his faithfulness to God. One final effort now occurs in this chapter. It serves as a salutary reminder to us that temptations to compromise are never isolated incidents in our spiritual life but are part of a larger strategy of Satan against us.

We see this supremely in Jesus. Satan assaulted Him in the wilderness. When he was repulsed he simply retreated in order to regroup and attack Him again when he could find an opportune time to do so (cf. Luke 4:13). Later Jesus was to refer to the intervening years as a whole as the time of his temptations, indicating that the Evil One had also endeavored to wear Him out by his persistent efforts to compromise Him (Luke 22:28). We cannot afford to be ignorant of these devices (2 Cor. 2:11). Many Christians, mistaking one battle for the whole war, have shielded themselves from one attack but then, assuming the enemy has permanently retreated, let their guard down and been defeated when the enemy comes in like a flood (Is. 59:19).

Daniel's experience runs counter to what we often assume is characteristic of Christian experience. In this respect it is like Christ's. His greatest test came toward the end of His spiritual pilgrimage, not at its beginning. We tend to assume that the great tests in Christian experience occur in its early stages. That perspective fails to see one of the chief functions of temptation in God's plans. He means to strengthen us through our successful resistance, to enable us to meet greater or more persistent tests in the future. God trains His children in the way they should go so that when they are old they will not depart from it (Prov. 22:6). That is the case with all the heroes of the faith whose victories are cataloged in Hebrews 11. Early success in trials strengthened their power to resist. Of course, their lives were not normally straight-line graphs of obedience. Sometimes they stumbled and fell (for example, Abraham). Like Abraham, however, they were "strengthened in faith, giving glory to God" (Rom. 4:20). Satan nevertheless persisted in his endeavors to wear out the saints. He did so with Daniel; he will do so with us too. Like Daniel we must not be taken by surprise.

A further marked feature of this new outbreak of hostility against the kingdom of God is the way in which the guile of the governors and satraps both contrasts with and illuminates the integrity of Daniel's character. It became public knowledge that Darius thought so highly of Daniel that he was contemplating promoting him to the office of prime minister.

In a manner reminiscent of contemporary character assassinations the governors and satraps tried to find some flaw in Daniel's life or work that would disqualify him from this supreme office. Their efforts to disqualify him, however, only underlined his outstanding qualifications for high honor: *"But they could find no charge or fault, because he was faithful; nor was there any error or fault found in him"* (v. 4). In all his relationships he had been faithful; in relationship to the law he had been faultless. Furthermore, in his devotion to the Lord they knew that he was utterly predictable. They realized that the only way to destroy Daniel was by manufacturing a conflict between the *"law of his God"* (v. 5) and the law of their land.

A recent magazine article reports the story of a similarly faithful pastor in Eastern Europe. A "friend" spent some time with him and asked if he would look after a couple of suitcases for him until he returned. Some time later the authorities arrived at his door, searched the cases, and found that they contained "stolen" material. The pastor now faces the possibility of imprisonment. Naturally, details of the situation are sketchy, but notice the similarity of this plot to the experience of Daniel. Satan—and those who work to further his purposes—recognizes that the graces of God's people can be used as leverage to destroy their influence. Just as the unrighteousness of man ultimately serves to show the righteousness of God, so the wicked plots of these evil and jealous men serve only as the dark cloth against which the jewel of Daniel's integrity sparkles.

So these supposed leaders duped Darius. They *"thronged before the king"* (v. 6), doubtless hoping to impress him with numbers rather than with integrity. The scene is reminiscent of the psalmist's description of the opposition to the kingdom of God:

> Why do the nations rage,
> And the people plot a vain thing? . . .
> The rulers take counsel together,
> Against the LORD and against His Anointed, saying,
> "Let us break Their bonds in pieces
> And cast away Their chords from us."
>
> —Psalm 2:1–3

What Herod and Pilate would fulfill in relation to Christ (Acts 4:25–27), the governors and satraps foreshadowed in their opposition to this man whom God had so evidently anointed with the Spirit of wisdom. All their personal jealousies were forgotten in their one great jealousy of Daniel. Doubtless all political party spirit was temporarily put aside as they closed ranks against the servant of God. Perhaps they sensed that his prime ministership would put a serious curb on their own sinfulness.

Notice their guile. First they lied in their presentation of the statistics: "*All the governors of the kingdom, the administrators and satraps, the counselors and advisers, have consulted together*" (v. 7). The "all" was no accidental slip of the tongue. They were fully conscious that the most significant person had been absent from their discussions. The foolish Darius should have had the courage and sense to say: "Wait a minute, what does Daniel have to say about this?" Instead, he was swept off his feet by their second ploy. They knew there was a price that Daniel would not pay for loyalty to the king; he would not set aside his devotion to his God. They knew their man, but they also knew Darius. They knew how to buy his interests: "*Whoever petitions any god or man for thirty days, except you, O king, shall be cast into the den of lions*" (v. 7). How they manipulated him! They assured him of his unique and exclusive position of power, but all the time they were using him as a puppet to fulfill their own wishes. They should not have been trusted for a moment.

We should notice two important lessons from this situation. (1) In the last analysis, opposition to God can never be consistently honest. There will always be an element of deceit because it is based on the principle of self-deceit. It is rooted in the lie that has been exchanged for the truth of God (Rom. 1:25). (2) We should not lose sight of the fact that this conflict in Daniel's life, which is to take him to the den of lions, is the expression of the greater conflict between the kingdoms of darkness and light. Some indication of this is given later in chapters 7—12 and especially in chapter 10. The lion pit into which Daniel will be thrown is only the instrument of the one who goes about like a roaring lion, seeking someone to devour (1 Pet. 5:8).

One of the characteristics of the laws of the Medes and the Persians was that, once made, such laws could not normally be revoked. Similar principles pertained elsewhere in the law codes of the ancient Near East. The famous law code of Hammurabi, for example, legislated that once a judge had pronounced his verdict in a case, he did not possess the power to reverse it. Presumably intoxicated by the apparent honor that his governors were prepared to bestow upon him, Darius fell to the temptation and *"signed the written decree"* (v. 9). He too exchanged the truth of God for the lie. That lie was the first one audibly uttered after the world's creation: "You will be like God" (Gen. 3:5). Now only Daniel stood firm before God, and on that account would be able to stand firm before his fellowmen.

FAITHFUL UNTO DEATH

10 Now when Daniel knew that the writing was signed, he went home. And in his upper room, with his windows open toward Jerusalem, he knelt down on his knees three times that day, and prayed and gave thanks before his God, as was his custom since early days.

11 Then these men assembled and found Daniel praying and making supplication before his God. 12 And they went before the king, and spoke concerning the king's decree: "Have you not signed a decree that every man who petitions any god or man within thirty days, except you, O king, shall be cast into the den of lions?"

The king answered and said, "The thing is true, according to the law of the Medes and Persians, which does not alter."

13 So they answered and said before the king, "That Daniel, who is one of the captives from Judah, does not show due regard for you, O king, or for the decree that you have signed, but makes his petition three times a day."

14 And the king, when he heard these words, was greatly displeased with himself, and set his heart on Daniel to deliver him; and he labored till the going down of the sun to deliver him. 15 Then these men approached the king, and said to the king, "Know, O king, that it is the law of the Medes and Persians that no decree or statute which the king establishes may be changed."

16 So the king gave the command, and they brought Daniel and cast him into the den of lions. But the king spoke, saying to Daniel, "Your God, whom you serve continually, He will deliver you." 17 Then a stone was brought and laid on the mouth of the den, and the king sealed it with his own signet ring and with the signets of his lords, that the purpose concerning Daniel might not be changed.

—Daniel 6:10–17

The forces of hell had assaulted the city of God and from all appearances had succeeded. Daniel was in a "Catch-22" situation. Yet the temptation to compromise was objectively a very great one. It was now the first year of the reign of Darius. Daniel's study of Jeremiah 25 and 29 had convinced him that the day of restoration was near (cf. Dan. 9:2). The seventy-year period that the prophet had described was on the verge of completion. Under such circumstances, did it make sense to lay his life on the line by continuing his practice of daily devotions and intercessions? From a purely human viewpoint such a sacrifice seems utterly pointless. Daniel would lose his life, and he would not live to see the day toward which his whole life had been directed.

Furthermore, Darius's decree had a duration of only thirty days. It was not as though Daniel was asked to deny his faith or worship an idol. The heroics of Shadrach, Meshach, and Abed-Nego might be understandable in the face of blatant idolatry and Nebuchadnezzar's insistence on public worship of his image. Darius's decree, though, made no such demands. It did not command idolatry, it only forbade the making of petitions to God, and that for only one month out of the year, one month out of an entire lifetime. It would not be too cynical to suggest that the presence or absence of such a decree would have made little or no difference to the lifestyle of some of Daniel's fellow exiles who had lost the heart to "sing the LORD's song in a foreign land" (Ps. 137:4).

We may well ask ourselves in this context if it would make any substantial difference in our lives or the lives of our church fellowship if prayer were banned for the next thirty days. Perhaps in many instances the answer would be both embarrassing and startling, for prayer has become a neglected discipline and a forgotten art in many Christian churches. Its centrality is certainly none too obvious. For years a debate has raged across the United States concerning prayer in the public schools and an interpretation of the U.S. Constitution that forbids involuntary prayer in these schools. Many combatants in this controversy are reminded of the days of Darius and Daniel. At the same time we need to ask ourselves if this concern for Christian civil rights and religious freedom has diverted us from an even more crucial issue. Is it not strange that there appears to have been more vociferous protest about this denial of our "right" than there has been prophetic protest about the deadly prayerlessness in our churches or homes? Could it be that Satan does not normally encourage Darius-style legislation in the West because he has no need to do so? Only elsewhere, where Christians have learned to pray like Daniel, where Christians have learned to sing the Lord's song in a foreign land, has that tactic been found necessary.

With equal degrees of wisdom and courage, Daniel saw through the wiles of his adversaries. Protected by the whole armor of God, he stood firm on the evil day for which all his previous tests had been a preparation. He understood that across the years God had graciously prepared him for moments such as this. Rather than view the situation as one in which he could excusably opt out of faithfulness, he saw it as a climax of his faithfulness. Past faithfulness was not meant to be a compensation for present unfaithfulness; it was a preparation for more faithfulness.

The lifestyle of the kingdom of God is contrasted once more with the kingdom of darkness. Daniel's sense of tranquility and rest in the Lord stand against the anxieties and feverish activity of his enemies. At one time they are thronging the king, disguising the truth from him; at another they are gathering at a vantage point from which to trap Daniel; at another they are anxiously maneuvering Darius into fulfilling his decree (cf. vv. 6, 11, 12, 15). Similarly, the picture we are given of Darius is of a man trapped in the power of a situation partly created by his own sin. For all his self-recrimination, his desire to do better, his efforts to change what has been accomplished, Darius is utterly powerless. On the other hand, Daniel alone has peace; he alone has access to the source of all power. He knows God, and he knows how to pray. Such people can never be made captives in any ultimate sense— they are already conquerors. While their fate may appear to be sealed by those who labor to reduce the kingdom of God to abject weakness and regard its principles as utter folly, their lives ultimately demonstrate that the weakness of God is stronger than the strength of men, and the foolishness of God is wiser than the wisdom of men. "God has chosen the foolish things of the world to put to shame the wise, and God has chosen the weak things of the world to put to shame the things which are mighty" (1 Cor. 1:27).

All this can be summarized in one statement about Daniel: He was a man of prayer. Three features of his praying emerge during the plot to end his influence and his life.

(1) It was his custom to pray *"with his windows open toward Jerusalem"* (v. 10). There may have been more than one reason for this. John Calvin suggested that it was simply an aid to prayer, and he made the sensible application: "Let us learn, therefore, when we feel ourselves to be too sluggish and cold in prayer, to

collect all the aids which can arouse our feelings and correct the torpor of which we are conscious."[1] How often Daniel must have echoed the words of Psalms 42 and 43 with their deep longing for the manifestation of God's presence. He may have looked to Jerusalem as a way of reminding himself of God's covenant promises. One of those promises was that God would dwell with His people and make Himself known to them. Through the centuries He had done this in Jerusalem; His holy hill was there. Jerusalem was the visible symbol of the kingdom of God that ultimately would never be destroyed. It was the city to which God would once again bring His people. Through the prophet Isaiah, God had promised a new exodus:

> "Comfort, yes, comfort My people!"
> Says your God.
> "Speak comfort to Jerusalem, and cry out to her,
> That her warfare is ended,
> That her iniquity is pardoned;
> For she has received from the LORD's hand
> Double for all her sins."
>
> —*Isaiah 40:1–2*

Whenever Daniel prayed, he instinctively knelt in the direction of Jerusalem. His mind, his emotions, and his will were focused on the power and the promises of God that were symbolized by that city.

Notice that Daniel's kneeling in the direction of Jerusalem was not a required ritual (there is no suggestion here that prayer must be made in this way or that Daniel encouraged others to follow the specifics of his example), nor was it merely emotional gymnastics. It was an attempt on Daniel's part to focus his attention on God's covenant word, which is the foundation of all true prayer. It reminded him that he was a stranger and an exile in Babylon. His citizenship and loyalties lay elsewhere. Jerusalem was a reminder of that covenant word. Whatever likewise reminds us of God's promises may legitimately be used to stir us to prayer. Are there Scripture passages that in some special way arouse our desire for God's blessing? Are there events in the history of God's people that encourage us to believe that He is a great prayer-hearing and answering God? Are there events that in reflection on our own lives invariably draw out our hearts in praise and petition? Let us use these as Daniel used Jerusalem, to encourage us to faithful and fervent prayer.

(2) Daniel's prayer life was characterized by discipline and regularity. It had been his lifelong custom to pray three times each day. It was well known that he served God *"continually"* (v. 16). There can never be spontaneity in any sphere without discipline. What seems so free and spontaneous in a musician's performance or an athlete's brilliance is always the fruit of hours, days, months, and years of regular discipline and practice. Discipline and regularity are vital keys to success. That is no less true of the spiritual life. It is certainly true of prayer, contrary to what so many people mistakenly assume. It is a fundamental mistake to pray only when one feels like it (otherwise, so this logic follows, it would not be true, spontaneous prayer). Instead the regular habit of prayer underlies spontaneous overflows of prayer. A healthy prayer life follows Daniel's example of regular seasons of prayer. It is this kind of patient commitment to meet with the Lord that bears rich fruit in our lives.

(3) Daniel's praying included both thanksgiving and intercession or supplication (vv. 10–11). His long years of disciplined praying meant that his spiritual focus was not destroyed by the sudden crisis in which he was placed. Yes, he made fervent supplication. The situation was critical. His cries for help, however, were prefaced by worship, adoration, and appreciation of his God. He *"gave thanks before his God, as was his custom since early days"* (v. 10).

One would give a great deal to know the content of this prayer. Although in chapter 9 we do have an extended illustration of Daniel's praying, there he came to God in confession. We can only guess the nature of his prayers of thanksgiving. No doubt they were nourished on the Psalms. It is tempting to think that Daniel would have turned to Psalm 92, "A Song for the Sabbath Day," to nourish his soul in those days of separation from Jerusalem and its temple worship. Already in this chapter we have seen the degree to which he exemplified that psalm's closing words. Did he not, in a time of great crisis, come in thanksgiving to God because he remembered that "It is a good thing to give thanks to the LORD" (Ps. 92:1)? Certainly the following psalm would have been especially appropriate to his situation.

> O LORD, how great are Your works!
> Your thoughts are very deep.
> A senseless man does not know,
> Nor does a fool understand this.
> When the wicked spring up like grass,
> And when all the workers of iniquity flourish,

It is that they may be destroyed forever.
But You, LORD, are on high forevermore.
For behold, Your enemies, O LORD,
For behold, Your enemies shall perish;
All the workers of iniquity shall be scattered.
But my horn You have exalted like a wild ox;
I have been anointed with fresh oil.

—Psalm 92:5–10

Did this theme form the burden of his supplication as well (v. 11)? These words sometimes appear to us as vindictive, but we need to set them in their proper context. Those who persecuted the psalmist and those who persecuted Daniel were the sworn enemies of the kingdom of God. They were not engaging in harmless pranks in the case of Daniel. They were deliberately and viciously seeking to destroy him because he was the Lord's anointed. With him they hoped to obliterate all trace of the kingdom of God. This was the hand of the kingdom of darkness seeking to annihilate the kingdom of God. No doubt, then, Daniel prayed that the kingdom of God would remain intact in whatever way God might choose to accomplish that. He also knew that the only way this could happen would involve the destruction of its enemies. In this respect, his petitions were early echoes of the final judgment on Babylon and on all for which it stood:

> Her sins have reached to heaven, and God has remembered her iniquities. Render to her just as she rendered to you, and repay her double according to her works; in the cup which she has mixed, mix double for her. In the measure that she glorified herself and lived luxuriously, in the same measure give her torment and sorrow. . . . Her plagues will come in one day—death and mourning and famine. And she will be utterly burned with fire, for strong is the Lord God who judges her.
>
> *—Revelation 18:5–8*

If we have no stomach for this, we appreciate far too little the severity of our sin in rebellion against the kingdom of God.

Daniel's fate was sealed by his adversaries: *"a stone was brought and laid on the mouth of the den, and the king sealed it with his own signet ring and with the signets of his lords, that the purpose concerning Daniel might not be changed"* (v. 17). The narrative bears an uncanny resemblance to an event centuries later when a greater conspiracy took place against another innocent who was declared guilty and condemned to death (Matt. 26:59–60). Jesus' tomb was also sealed as a preventive measure by his opponents: "On the next day . . . the chief priests and Pharisees gathered together to Pilate, saying, 'Sir, we remember, while he was still alive, how that deceiver [cf. "one of the captives" in Dan. 6:13] said, "After three days I will rise." Therefore command that the tomb be made secure. . . .' So they went and made the tomb secure, sealing the stone and setting the guard" (Matt. 27:62–66). Their efforts to prevent the Resurrection were in vain—just as were the efforts of the governors and satraps of Babylon to prevent the "resurrection" of Daniel from the den of lions. Work done for the kingdom of God, however, is never in vain in the Lord (1 Cor. 15:58).

SHUT YOUR MOUTH!

18 Now the king went to his palace and spent the night fasting; and no musicians were brought before him. Also his sleep went from him. 19 Then the king arose very early in the morning and went in haste to the den of lions. 20 And when he came to the den, he cried out with a lamenting voice to Daniel. The king spoke, saying to Daniel, "Daniel, servant of the living God, has your God, whom you serve continually, been able to deliver you from the lions?"

21 Then Daniel said to the king, "O king, live forever! 22 My God sent His angel and shut the lions' mouths, so that they have not hurt me, because I was found innocent before Him; and also, O king, I have done no wrong before you."

23 Now the king was exceedingly glad for him, and commanded that they should take Daniel up out of the den. So Daniel was taken up out of the den, and no injury whatever was found on him, because he believed in his God.

24 And the king gave the command, and they brought those men who had accused Daniel, and they cast them into the den of lions—them, their children, and their wives; and the lions overpowered them, and broke all their bones in pieces before they ever came to the bottom of the den.

25 Then King Darius wrote:

To all peoples, nations, and languages that dwell in all the earth:

Peace be multiplied to you.

26 I make a decree that in every dominion of my kingdom men must tremble and fear before the God of
Daniel.

For He is the living God,
And steadfast forever;
His kingdom is the one which shall not be destroyed,
And His dominion shall endure to the end.

27 He delivers and rescues,
And He works signs and wonders
In heaven and on earth,
Who has delivered Daniel from the power of the lions.

28 So this Daniel prospered in the reign of Darius and
in the reign of Cyrus the Persian.

—Daniel 6:18–28

Poor Darius. He goes without food, entertainment, and sleep.
He is powerless to help and driven to despair. His helplessness suggests to us that it is better to be a child of faith in a den of lions
than a king in a palace without faith. Early in the morning he vis-
its the den, obviously expecting it to have become a tomb. With
a *"lamenting voice"* (v. 20) he calls out: *"'Has your God . . . been able
to deliver you from the lions?'"* (v. 20). To his amazement the answer
is a resounding "Yes!" Daniel has been delivered. His faith has shut
the mouths of the lions (Heb. 11:33). In answer to his prayers, the
angel of God had delivered him. His righteousness was vindicated
by divine intervention.

It is not surprising that the early church saw in this event a foretaste of the resurrection of Christ. Daniel's life story is intended to
illustrate in Old Testament terms the meaning of faith in the promised Messiah. It means being conformed to His image. Through
Daniel's experience God gave hints of what would occur when
Christ came to deal with the powers of darkness. By exposing Himself to the power of death, He conquered all His and our enemies.

Daniel experienced nothing less than the powers of the age to
come (Heb. 6:5). In the Old Testament, the destructive power of lions
metaphorically expressed the disharmony and chaos of the universe.
In the promised age, the chaos of creation will be restored to order
and harmony so that all the creatures of nature will live together in
peace (Is. 11:6–7). Thus Daniel's deliverance in the lions' den is a
foretaste of that promised universal renovation. This is a clue to understanding all the Old Testament miracles. In order to preserve His

kingdom in times of special crisis, God brings the power of the fulfilled kingdom to the time of adversity. That is why (as in 3:27) Daniel's deliverance is so wonderfully complete: *"No injury whatever was found on him, because he believed in his God"* (v. 23). The power of God that ensured that not a bone of Christ's body was broken guarded Daniel, too, in order that he would be a powerful testimony to the coming Savior. A servant of God is immortal until his work has been completed.

In a fallen and sinful world there is a somber side to the salvation of God's people. The deliverance of Eve's seed is always accompanied by the bruising of the head of the serpent (Gen. 3:15). Christ delivers those who were subject to a lifelong fear of death by destroying the one who had the power of death (Heb. 2:14–15). The dark side to Daniel's deliverance is the judgment that falls on those who had sought to destroy the kingdom of God. They and their entire families, even wives and children, were cast into the den of lions and immediately attacked and devoured. Herodotus informs us that such punishment of entire families was meted out according to Persian law. It was a terrible end. Their gods were unable to deliver them from the lions, whereas Daniel's God had delivered him. The One who was in Daniel was stronger than the one who was in the world (cf. 1 John 4:4).

The closing verses of this chapter provide an appropriate climax to the first section of the book as well as to the miracle of Daniel's deliverance. Darius, whatever his ultimate spiritual condition, confessed the supreme authority of *"the God of Daniel"* (v. 25).

By bitter experience Darius had learned vital lessons about the character and activity of Daniel's God. He is the "living God" in contrast to the dumb idols of the nations. He is a "steadfast" God who keeps His promises to His people because He cares for them. His kingdom is indestructible and "shall endure to the end," unlike the kingdoms and empires that men build. The kingdom of God "cannot be shaken" (Heb. 12:28). Daniel's God is a saving God. Under His hand Daniel continued to prosper (v. 28). The lyrics of Martin Luther's dynamic Reformation hymn give voice to this notion:

> A mighty fortress is our God,
> A bulwark never failing;
> Our helper He, amid the flood
> Of mortal ills prevailing:
> For still our ancient foe
> Doth seek to work us woe;

His craft and power are great,
And, armed with cruel hate,
On earth is not his equal.

Did we in our own strength confide,
Our striving would be losing;
Were not the right Man on our side,
The Man of God's own choosing:
Dost ask who that may be?
Christ Jesus, it is He;
Lord Sabaoth, His name,
From age to age the same,
And He must win the battle.

And tho' this world, with devils filled,
Should threaten to undo us,
We will not fear, for God hath willed
His truth to triumph through us.
The Prince of Darkness grim,
We tremble not for him;
His rage we can endure,
For lo, his doom is sure,
One little word shall fell him.

That word above all earthly powers,
No thanks to them, abideth;
The Spirit and the gifts are ours
Thro' Him who with us sideth;
Let goods and kindred go,
This mortal life also;
The body they may kill:
God's truth abideth still,
His kingdom is forever.[2]

NOTES

1.   John Calvin, *Commentaries on the Book of the Prophet Daniel,* tr. Thomas Myers, 2 vols. (Edinburgh: Calvin Translation Society, 1852–53), 1:361.

2.   Martin Luther, "A Mighty Fortress Is Our God" (1521), tr. Frederick H. Hedge (1853).

CHAPTER SEVEN—APOCALYPSE!
DANIEL 7:1-28

Scripture Outline
   Jungle Book (7:1–8)
   The Vision of God (7:9–14)
   The Everlasting Kingdom (7:15–28)

Chapter 7 is at one and the same time perhaps the most exhilarating and the most puzzling of all the chapters in this remarkable book. It is also, in a variety of ways, the central chapter. The seventh chapter introduces the second half of Daniel, but it does so in a way that links the two sections. It takes us back in time from the point reached at the end of chapter 6. Once again we are in the reign of Belshazzar, prior to the night of the feast that is the background for chapter 5. Furthermore, as we saw before, the Aramaic section of the book concludes not at the end of chapter 6 (the close of the historical section) but at the end of chapter 7. Whatever else this may be intended to signify, it serves the function of linking the two different sections. It indicates that there is an important connection between them that the reader should not ignore.

What is this connection? There seems to be an obvious relationship between Daniel's vision in this chapter and Nebuchadnezzar's dream in chapter 2. In both cases there is a fourfold progression of the kingdoms of this world; in both cases God establishes His kingdom in a dramatic fashion. Can it be that in chapters 2 and 7 the same revelation is being given through different means, for different purposes, and perhaps with slightly different messages to the recipients? In Nebuchadnezzar's dream the focus is on the power of the various kingdoms that are eventually overpowered by the kingdom of God. In Daniel's vision the focus is on the depravity of the various kingdoms that are outlasted by the righteous kingdom of God. What we seem to be given in the latter half of Daniel is divine insight into the ultimate significance and implications of the events of history. Here we learn that the events of history are not isolated from events beyond history. The conflict with the people of God is an expression of an older, deeper, more sinister conflict between the powers of darkness, the spiritual hosts of wickedness (Eph. 6:12), and the throne of God and His kingdom.

This is not a unique pattern in Scripture. It reappears in the Book of Revelation where ever-clearer insights are given into the perpetual conflict between Babylon and Jerusalem. Already the kingdoms of the world have become the kingdom of the Lord (Rev. 11:15). The beginning of Revelation 12 describes more fully the nature of the conflict and the reasons for such a glorious victory. A similar pattern can be detected in the Book of Daniel. This is the central lesson we ought to take from chapter 7. Yet much energy and attention have been devoted to tracking down the identity of the ten horns and the little horn (vv. 7–8) and to investigating other minutiae of interpretation. Such study should not be downplayed (after all, even Daniel seems to have a special interest in the fourth beast, the ten horns, and the little horn [vv. 19–20]). It is possible, however, to miss the woods for the trees and fail to see that this chapter was first written to help those who were incapable of dogmatically identifying these symbols. Whatever our own identification may be, we surely miss a basic thrust of this part of God's Word if we regard our task as finished when we have solved the identification problem. We could conceivably do that (at least to our own satisfaction) and fail to hear what God is really saying to His people through this chapter.

If the Lord had simply wanted Daniel to know the facts of history ahead of time, why did He give him such a complex, curious, multicolored, sense-appealing revelation? To ask the question is to answer it. God not only revealed facts about history in advance; He revealed Himself to Daniel, impressing on him something of His own awesome and glorious purposes. Miss this and we miss almost everything.

We have already hinted that, like Revelation, Daniel is essentially a book of pictures, appealing to our senses. We are meant to see, hear, and smell the strange beasts that appear throughout this chapter. We are meant to be overwhelmed as Daniel was by the revelation of the Ancient of Days and the coming of the Son of Man. We do well to remember the wise words that G. K. Chesterton wrote in a child's picture book:

Stand up, and keep your childishness,
Read all the pedant's creeds and strictures
But don't believe in anything
That can't be told in colored pictures!

This is why the visual dominates Daniel's record: "I saw" (vv. 2, 7); "I watched" (vv. 4, 9, 11); "I looked" (v. 6); "I was considering" (v. 8); "I was watching" (vv. 13, 21). It is surely tragic if we read this chapter or hear it expounded and show only a myopic interest in the identification of a few details rather than experience Daniel's vision: "I was grieved in my spirit within my body, and the visions . . . troubled me . . . my thoughts greatly troubled me, and my countenance changed" (vv. 15, 28). This section of God's Word is not meant to be an amusement for armchair theological sleuths. It is intended to give an overwhelming impression of the mysteries of God's purposes and the awful conflict that lies behind and beneath history. Here is true apocalyptic. Our depravity is unveiled, and the curtain that hides the glory of God is momentarily drawn back. We are given a brief look into the throne room of the universe and the sovereignty of God.

Verses 1–8 describe Daniel's vision of four beasts or empires. The centerpiece (vv. 9–14) records his vision of the throne of God and the One like the Son of Man. Verses 15–28 note the interpretation of these scenes.

JUNGLE BOOK

7:1 In the first year of Belshazzar king of Babylon, Daniel had a dream and visions of his head while on his bed. Then he wrote down the dream, telling the main facts.

² Daniel spoke, saying, "I saw in my vision by night, and behold, the four winds of heaven were stirring up the Great Sea. ³ And four great beasts came up from the sea, each different from the other. ⁴ The first was like a lion, and had eagle's wings. I watched till its wings were plucked off; and it was lifted up from the earth and made to stand on two feet like a man, and a man's heart was given to it.

⁵ "And suddenly another beast, a second, like a bear. It was raised up on one side, and had three ribs in its mouth between its teeth. And they said thus to it: 'Arise, devour much flesh!'

6 "After this I looked, and there was another, like a leopard, which had on its back four wings of a bird. The beast also had four heads, and dominion was given to it.

7 "After this I saw in the night visions, and behold, a fourth beast, dreadful and terrible, exceedingly strong. It had huge iron teeth; it was devouring, breaking in pieces, and trampling the residue with its feet. It was different from all the beasts that were before it, and it had ten horns. 8 I was considering the horns, and there was another horn, a little one, coming up among them, before whom three of the first horns were plucked out by the roots. And there, in this horn, were eyes like the eyes of a man, and a mouth speaking pompous words.

—Daniel 7:1–8

With great care the opening verse of this chapter dates the events that it describes. Knowing what we do from the earlier chapters, that dating takes on special significance. It seems highly likely, in view of Daniel's long familiarity with the royal court (cf. 1:21), that he knew quite well the kind of man Belshazzar was and the kind of ruler he would prove to be. Under those circumstances he no doubt feared for the stability of Babylon and, perhaps, for the people of God. Since the time was also drawing near in which God had promised to restore His people to Jerusalem, we can imagine the mixture of expectation and apprehension that filled Daniel's heart. Now, however, God was going to set his expectations in a deeper and broader context. He would give Daniel a panoramic vision of the world empires. For all their power, majesty, and brutality, they would simply form the background against which the glorious kingdom of God would be inaugurated and later fully and finally established. The summary of this vision dominates chapter 7. Daniel *"wrote down the dream, telling the main facts"* (v. 1).

We have already stressed the central importance in studying Daniel's vision of doing what he did, that is, watching the scenes that unfold (vv. 2, 6, 7, 8, 9, 11, 13, 21). We should note that Daniel's narrative employs a style of communication that has become a classic movie technique: One scene fills the screen and begins to fade as the next scene takes its place. Thus a whole series of impressions is made upon the mind of the viewer.

The vision begins with a picture of universal chaos. *"The four winds of heaven were stirring up the Great Sea"* (v. 2). The "Great Sea" is a picture of the world in its godlessness and instability. The significance of the phrase "of heaven" is intriguing. Is there a hint here that not even the chaos caused by the emergence of the kingdoms of this world is outside the sovereign control of God as He rules history in His sovereign providence? That would be in keeping with the opening words of the book, which reminded us that "the Lord gave Jehoiakim king of Judah into [Nebuchadnezzar's] hand" (1:2). For all the apparent chaos, it is always the Lord who "removes kings and raises up kings" (2:21). This is an awe-inspiring and yet comforting truth to learn. When it must have seemed to Daniel that Babylon was reaching a crisis point, he was reminded of this truth. Nothing is accidental in God's world.

A quick succession of scenes follows in which four beasts hold center stage, or so it seems. There are hints that these beasts—clearly four empires—do not possess autonomous power. The descriptions of the first three hint that they do not hold ultimate sovereignty: The lion *"was lifted up . . . and made to stand; . . . a man's heart was given to it"* (v. 4); the bearlike creature was given a command to *"Arise, devour much flesh!"* (v. 5); and the leopard-like creature was given *"dominion"* (v. 6). Only the fourth creature, the one understood to be the most terrible of the beasts, gives no immediate sign of dependence. Perhaps this is what is meant by the enigmatic statement, *"It was different from all the beasts that were before it"* (v. 7). We have to wait for verses 21–22 for the final bestial kingdom to be overthrown by sovereign, divine intervention.

Of course the question is: Who are these strange beasts? An answer, however, may need to be built in stages, beginning with the elements on which interpreters have reached general agreement.

Obviously these beasts represent kingdoms or empires. We are told that "Those great beasts, which are four, *are* four kings *which* arise out of the earth" (v. 17). It has been common throughout the ages for animals to be used to represent nations or empires. Even in our time, the eagle and the bear have been used as symbols for the U.S. and Russia. We generally understand that superpowers are represented by beasts of prey. It would indeed seem strange if a superpower were represented by an animal perceived to symbolize peace and gentleness. Instead of the eagle, would not the average American be embarrassed had his forefathers accepted Benjamin Franklin's urging that the harmless turkey should be the symbol of the nation? Perhaps that says something about how easily the spirit of nationalism can become a sinister power.

There are four beasts just as there were four parts to the image that Nebuchadnezzar had seen in his dream in chapter 2. Because of the connection between chapters 2 and 7 (that is, they are the first and last chapters of the Aramaic section), it seems likely that the beasts should be representative of the same empires. Some commentators delineate the figures as follows: the lion as symbolic of Babylon, the bear as Medo-Persia, the leopard as Greece, and the fourth beast as Rome. An alternative view is that the four successive empires are Babylon, Media, Persia, and Greece. This interpretation has been held by some who were quite uninfluenced by the presuppositions of contemporary scholarship—that it was written in the second century B.C., that its contents are nonhistorical, and that its purpose was to speak to the days of Antiochus Epiphanes (who is identified as the little horn of vv. 8, 11, 20, and 21). Similar views have been held by some who have not shared the critical presuppositions. John Calvin, while rejecting this interpretation, nonetheless conceded that the identification of the little horn with Antiochus Epiphanes was plausible. If this interpretation is correct, then it would follow that the basic application of Daniel 7 would lie in the second century B.C. From the New Testament point of view, however, the coming of the Son of Man (v. 13) and the events associated with His coming are fulfilled only through Christ. It is necessary, therefore, to see the fourth empire as (in one sense or another—evangelical commentators differ greatly) stretching into the time of Christ's advent.

The first beast, like the head of gold in Nebuchadnezzar's dream, has a certain preeminence. It *was like a lion and had eagle's wings"* (v. 4), a combination of two creatures, each magnificent in its own right. It is significant that Nebuchadnezzar was compared by Jeremiah and Ezekiel to both the lion and the eagle:

> The lion has come up from his thicket,
> And the destroyer of nations is on his way.
> He has gone forth from his place
> To make your land desolate.
> Your cities will be laid waste,
> Without inhabitant.
>
> —*Jeremiah 4:7; cf. 49:19; 50:44*

> 'Thus says the Lord GOD:
> "A great eagle with large wings and long pinions,
> Full of feathers of various colors,
> Came to Lebanon
> And took from the cedar the highest branch.

> He cropped off its topmost young twig
> And carried it to a land of trade;
> He set it in a city of merchants. . . ."Moreover the
> word of the LORD came to me, saying, "Say now to the
> rebellious house: 'Do you not know what these things
> mean?' Tell them, 'Indeed the king of Babylon went to
> Jerusalem and took its king and princes, and led them
> with him to Babylon.'"
>
> —*Ezekiel 17:3, 11–12*

Yet such power is not autonomous, as the prophets made clear and as Daniel is about to witness. The wings of the eagle are *"plucked off"* before Daniel's astonished eyes; the mighty lion is *"lifted up from the earth and made to stand . . . like a man"* (v. 4). The great beast is reduced in size by some invisible, but not unfamiliar, hand. It is unclear whether the beast's reception of *"a man's heart"* refers directly to Nebuchadnezzar's restoration (4:34–37) or to the comparatively humane elements in the Babylonian Empire (for example, Nebuchadnezzar's vast building program). The first view seems the more likely.

None of this was new to Daniel. He was already living in the era depicted by the lion with eagle's wings. Indeed that era was soon to close. Why, then, did God show him what he already knew to be true? Perhaps the vision begins here to encourage Daniel to believe that what follows was no less God-given and reliable than what he had already experienced from God. He certainly would need such assurance, because the unfolding vision was to leave him grieved, greatly troubled, and crestfallen (vv. 15, 28).

Without warning Daniel began to see *"another beast, a second, like a bear"* (v. 5). It appeared "suddenly"—possibly an intimation of the swift judgment that was to fall on Belshazzar (*ch. 5*). Three things about the bear caught Daniel's attention. The first was that *"It was raised up on one side."* Exactly what this signifies is not clear. Some commentators suggest that the bear was stirring itself from a lying position in preparation for action; others suggest that this symbolizes the imbalance of power in the Medo-Persian Empire; and others suggest that "side" might better be translated as "end" so that Daniel saw the bear standing on its hind legs. This last view certainly pictures the bear in a common position. It would also suggest that the vision of the first beast gave way rather naturally (from a visual perspective) to that of the second, that is, both picture beasts in a quasi-human position.

The bear has *"three ribs in its mouth"*; already it has begun to destroy. There is, however, a third feature: Voices command the bear to *"Arise, devour much flesh."* The detail here of three ribs should not be pressed further. It is merely an indication of the savage power of the lust for empire-building. The voice serves as a further reminder that in the mystery of His will, God sometimes gives kingdoms to "the lowest of men" (Dan. 4:17) who flout His commands of justice and mercy. While we noted a similarity in structure between Nebuchadnezzar's dream and Daniel's vision, it is clear that there are significant differences. Nebuchadnezzar was impressed by the pursuit of power; Daniel was alarmed by the lust for power and glory in all its brutality. He is left under no illusion about the so-called glory that was Babylon, Medo-Persia, Greece, and Rome.

The third empire is represented by *"a leopard, which had on its back four wings of a bird. The beast also had four heads"* (v. 6). Again we are reminded of the complete sovereignty of God— "dominion was given to it." Here "four" (as in the "four winds" of v. 2) appears to suggest the idea of universality rather than specific historic details (such as the four divisions of the Hellenistic Empire following the death of Alexander the Great). The symbolism—a leopard, an animal of lethal swiftness and power—is only too appropriate as representative of the advance of the Greek Empire. Later, in chapter 8, Alexander is also represented by a ram, but that should pose no difficulty for the student of Scripture. Symbols are not the realities they represent, and in different visions the same reality may be depicted by different but equally appropriate symbols. A map of Alexander's conquests—achieved in the same life span as that of Jesus—is enough to take one's breath away. Alexander was indeed a leopard with the wings of a bird. His lust to be ruler of the world is legendary. Daniel, however, was given a perspective on his life that is not to be found in the historical record of the fourth century B.C. According to Daniel, not even Alexander achieved his ambition in his own strength—dominion was given to him by God.

The final beast to rise is the most terrible of all. There is something unique about it: *"It was different from all the beasts that were before it"* (v. 7). Unlike the first three, it is not likened to any creature or combination of creatures. Daniel describes it first in general terms: *"dreadful and terrible, exceedingly strong."* Then he draws attention to its *"iron teeth"* and the way it devoured, broke in pieces, and then trampled whatever was left under its feet. Here is orderly, monotonous, ruthless expansion. It was said of the Roman Empire, "They make a desert and call it 'peace.'" If what Daniel here envisions is Rome, the description is altogether appropriate.

Ten horns appeared on this monster (v. 8). Suddenly Daniel's gaze was drawn to *"another horn, a little one, coming up among them."* Three of the original ten horns were *"plucked out"* before it. We are probably not intended to trace specific identifications for these numbers. Ten could be a symbol of completeness here. Three, in this instance, could represent a sizable segment. What fascinates Daniel, however, is the little horn. It has *"eyes like the eyes of a man, and a mouth speaking pompous words."* For all its inordinate power, this horn represents an individual; for all its real humanity, it is dominated by pride and self-glory. Nothing is said at this point about the sovereign will of God in relation to this beast or to the enigmatic little horn. Here it seems that we encounter autonomous humanity. The outcome is certain to be a cataclysmic conflict with the sovereign God. Then, dramatically, the scene changes once again. We have seen an unfinished portrait, and—as we shall see—there is a powerful, important, but unspoken message in this too.

THE VISION OF GOD

9 "I watched till thrones were put in place,
And the Ancient of Days was seated;
His garment was white as snow,
And the hair of His head was like pure wool.
His throne was a fiery flame,
Its wheels a burning fire;
10 A fiery stream issued
And came forth from before Him.
A thousand thousands ministered to Him;
Ten thousand times ten thousand stood before Him.
The court was seated,
And the books were opened.
11 "I watched then because of the sound of the
pompous words which the horn was speaking; I watched
till the beast was slain, and its body destroyed and given
to the burning flame. 12 As for the rest of the beasts, they
had their dominion taken away, yet their lives were prolonged for a season and a time.
13 "I was watching in the night visions,
And behold, One like the Son of Man,

Coming with the clouds of heaven!
He came to the Ancient of Days,
And they brought Him near before Him.
14 Then to Him was given dominion and glory and a
     kingdom,
That all peoples, nations, and languages should serve
     Him.
His dominion is an everlasting dominion,
Which shall not pass away,
And His kingdom the one
Which shall not be destroyed.

—Daniel 7:9–14

As one part of the vision faded into another, Daniel stood and *"watched"* (v. 9). Three scenes followed in rapid succession.

The first contrasts strongly with the confusion and noise of the opening scene (v. 2). Here, as in the Book of Revelation, all is calm and orderly in the presence of God (cf. Rev. 4:6 where the sea is as calm as glass in God's presence and the four creatures are devoted to worship). The heavenly court was assembled, and God sat in judgment. In contrast to the hectic and often demoniacally inspired activity of the earthly kingdoms, God sits on the universal throne. The little kingdoms have their day; however, God is *"the Ancient of Days."* The kingdoms rise and fall, but Daniel sees a God whose ways are everlasting. His plans stretch into eternity whereas the plans of a Nebuchadnezzar or an Alexander or a Caesar are ephemeral.

God wears a garment *"white as snow "*—He has never compromised His righteous dealings in establishing His kingdom, as humans have in gaining their kingdoms. Human kingdoms are always caught up in feverish activity, military or diplomatic, but *"the Ancient of Days was seated."* He is never taken by surprise, never undecided, never in a panic about His world. He reigns. In the face of the terrible havoc that people are able to cause, Daniel is reminded that ultimate authority does not reside in Babylon, Persia, Greece, or Rome. It is in the hands of God. It is Isaiah's age-old lesson that Daniel is to learn and we with him: "You will keep him in perfect peace, whose mind is stayed on You, because he trusts in You. Trust in the Lord forever. . . For He brings down those who dwell on high" (Is. 26:3–5). Ultimate power is not centered in Washington, D.C., or London or Beijing or Moscow. It lies in the hands of God.

There is even more to this vision of God than His sovereign tranquility. There is the element of judgment. God's throne is ablaze and from it flows a stream of flame. This is the imagery of divine judgment; compare it with the psalm:

> Our God shall come, and shall not keep silent;
> A fire shall devour before Him,
> And it shall be very tempestuous all around Him.
> He shall call to the heavens from above,
> And to the earth, that He may judge His people.
>
> —*Psalm 50:3–4*

In Daniel's vision the judgment of the divine court will go in favor of the saints of God. It will mean the destruction of the powers of darkness and of the kingdoms of this world order. All this is intimated when *"The court was seated, and the books were opened"* (v. 10).

Daniel is also given an overwhelming picture of the triumph of God: *"A thousand thousands ministered to Him; ten thousand times ten thousand stood before Him"* (v. 10). In a new way, Daniel, who had so often dared to stand alone, must have realized, "I am not alone." Myriads of others served the Lord with him. He was an earthly outpost of the heavenly garrison. He was learning some of the implications of Paul's later words, "Seek those things which are above, where Christ is, sitting at the right hand of God. Set your mind on things above, not on things on the earth. For you have died, and your life is hidden with Christ in God. When Christ who is our life appears, then you also will appear with Him in glory" (Col. 3:1–4).

Christians who have this vision of God and His throne will never feel alone and isolated. They will find their point of orientation not on earth but in heaven (Phil. 3:20–21). Their perspective on history will not arise from below (that is, from "the Great Sea" of v. 2) but from above, from the throne of God. Others may claim to see things realistically rather than idealistically; Christians, on the other hand, will try to gain God's perspective in order to see them as they really are.

A missionary returning to the United States, in the days when all overseas travel was by ship, found himself arriving in New York Harbor on the same vessel as an acclaimed national figure. Crowds waited on the quay to greet this person. The missionary could not help but feel the contrast. He had been laboring for the treasure that does not perish, pouring his life's blood into sowing the seed of the gospel. As he scanned the faces on the dock, he realized that no one had come to welcome him "home." As he began to submerge in a wave of self-pity he realized the truth as clearly as if a voice had spoken to him from heaven: "Do not be discouraged; you have not yet reached home." This was a new perspective for Daniel, too. It is the perspective to which we are all exhorted:

> You have come to Mount Zion and to the city of the living God, the heavenly Jerusalem, to an innumerable company of angels, to the general assembly and church of the firstborn who are registered in heaven, to God the Judge of all, to the spirits of just men made perfect, to Jesus the Mediator of the new covenant, and to the blood of sprinkling that speaks better things than that of Abel.
>
> —*Hebrews 12:22–24*

If we succeed in absorbing the impact of the vision of the Ancient of Days, what follows will seem the less surprising; indeed, it possesses a certain inevitability. Daniel's attention is drawn back from heaven to earth *"because of the sound of the pompous words which the horn was speaking"* (v. 11). What did he see? He briefly describes the death of the beast and the destruction of its body. It is an amazing anticlimax, but it is intended to be so. True world dominion belongs exclusively to God; all others who seek it will be cut short in their path. The other beasts lose their dominion although their days are prolonged in some sense *"for a season and a time,"* presumably meaning an extended period that continues but is brought definitely to an end. The books that were opened (v. 10) are closed. God sets things in final order.

The picture changes again, and a third element of the second part of Daniel's vision now unfolds. It brings us to one of the peaks of Old Testament revelation. Daniel sees *"One like the Son of Man, coming with the clouds of heaven"* (v. 13). This figure comes to the Ancient of Days and receives dominion from Him. Verse 14 describes His dominion as glorious (*"to Him was given dominion and glory"*), universal (*"That all peoples, nations, and languages should serve Him"*), and everlasting (*"His dominion is an everlasting dominion, which shall not pass away, and His kingdom the one which shall not be destroyed"*; notice the threefold statement).

These two verses are weighted with theological nuances, and it is important for us to recognize them. The expression "Son of

Man" appears to be the virtual equivalent of "man," but when "One like the Son of Man" appears, the title has particular rather than general significance. This is True Man in contrast to the man-become-beast in the earlier elements in the vision. This is the one who is able to stand in the presence of the God whose throne is made of the fire of His judgment. This is the one who is worthy to receive *"dominion and glory and a kingdom, that all peoples, nations, and languages should serve Him. His dominion is an everlasting dominion"* (v. 14). This True Man is all that humans as God's image were meant to be but failed to be.

Adam was made to rule as God's vice-gerent and obediently exercise his God-given dominion (Gen. 1:26–28). He sinned, lost his dominion, and fell short of God's glory (Rom. 8:23). Since then, we have sought rapaciously to recover that lost dominion without letting go of our sin. When the Son of Man came, however, He became the servant Adam had failed to be; He reflected the glory of God in His obedience to Him. He has consequently been highly exalted. Another messianic promise has been fulfilled in Him: "Ask of Me, and I will give You the nations for Your inheritance" (Ps. 2:8).

When we remember that just before He was taken up in the clouds to the throne of God Jesus said, "All authority has been given to Me in heaven and on earth" (Matt. 28:18), we are left in no doubt as to the identity of this One like the Son of Man in Daniel. It is all the more significant that this title is used in the New Testament almost exclusively by Jesus in referring to Himself. What has been true of no other kingdom—certainly not the Babylonian, Medo-Persian, Greek, or Roman empires—is true of His: it is *"an everlasting dominion,"* it *"shall not pass away,"* it *"shall not be destroyed."*

> His large and great dominion shall
> From sea to sea extend:
> It from the river shall reach forth
> Unto earth's utmost end.
>
> Yea, all the mighty kings on earth
> Before him down shall fall;
> And all the nations of the world
> Do service to him shall.
>
> His Name for ever shall endure;

Last like the sun it shall:
Men shall be blest in him, and blest
All nations shall him call.
—*Psalm 72:8, 11, 17 (Scottish Paraphrases)*[1]

THE EVERLASTING KINGDOM

[15] "I, Daniel, was grieved in my spirit within my body, and the visions of my head troubled me. [16] I came near to one of those who stood by, and asked him the truth of all this. So he told me and made known to me the interpretation of these things: [17] 'Those great beasts, which are four, are four kings which arise out of the earth. [18] But the saints of the Most High shall receive the kingdom, and possess the kingdom forever, even forever and ever.'

[19] "Then I wished to know the truth about the fourth beast, which was different from all the others, exceedingly dreadful, with its teeth of iron and its nails of bronze, which devoured, broke in pieces, and trampled the residue with its feet; [20] and the ten horns that were on its head, and the other horn which came up, before which three fell, namely, that horn which had eyes and a mouth which spoke pompous words, whose appearance was greater than his fellows.

[21] "I was watching; and the same horn was making war against the saints, and prevailing against them, [22] until the Ancient of Days came, and a judgment was made in favor of the saints of the Most High, and the time came for the saints to possess the kingdom.

[23] "Thus he said:
'The fourth beast shall be
A fourth kingdom on earth,
Which shall be different from all other kingdoms,
And shall devour the whole earth,
Trample it and break it in pieces.
[24] The ten horns are ten kings
Who shall arise from this kingdom.
And another shall rise after them;
He shall be different from the first ones,
And shall subdue three kings.

²⁵ He shall speak pompous words against the Most
High,
> Shall persecute the saints of the Most High,
> And shall intend to change times and law.
> Then the saints shall be given into his hand
> For a time and times and half a time.
²⁶ 'But the court shall be seated,
> And they shall take away his dominion,
> To consume and destroy it forever.
²⁷ Then the kingdom and dominion,
> And the greatness of the kingdoms under the whole
heaven,
> Shall be given to the people, the saints of the Most
High.
> His kingdom is an everlasting kingdom,
> And all dominions shall serve and obey Him.'
²⁸ "This is the end of the account. As for me, Daniel,
my thoughts greatly troubled me, and my countenance
changed; but I kept the matter in my heart."

—Daniel 7:15–28

Daniel was deeply disturbed by all that he saw. In his vision,
he approached *"one of those who stood by"* (v. 16) seeking an explanation of the things he had seen. The clues he was given (and we
through him) have governed our own exposition to this point.
"Those great beasts . . . are four kings" (v. 17). To this, however, is
added, *"But the saints of the Most High shall receive the kingdom and
possess the kingdom forever, even forever and ever"* (v. 18). Particularly
intriguing here is that "the saints of the Most High" have not as
yet been mentioned in Daniel's vision. To whom, then, do these
words refer? The most satisfactory answer is that the One like the
Son of Man is related in some special way to "the saints of the
Most High" so that they share in His dominion.

The correctness of this view is underlined by the way in which
the One like the Son of Man here appears to be all that Adam
failed to be. Adam was a historical individual according to
Scripture, but he was also an individual whose actions carried
unique consequences for others. Paul expounds this in great detail
(Rom. 5:12–21; 1 Cor. 15:47ff.). In and through Adam's fall, sin
and death came to all who followed. His actions had consequences for a whole species. So, too, with the One like the Son of
Man. His conquest means that all those who belong to Him share

in the victory. This teaching is also examined in Hebrews (Heb. 2:5–18). Taking up the words of Psalm 2 that all things are under human dominion (cf. Gen. 1:28), the author reflects on the contrast between the promise and the reality. We do not yet see everything in subjection to ourselves, but, says Hebrews, "We see Jesus, who was made a little lower than the angels, for the suffering of death crowned with glory and honor, that He, by the grace of God, might taste death for everyone" (Heb. 2:9). This is what Daniel perceived so vividly, if puzzlingly, in chapter 7. The coronation of the One like the Son of Man is the assurance that those who belong to Him will share in His dominion (cf. Rev. 20:6).

Daniel, however, like Elijah, was "a man with a nature like ours" (James 5:17). He confesses, *"Then I wished to know the truth about the fourth beast . . . and the ten horns . . . and the other horn . . . namely, that horn which had eyes and a mouth which spoke pompous words, whose appearance was greater than his fellows"* (vv. 19–20). He also justifies his concern, one which has not yet been mentioned in the vision: *"the same horn was making war against the saints, and prevailing against them"* (v. 21). The victory of God's people is not in doubt, *"a judgment was made in favor of the saints of the Most High, and the time came for the saints to possess the kingdom"* (v. 22). Daniel is, however, a realist. The assurance of ultimate victory does not blind him to the travail and anguish that many of the people of God will suffer under the persecution of the little horn. This concern for the people of God in an age other than his own is deeply impressive. It must have been obvious to him that he himself would not live to see these events. We shall see again, before the book is concluded, that this catholic concern for the kingdom of God in another place and time was characteristic of the spirit of his latter years. It is one of the finest evidences of a truly God-centered, kingdom-dominated life.

What does Daniel learn about the little horn and its conflict with the people of God? Daniel's interpreter explains in verses 23–27. In brief he paints a sobering picture of a kingdom of immense power and influence that conquers the whole earth, destroying everything that stands in the way of its goal of world dominion (v. 23). From this empire ten kings (the ten horns) arise. We have already suggested that the number ten here should be taken generally rather than identified particularly. Unlike the four great beasts of verse 8, no specific point is made about any of the ten horns or even the three horns that suffer defeat. Much study of this section has been based on the assumption that these ten horns are to be identified.

Thus, for example, concern was expressed about the entry of the United Kingdom into the European Economic Community (the Common Market) because this would bring the membership to ten nations. The fear was that such an event might be the fulfillment of Daniel's vision.

Such anticipations of fulfillment of the details of visionary teaching may be fundamentally mistaken. It would be like looking for exact doctrinal equivalents to the father's kiss, the robe, the ring, and the fatted calf in the Parable of the Prodigal Son, or for the donkey, the innkeeper, and the coins in the Parable of the Good Samaritan. This is to fail to grasp the genre of the passage whose details do not have one-to-one equivalents. Where details of the symbolism of the vision are not given further weight, the symbolism probably has general significance. Where that symbolism is underscored and elaborated (for example, the four beasts, the little horn, etc.), then it is fitting that we pursue the matter further. It is clear from Daniel's questions and the interpreter's carefully weighed answer that this is true here.

Ten horns grew out of the beast. If the beast represents the Roman Empire, then the ten horns are best taken as the continuation of the spirit that was so powerfully expressed in that empire. The little horn arises in this context and engages in hostile activity against three of the horns.

Earlier Protestant commentators often saw a reflection of the little horn in the power of the papacy. Calvin, on the other hand, saw its fulfillment in the Roman Empire itself. In Daniel's vision, however, the little horn represents the final consummation of evil. It belongs to the final days. Therefore, it ought not be given a specific identification in any historical figure. Notice, however, that the little horn emerges in the context of the beast and the ten horns. It should not surprise us that there will be continual expressions of the characteristics of the little horn that will reach their apex in appearances of the little horn in the last days as described in Daniel's conclusion. Nevertheless, it is not surprising that many dictators and empire-builders have been identified with the little horn and have shared some of its worst features. We have been told that the Antichrist will come in the final days, but that does not preclude our recognizing that many antichrists have already strutted across the pages of history (1 John 2:18).

What are the characteristics of the little horn? In verse 25 Daniel mentions three which appear in all antichrists and will be revealed fully in the final one. The little horn:

1. *"shall speak pompous words against the Most High";*
2. *"shall persecute the saints of the Most High";*
3. *"shall intend to change times and the law."*

As a result, the people of God will suffer under its influence for *"a time and times and half a time"* (v. 25). Students of this chapter have attempted to pinpoint this length of time, usually concluding that it should be understood as three and a half years. This is as unnecessary as was the determination that Nebuchadnezzar's mania (which was to span seven times [2:16, 23, 25, 32]) lasted seven years. The little horn's dominion is taken away by the judgment of God (v. 26), and God's people reign.

The charges against the little horn are blasphemy, persecution of the church, and some form of self-deification. God alone "changes the times and the seasons" (Dan. 2:21). The little horn even seeks to subvert the law and thus transform society into a godless mass (v. 25). It is a picture of blatant and sinister opposition to God and His rule of the world. His influence will last *"for a time,"* then it will strengthen and be consolidated for *"times."* Just when one would expect its ever-increasing power to reach its zenith, it will be destroyed and survive only for *"half a time."* The Ancient of Days will bring its activity to a halt by His righteous decree.

Who or what is this little horn? To those who identify the fourth monarchy with Greece and set the writing of Daniel in the second century B.C., there can be only one answer: Antiochus Epiphanes. Those who see the final kingdom as the Roman Empire and its successors are likely to provide numerous answers. Calvin saw the little horn in terms of the persecuting Caesars and the giving of the kingdom to the saints of the Most High (v. 27) taking place at the end of that period. Others have concentrated their interpretation on the rise of the papacy. Some see the era of the ten horns stretching from the past into the future. In this case, the little horn represents the final antichrist, the man of sin. This is the view adopted here.

One variation of this view sees a gap between the ancient Roman Empire and a revived Roman Empire on the ground that the ten horns must represent ten contemporaneous rulers, a situation not found in ancient Rome. It is further argued that the kingdom is given to the One like the Son of Man when the little horn is destroyed. This must refer to the coming millennial kingdom of Christ. Thus the beast of Daniel 7 is linked with the beast of Revelation 17 which also had ten horns (Rev. 17:12). Even within this framework, an abundance of nuances exists.

All this can be extremely confusing. We must therefore ask one or two questions. Are there any statements in the Book of Daniel that give us controls on our interpretation of this vision? Are there practical applications of his vision that help us to do what Daniel himself did—sing the Lord's song in a strange land?

Several factors arise. (1) The overarching concern of this chapter is to focus our attention on the age-long conflict between two kingdoms: the kingdom of God and the kingdoms of this world. Just when Daniel is anticipating the deliverance of the kingdom of God from its oppression in the form of the return from exile, he learns an important lesson: This conflict is endemic to world history until the end. Rather than decrease, it will be perpetuated until it reaches its zenith in the ferocious blasphemies of the little horn.

(2) Daniel sees two things: (a) the first is the throne room of God, the Lord and judge of all the earth. This enables him to face the perpetual conflict in the knowledge that the Lord reigns. The ultimate issue in the conflict is not in doubt. God has already issued His decree of judgment. Furthermore, he sees (b) the destruction of the beast. This appears to be linked with the Son of Man coming to the Ancient of Days with the clouds of heaven to receive His kingdom. This is not the final return of the Son of Man but His approach to the Ancient of Days to receive His kingdom. In all likelihood this should be seen as fulfilled in the death, resurrection, ascension, and coronation of the Son of Man—an event publicized on the day of Pentecost by the outpouring of His Spirit (Acts 2:33–36). In this way the kingdom of God is extended. Our Lord claimed at the time of His Ascension that all dominion in heaven and earth was already His; the apostles were to make that a reality by the preaching of the gospel (Matt. 28:18–20). Here, as in Nebuchadnezzar's dream, the God of heaven sets up His kingdom among us in time and not just at the end of time.

(3) Although the beast is destroyed, all that it represented appears to live on in the ten horns and to reach a climax in the little horn (which was *"making war against the saints, and prevailing against them"* [v. 21]). It exercises this power for a *"time,"* and then consolidates it with increased authority for *"times."* Suddenly it is cut down by the Ancient of Days who executes judgment *"in favor of the saints"* (v. 22). The kingdom is thus given to the saints in verse 27.

We have a picture of the entire history of the Christian church. Just as the character of the beast reaches its apex in the little horn (although the beast itself is slain), so the kingdom of God will reach its climax in the destruction of the Antichrist (even though the kingdom of God has already been established by the Son of Man). Then the kingdom of God will fill the whole earth, just as Nebuchadnezzar had seen (2:35). The kingdoms of this world will become the kingdom of our God and of His Christ, and He will reign forever, sharing His rule with His saints. Throughout the chapter, kingdom wars against kingdom until one kingdom finally conquers and becomes the one and only kingdom in the world—the everlasting kingdom of God.

(4) It is perhaps a mistake for us to see verses 9–10, 10–12, and 13–14 as pointing to successive events. Rather, they are three aspects of one event, the outworking of which is not necessarily limited to a single point in time. The sovereign judgment of God on the empires and their successors, the establishing of the kingdom of Christ, and the ultimate destruction of the little horn have all been put in motion. We are now in the last days because Christ has already established His kingdom. Judgment has already been made in favor of the saints, in Christ, and they already experience the kingdom (cf. Rom. 5:1; 8:1; Matt. 5:8, 10). The best interpretation of this passage views the courtroom scene of verses 9–10 as an illumination into God's sure and sovereign judgment of evil: the destruction of the beast and the rise of the ten horns as events stretching over the years, the centuries, the millennia (for the symbols represent empires, not merely individuals). The *consequence* of the first scene and the *cause* of the second is the *content* of the third: the fact that the Son of Man has accomplished all that is necessary to establish His kingdom.

What are the implications for us of this strange vision? (1) The people of God must never be naive about the reality, strength, or durability of evil. Daniel's sense of horror and his resulting concern for God's people are an example to us all. We may live in a day and a place where life is relatively tranquil for Christians. Do we remember to pray for those who know evil's full force? Are we concerned, as Daniel clearly was, for the saints of God in the future who will face such trials? If this vision does not produce a like spirit in us, we have not really understood its message. (2) The people of God must learn that the kingdom of God is a kingdom of suffering. The forces of hell will not prevail against it, but they will do all in their limited power to overwhelm the saints. Suffering of one kind or another is integral to being a Christian (Rom. 8:16–17). That thought may devastate us, but if we learn to accept it, it may also stabilize us. (3) Our gaze must always penetrate beyond the terrible events of history to the throne of God. Only in the assurance that He reigns will we be able to live triumphantly when we cannot trace or understand His plan of victory. (4) Our great hope as the people of God does not lie in the centers of world power. Our aim is not to build the kingdoms of this world but to share in the triumph of Christ. He has already established His everlasting kingdom among men. He reigns now. All kingdoms that stand against His have been judged in the courtroom of God and are destined to fail. Even the little horn cannot overthrow His rule.

We live in the age when we already reign in Christ. Such is the opposition to His reign, however, that often His splendor and ours may be hidden (Col. 3:3). When the little horn appears to wear out the people of God, the reign of Christ will not have high visibility. The little horn does not reign; Jesus Christ is Lord and His saints reign with Him until the day when they will reign publicly and finally. That was Daniel's vision. As Daniel thought of what the people of God would suffer in the centuries after his own death, he was deeply concerned. If we are not, we have missed the point of the vision.

NOTE

1. Douglas J. Maclagan, *Scottish Paraphrases: Being the Translations and Paraphrases in Verse of Several Passages of Sacred Scripture* (Edinburgh: A. Elliot, 1889).

CHAPTER EIGHT—THE RAM, THE GOAT, AND THE LITTLE HORN

DANIEL 8:1-27

Scripture Outline

The Ram with Two Horns (8:1–4, 15–20)

The Goat with the Horn Between His Eyes (8:5–8, 21–22)

The Little Horn (8:9–14, 23–27)

During Belshazzar's reign God enlarged Daniel's understanding of the nature of reality and historical development. Daniel had seen himself all along as an exile from Jerusalem and an alien in Babylon. Both God's Word and his own experience had taught him that there could be no negotiation between the kingdom of God and the kingdoms of the world. We may well imagine then that Daniel's great hope was in the prospect of restoration. God had promised that through Isaiah. Daniel must also have wrestled with the promise God gave through Jeremiah; namely, that the period of exile would last for only seventy years. Yet even during Belshazzar's reign Daniel found his spiritual horizons transformed and the borders of his spiritual concerns widened. He discovered that the conflict in which he was involved as a citizen of God's kingdom would stretch throughout the ages and reach heights of severity and depths of depravity of which he could not have dreamed.

Chapter 7 introduced us to this new dimension, and chapter 8 is directly linked with it. Daniel notes that although his second vision was two years later, it clearly reminded him of *the one that appeared to me the first time* (v. 1). In this second vision, Daniel sees himself on the banks of the River Ulai—he is in Susa (*Shusan*[v. 2]), the capital of Persia. No explanation is given for the location, but this setting in Persia sets the stage for the power struggle that unfolds throughout the chapter. Verses 3–14 recall the content of Daniel's vision; verses 15–27 record the interpretation of it given by Gabriel. Hence, the most convenient way to study the chapter is by taking content and interpretation together. Three figures participate in the drama.

THE RAM WITH TWO HORNS

8:1 In the third year of the reign of King Belshazzar a vision appeared to me—to me, Daniel—after the one that appeared to me the first time. ² I saw in the vision, and it so happened while I was looking, that I was in Shushan, the citadel, which is in the province of Elam; and I saw in the vision that I was by the River Ulai. ³ Then I lifted my eyes and saw, and there, standing beside the river, was a ram which had two horns, and the two horns were high; but one was higher than the other, and the higher one came up last. ⁴ I saw the ram pushing westward, northward, and southward, so that no animal could withstand him; nor was there any that could deliver from his hand, but he did according to his will and became great.

¹⁵ Then it happened, when I, Daniel, had seen the vision and was seeking the meaning, that suddenly there stood before me one having the appearance of a man. ¹⁶ And I heard a man's voice between the banks of the Ulai, who called, and said, "Gabriel, make this man understand the vision." ¹⁷ So he came near where I stood, and when he came I was afraid and fell on my face; but he said to me, "Understand, son of man, that the vision refers to the time of the end."

¹⁸ Now, as he was speaking with me, I was in a deep sleep with my face to the ground; but he touched me, and stood me upright. ¹⁹ And he said, "Look, I am making known to you what shall happen in the latter time of the indignation; for at the appointed time the end shall be. ²⁰ The ram which you saw, having the two horns—they are the kings of Media and Persia.

—Daniel 8:1-4, 15–20

As Daniel's gaze came into focus he saw a two-horned ram. Its horns grew up, one after the other. The second one grew taller than the first. The identity of the ram is revealed in verse 20: *"the ram which you saw, having the two horns—they are the kings of Media and Persia."* The second, higher horn, represents the Persian kingdom, perhaps expressing the same idea as the bear raised on one side (Dan. 7:5). Indeed, there is some evidence that the ram was sometimes used in the ancient world to depict the Persian Empire.

Daniel saw the ram butting its way *"westward, northward, and southward . . . no animal could withstand him . . . he did according to his will and became great"* (v. 4). Its conquest was all-embracing and irresistible. The Persian Empire was to spread to Babylonia, Syria, and Asia Minor in the west, to Armenia and the area of the Caspian Sea in the north, and into Africa in the south.

In all likelihood it is the authoritative interpretation of this vision that helps to explain the boldness of Daniel's words to Belshazzar on the last day of his reign (Dan. 5:17–28). For some time before that day Daniel had already known (at least in general terms) that the Babylonian Empire would collapse. The writing on the wall was simply an indication to him of the divine timing. He was not taken by surprise. He spoke boldly because he knew that his God was ruling over the affairs of the world.

This is one of the secrets of singing the Lord's song in a strange land (Ps. 137:4). We do not know the details of individual biographies nor God's exact plan for the future, but we do know that neither biography nor history is governed by individuals alone or by chance. We know that God will bring history to a conclusion. It has direction and purpose that is fully revealed in Christ. With such confidence, we can speak boldly and plainly to the darkness and confusion of our times. We do not know everything, but we know something that those apart from God do not know or understand: God rules history in righteousness. We are not surprised by God's judgments.

THE GOAT WITH THE HORN BETWEEN HIS EYES

5 And as I was considering, suddenly a male goat
came from the west, across the surface of the whole earth,
without touching the ground; and the goat had a notable
horn between his eyes. 6 Then he came to the ram that
had two horns, which I had seen standing beside the
river, and ran at him with furious power. 7 And I saw him
confronting the ram; he was moved with rage against
him, attacked the ram, and broke his two horns. There
was no power in the ram to withstand him, but he cast

him down to the ground and trampled him; and there was no one that could deliver the ram from his hand. 8 Therefore the male goat grew very great; but when he became strong, the large horn was broken, and in place of it four notable ones came up toward the four winds of heaven.

21 And the male goat is the kingdom of Greece. The large horn that is between its eyes is the first king. 22 As for the broken horn and the four that stood up in its place, four kingdoms shall arise out of that nation, but not with its power.

—Daniel 8:5–8, 21–22

As Daniel observed the ram another animal came into view—a goat. It *"came from the west across the surface of the whole earth, without touching the ground"* (v. 5). This second beast obviously represented an empire achieving tremendous expansion swiftly. It is, Gabriel reveals, *"the kingdom of Greece"* (v. 21). The *"notable horn"* is a clear reference to Alexander the Great. The vision describes the totality and speed of his conquest of the nations prior to his early and debauched death at the age of thirty-three. A general of the Greek army at twenty-one, he had virtually conquered the world by the age of twenty-six.

In his vision Daniel witnessed the confrontation between the ram and the goat. The goat *"ran at [the ram] with furious power. . . . There was no power in the ram to withstand him"* (vv. 6–7). Nothing could more eloquently summarize the overwhelming defeat Alexander visited upon the Persian forces in a battle at the Granicus River in 334 B.C. With only thirty-five thousand men, Alexander's forces plunged through the river attacking Darius's one hundred thousand footmen and ten thousand horsemen, reportedly killing twenty thousand at a loss of only one hundred Greek troops. Complete victory was assured at the battles of Issus the following year and at Guagamela in 331 B.C.

The *"large horn was broken"* (v. 8), however, suddenly and unexpectedly. Alexander's empire was divided into four regions (cf. v. 22: *"four kingdoms shall arise out of that nation, but not with its power"*), although it is possible that the expression *"four notable ones came up toward the four winds of heaven"* (v. 8) indicates simply that the empire was fragmented (as we might say, "to the four winds").

Of these four kingdoms, one takes center stage in Daniel's vision. It is the "little horn which grew exceedingly great toward the south, toward the east, and toward the Glorious Land" (v. 9). The little horn not only takes a position of prominence; it becomes the centerpiece of the vision, and its activity is described in great detail. Clearly this little horn represents the climax of the revelation.

Why should this kingdom—which confessedly does not have the power of Alexander's empire (v. 22)—be given top billing instead of Alexander? Is there not a distortion of history here? No. What we have here is history viewed from a particular point of view (in the last analysis, of course, there is no other history). World events and people's lives are always researched and understood from a particular perspective. The point of view envisaged here is God's. What is significant about the little horn is that it turns "toward the Glorious Land," that is, the land of God's covenant people.

This understanding of history focuses the judgment of God on one issue: How did that nation respond to My chosen people? Jesus intimates that this will be the perspective of the final judgment of the nations (Matt. 25:31–46). Alexander proved to be a confused and evil man, but the little horn here is singled out because its evil is directed with demonic hatred against the people of God and all that they represent. Who is the little horn?

THE LITTLE HORN

9 And out of one of them came a little horn which grew exceedingly great toward the south, toward the east, and toward the Glorious Land. 10 And it grew up to the host of heaven; and it cast down some of the host and some of the stars to the ground, and trampled them. 11 He even exalted himself as high as the Prince of the host; and by him the daily sacrifices were taken away, and the place of His sanctuary was cast down. 12 Because of transgression, an army was given over to the horn to oppose the daily sacrifices; and he cast truth down to the ground. He did all this and prospered.

13 Then I heard a holy one speaking; and another holy one said to that certain one who was speaking, "How long will the vision be, concerning the daily sacrifices and the transgression of desolation, the giving of both the sanctuary and the host to be trampled underfoot?"

14 And he said to me, "For two thousand three hundred days; then the sanctuary shall be cleansed."

23 "And in the latter time of their kingdom,
When the transgressors have reached their fullness,
A king shall arise,
Having fierce features,
Who understands sinister schemes.
24 His power shall be mighty, but not by his own power;
He shall destroy fearfully,
And shall prosper and thrive;
He shall destroy the mighty, and also the holy people.
25 "Through his cunning
He shall cause deceit to prosper under his rule;
And he shall exalt himself in his heart.
He shall destroy many in their prosperity.
He shall even rise against the Prince of princes;
But he shall be broken without human means.
26 "And the vision of the evenings and mornings
Which was told is true;
Therefore seal up the vision,
For it refers to many days in the future."
27 And I, Daniel, fainted and was sick for days; afterward I arose and went about the king's business. I was astonished by the vision, but no one understood it.

—Daniel 8:9–14, 23–27

We have already noted in connection with chapter 7 that the little horn that emerged from the fourth beast is not identical with the little horn that emerges out of the fragmented empire of the goat. The former appears to represent the final antichrist; the latter clearly represents antiochus Epiphanes. One of the four horns (or divisions) of the Alexandrian Empire was that of Syria, which was governed by one of Alexander's generals, Seleucus Nicantor, progenitor of the Seleucid dynasty. Antiochus Epiphanes emerged within this dynasty bearing all the demonic characteristics of the little horn of Daniel's vision.

It may well be that there is some significance in the common designation of a little horn for Antiochus Epiphanes and the antichrist. The final antichrist will not appear on the scene of world history without predecessors. Its personal characteristics have long been shared by others who may be seen as the "many antichrists" who have already appeared (cf. 1 John 2:18). Later in Daniel reference is made to the "abomination of desolation"(11:31, cf. 9:27). This refers in the first instance to an activity of Antiochus Epiphanes, but that activity is the embryonic form of an evil that all antichrists perpetrate in one form or another. Hence Jesus uses the expression in Mark 13:14, and further allusions to it appear in the New Testament's teachings on the last things.

What then of Antiochus? He came to power in 175 B.C., succeeding his brother, Seleucus Philopater. He was in fact Antiochus IV. Epiphanes was a blasphemous title he arrogated to himself later in his reign—Theos Antiochus Epiphanes, meaning "The Illustrious God"—although others called him Epimanes, meaning "the Madman."

Power hungry, Antiochus sought to expand his dominion to include Palestine. This brought him into conflict with the Ptolemaic dynasty in Egypt. In Jerusalem he replaced the high priest with a man of his own choosing. He then invaded Egypt, and while there a rumor of his death circulated among the Jews (much to their joy). Efforts were made to reinstate the genuine high priest. Antiochus accused the people of rebellion, savagely attacked and sacked Jerusalem, and executed tens of thousands of its inhabitants—forty thousand apparently dying within the space of three days—while others were taken captive. He entered the holy of holies in the temple, sacrificed a pig on the altar of burnt offering, defiled the temple precincts, took the sacred furniture, and established a traitor, Menelaus, as high priest.

In 168 B.C., when Antiochus's efforts to take Egypt were foiled by the Romans, he again vented his revenge on the Jews. More than twenty thousand of his soldiers massacred the Jews assembled for worship on a Sabbath day and committed further atrocities and vandalism. The temple was left without the daily sacrifices, religious practices were nonexistent, and a statue of Zeus was placed in the temple and human sacrifices were made on the altar. Circumcision was forbidden, unclean meat was mandatory fare, and the Sabbath and other feast days were profaned. The psalmist describes a similar (but perhaps less awful) situation:

> O God, the nations have come into Your inheri-
>   tance;
> Your holy temple they have defiled;
> They have laid Jerusalem in heaps.
> The dead bodies of Your servants
> They have given as food for the birds of the heavens,
> The flesh of Your saints to the beasts of the earth.

Their blood they have shed like water all around
   Jerusalem,
And there was no one to bury them.
We have become a reproach to our neighbors,
A scorn and derision to those who are around us.
                                             —*Psalm 79:1–4*

It was in this context that Judas Maccabeus and his followers began their nationalist exploits. Antiochus Epiphanes died under mysterious circumstances while returning from Persia. He contracted an exceedingly painful disease, which according to the account of 1 Maccabees was accompanied by deep and unmitigated psychological anguish.

Daniel's vision of the little horn is a prophetic anticipation of these events. He saw that it *"grew up to the host of heaven"*; that is, it rivaled other kings and overcame them. It *"cast down some of the host and some of the stars to the ground, and trampled them"* (v. 10). Daniel saw that the horn attacked the Glorious Land (v. 9, cf. Jer. 3:19 and Ezek. 20:6, 14) and blasphemed the name of the Lord as though he were God himself (*Theos* Antiochus Epiphanes). He saw the horn bringing the daily sacrifices to an end and desecrating the temple and the truth of God (vv. 11–12). Yet *"he prospered"* (v. 12). Daniel learned that this was to be a lengthy persecution. As one eavesdropping on a great secret, Daniel overheard two heavenly beings discussing *"how long"* this terrible evil would last. It would endure for *"two thousand three hundred days"* (v. 14), and only then would the temple be restored. As the NKJV footnote suggests, the Hebrew here is literally "two thousand three hundred evening-mornings." This of course may indicate "days"; another possibility is that it refers to the evening and morning sacrifices and therefore denotes a period of around three years. Soon after that time, the sacrificial system would be restored. If the reference is to days, then its fulfillment would cover the whole period of Antiochus's blasphemous activities; if the reference is to the evening and morning sacrifices, then the period envisaged is a shorter time of three and a half years—the period between the desecration of the temple by the statue of Zeus and its ultimate cleansing.

Three further aspects of the vision and its meaning call for comment before some contemporary lessons are underlined. (1) It is of central importance that Daniel should "understand the vision" (v. 16). This is emphasized several times: by the man's voice (v. 16) and by the appearance of Gabriel and his exhortation ("Understand, son of man, that the vision refers to the time of the end" [v. 17]) and his insistence that Daniel be aware that the vision reveals to him "what shall happen in the latter time of the indignation; for at the appointed time the end shall be" (v. 19).

What is the "end" to which Gabriel refers (vv. 17, 19)? A common view is that it must be the end of the age and the return of Christ. If this is the case, however, then the vision not only foresees nations and rulers displaying some of the characteristics of the Antichrist, but it actually envisages the time of the final Antichrist. There is good reason for thinking that this interpretation reads back into Daniel the full and final significance of the expression "the end" when it occurs in the New Testament. "The end" in the Old Testament refers to the conclusion of the problem then at hand. Here it refers to "the latter time of the indignation," that is, the days of Antiochus (v. 19). Gabriel has been sent to assure Daniel that there will be an end; God will step in to preserve His people and to halt this inordinate time of stress. God's destruction of Antiochus will be a foretaste of His final destruction of the Antichrist.

(2) What did it mean for Daniel to "understand the vision" (v. 16)? Clearly it could not mean that he would be able to see the future as though he were reading an advance copy of a history book. No names are given and no dates are set. The timetable for the events contains very little specific chronology. Therefore, to "understand the vision" must have some other connotation. The description of the little horn's psychology in verses 23–27 gives us the answer. It means to have some insight into the nature and causes of the conflict. Thus Daniel's vision will give him some understanding of the nature of evil and the reasons that it must be destroyed if the kingdom of God is to last forever.

The little horn has *"fierce features"* (it is what we might call "hard-nosed"). There is a streak of insolence about it, not unrelated to its intellectual abilities, for it *"understands sinister schemes"* (v. 23). Its God-given ability to reason and plan is twisted so that it finds intellectual stimulation and pleasure in evil. It is often assumed that we do evil only against our better judgment. That is not the case with the little horn. It has called evil its good and finds attractive what is offensive to God precisely because it is an offense to God. It is in its own way an apocalyptic figure because the real nature of sin is unveiled in it. It is here a figure for humanity, twisted out of its original character and direction, standing unrepentantly in opposition to God.

The little horn also expresses the power of sin. Yet not even its power to sin or the power of its sin is autonomous. *"His power shall be mighty,"* but it will not be *"by his own power"* (v. 24). Even for the breath it breathes to sin against God it is dependent upon the One against whom it sins. We can never escape the fact that we are created, dependent beings. The little horn's desire to attain autonomy only reveals that there is no such thing as human autonomy. It may appear to possess a measure of autonomy—to the point of being able to *"destroy the mighty, and also the holy people"* (v. 24)—but nowhere does it step beyond the borders God has set for its activity. What is true of this antichrist is true of all antichrists. It will also be true of the final antichrist.

There is no integrity in the little horn: *"He shall cause deceit to prosper"* (v. 25). What would be true of the little horn of chapter 7 is also true here: Its sin corrupts the very foundation of all human relations, namely, honesty and integrity. In Scripture, the great deceiver is Satan himself (Gen. 3:13; 1 Tim. 2:14; Rev. 12:9), and all who belong to the kingdom of the dragon share in this moral corruption. The unveiling of sin in all its evil also underscores the fact that sin is essentially self-centered and self-glorifying, never God-centered or God-glorifying. The horn *"shall magnify himself in his heart"* (v. 25). It not only deceives others; ultimately it will deceive itself. It is against God. It exchanges the truth of God for the lie (Rom. 1:25) and falls foul of the oldest of all temptations: "You will be like God" (Gen. 3:5). It *"shall even rise against the Prince of princes"* (v. 25). The folly of its sin lies in the fact that it could do none of this *"by [its] own power"* (v. 24). This is the true nature of sin.

Daniel sees what we might call a negative apocalypse in which sin stands revealed. God does not often allow sin its prerogatives in quite this way, but we may be assured that this is the essence of all sin—even our sin. This is what we would become were it not for the restraints God places on our lives.

(3) Daniel was told clearly that his vision related to events *"many days in the future"* (v. 26). His reaction was twofold. He was overwhelmed by what he had seen and heard: *"I . . . fainted and was sick for days. . . . I was astonished by the vision"* (v. 27). He did not respond indifferently just because he had learned that he would not personally face these days of unmitigated evil. Instead he was deeply burdened for the future of the kingdom of God, just as he was grieved and troubled by his earlier vision (7:15). Here was a man whose zeal for the kingdom of God was not—as zeal so easily can be—restricted to his own time frame and the events in

which he himself would participate. What distinguishes Daniel's spiritual leadership from so many spiritual leaders of our own day is very simple: He was seeking to build God's kingdom, not his own kingdom. From a personal point of view he would have been satisfied with obscurity so long as the work of God was not obscured. In fact, that was all he really treasured, and this explains why he was so distressed in the face of the unfolding vision. His life was physically and emotionally bound up with the lasting prosperity of the kingdom of God. Like Charles H. Spurgeon, he could say: "Let my name perish; but let the Name of Jesus Christ endure." This is reflected in the brief but illuminating statement with which the chapter closes: *afterward I arose and went about the king's business* (v. 27). He returned to the duties to which God had called him. He did not retire from the world in view of the evil days that were coming. Nor did he go to the opposite extreme and live on a "high" of visionary excitement. Instead he did his duty.

Daniel's attitude illustrates an important biblical principle: In view of what the future holds, we must live holy lives now. He caught a glimpse of realities that would take place centuries later. Those events were shadows of the last conflict between the kingdom of Christ and the kingdoms of the world. One day Christ will return and the Antichrist "shall be broken without human hand" just as Antiochus was. We know this from the New Testament. How then should we live? Passage after passage gives the same answer: Do the King's business; walk in obedience; live in holiness; purify yourself as He is pure. While riding to a preaching engagement one day, John Wesley was stopped by a stranger who asked him what he would do if he knew that Christ was going to return at noon the next day. Wesley reached into his saddlebag, retrieved his diary, read out his engagements for the rest of the day and for the morning of the next day, and said, "That, dear sir, is what I would do." His knowledge of the Lord's future kingdom allowed him to live already for that kingdom. That was the spirit of Daniel. Is it so surprising that his life made such a lasting impression on the queen (5:11)? The tragedy is that Belshazzar allowed it to make so little impression on him.

Our forefathers included in their sermons a section entitled "Uses." Having given the exposition of their text, they would stand back from its teaching to ask whether there were any general principles that might apply to the people of God in every age. This chapter in Daniel is susceptible to many interpretations. Therefore, it is particularly important for us to ask: What are the uses of this chapter for the church and for Christians today? Are there general spiritual principles of common importance enshrined here? Three may be suggested.

(1) *Evil always and inevitably has a tendency to overstep itself.* Gabriel explained to Daniel that the little horn would arise *"When the transgressors* [perhaps "transgressions"] *have reached their fullness."* The statement is reminiscent of the statement that "the iniquity of the Amorites is not yet complete" (Gen. 15:16). When it was, judgment fell. Sin in individuals, nations, or rulers persists in stretching itself only to fall under the judgment of God. The kingdom that is built on principles that are contrary to the kingdom of God will always be toppled by another similar kingdom. We see that here in verses 4-5, 8, and 11-12. The same is true of individuals (for example, compare the lives of Nebuchadnezzar and Belshazzar). Sin is transgression. It involves overstepping the boundaries God has set. It leads to our lives being broken by forces we cannot control—or more accurately—being broken against the laws of God.

Sometimes the wicked prosper. That was a problem with which the Old Testament saints often wrestled. In Psalm 73, Asaph recalls how he envied the prosperity of the wicked (v. 3). They seemed to sin and profit, contrary to all he felt to be right. Yet he observed, "I went into the sanctuary of God; then I understood their end. Surely you set them in slippery places; You cast them down to destruction" (Ps. 73:17-18). He realized that the wicked eventually overstep themselves. Just when they think they have the world at their feet, everything is lost. They hear the terrible words: "Fool, this night your soul will be required of you; then whose will those things be which you have provided?" (Luke 12:20).

We see the same principle at work in the New Testament. In the Great Sin—Satan's plot to destroy Jesus—it must have seemed as though evil was victorious. Jesus died in the hour of the power of darkness (Luke 22:53), but Satan had overstepped himself. Through the death in which he sought to destroy the Christ, Jesus was able to "destroy him who had the power of death, that is, the devil, and release those who through fear of death were all their lifetime subject to bondage" (Heb. 2:14-15).

The same principle is illustrated in Paul's life. During his ministry he was frequently imprisoned. No doubt the powers of darkness against which he constantly wrestled believed that they had overcome him. With their leader silenced, surely Christians throughout the Roman world would become discouraged. Paul knew that some might be and wrote to them: "I ask that you do not lose heart at my tribulations for you" (Eph. 3:13). Evil appeared to be prospering, but Paul knew that it was overstepping itself. One day that would become clear.

Paul did not have to wait too long. When he penned other prison letters to the Philippians, to Philemon, and to the Colossians, it was clear that God had allowed the forces of evil to overstep themselves once again. As a result of his imprisonment, Paul had been able to share the gospel with the entire prison guard, and his fellow believers had taken such heart from his example that they were witnessing with even greater boldness (Phil. 1:12–14). Satan should have learned his lesson from the Damascus Road, when under his inspiration the young Saul had been breathing out the fire of slaughter and persecution against the early Christians, only to discover that his chief agent was actually marked for the service of the Lord. The knowledge that evil will inevitably overstep itself also has a vital role to play in our contemporary Christian lives. It is the groundwork of a spirit of patience in the face of trial, unrighteousness, and persecution. Evil will always overstep itself. We can therefore wait patiently on the Lord's judgment without seeking vengeance ourselves.

The prophet Habakkuk learned this in the face of the evil of his day. The Lord urged him to be patient until the day of His judgment (Hab. 2:8). This brought not only patience but a fresh perspective on life. Habakkuk anticipated the Pauline injunction to "glory in tribulations, knowing that tribulation produces perseverance [patience]" (Rom. 5:3). This enabled him to say:

> Though the fig tree may not blossom,
> Nor fruit be on the vines;
> Though the labor of the olive may fail,
> And the fields yield no food;
> Though the flock may be cut off from the fold,
> And there be no herd in the stalls—
> Yet I will rejoice in the LORD,
> I will joy in the God of my salvation.
> —*Habakkuk 3:17–18*

(2) *Daniel's vision underlines the weakness of the strongest and greatest of men without God.* Alexander the Great was the paramount empire builder of his day; Antiochus exerted ruthless and irresistible power against the Jews of his kingdom. Yet these ambitious men

were not masters of themselves; neither was able to control his fate. Alexander was the victim of a fever, Antiochus of his uncontrolled passions that flared in hatred first against the people of God and ultimately against God Himself.

We are never so vulnerable as when we believe ourselves to be strong by our own strength. Uzziah, the eleventh king of Judah, was an example of this: "When he was strong his heart was lifted up, to his destruction, for he transgressed [notice that word again] against the LORD his God by entering the temple of the LORD to burn incense on the altar of incense" (2 Chr. 26:16). When he was discovered, "Uzziah became furious" (2 Chr. 26:19), and was smitten with leprosy. Sin and guilt render us incapable of self-control.

Daniel stands in marked contrast. He confesses freely that he is nothing apart from God (2:27–28). With God's power, however, his whole life is one of remarkable self-control under the most arduous tests. Why is this? It is because the Spirit of God that dwells in him (5:11) is a spirit of self-discipline (2 Tim. 1:7 [NIV]). Only those who are submitted to God's Spirit can ever ultimately be in control of their own lives.

This is because only those whose whole lives are controlled by the Lord will be motivated to grow in control of the whole of their lives (Rom. 8:5–18). When we are motivated by self-glory we will be prepared to make considerable sacrifices to control certain aspects of our lives. It is impressive to see the discipline involved in the nurturing of a great athlete or musician. The days and months and years of monotonous practice involved in learning to control different parts of the body are not lightly spent. Yet the development of such skills sometimes goes hand-in-hand with a debilitating lifestyle. Control of only part of life for the glory of self is not self-control at all. It is self-serving and ultimately becomes self-slavery. Pride can motivate us to have a well-controlled body, but only grace can produce a self-controlled life.

(3) *Daniel's vision of the little horn teaches us a consistent pattern of satanic opposition to the work of God among His people.* The little horn's activities are summarized in a threefold manner: *"By him the daily sacrifices were taken away"; "the place of [the Lord's] sanctuary was cast down";* and it *"cast truth down to the ground"* (vv. 11–12). These were prophecies of specific historical acts on the part of Antiochus, but they also illustrate three areas of spiritual life that Satan consistently attacks in the Lord's people.

1. The daily sacrifices were part of the liturgical discipline of the Mosaic covenant. They no longer exist for Christians, but they

were inaugurated on a daily basis in order to teach the necessity of sacrifice if the people were to enjoy fellowship with God. They may have also taught the people that sacrifice was a daily part of their lives before God. No wonder Antiochus—as the enemy of God and His people—sought to put an end to this.

Satan continues to see this area as crucial if he is to pull down the children of God. That is why it is so important for us to remember daily that only in Christ's sacrifice are our sins forgiven; only through Him may we enjoy full fellowship with God. Let Satan draw us away from Christ's sacrifice, and our consciences will cloud over with guilt, and the joy and assurance of fellowship with God will be dissipated. That is one reason that Jesus taught us to pray on a daily basis "Forgive us our debts" (Matt. 6:11–12). It is also important for us to remember that sacrifice continues to be a principle that regulates our daily Christian lives. We no longer bring sacrifices in order to expiate our sin, but we should bring a sacrificial lifestyle in thanksgiving to our Lord (Rom. 12:1; 1 Pet. 2:5). If we do not deny ourselves and take up the cross daily, we cannot be His disciples (Matt. 16:24). How often Satan tempts us away from this just as he did with our Lord. He encourages us to conform to different standards, all of which involve the repudiation of the cross or the principle of sacrificial self-denial (Luke 4:1–13). Beware of anything purporting to be biblical Christianity that does not emphasize the necessity of Christ's sacrifice for our forgiveness or teaches a style of discipleship that avoids the daily bearing of the cross. Such teaching does not come from above but from below.

2. Just as Antiochus sought to cast down the sanctuary, Satan seeks to destroy the new temple of God, the living fellowship of God's people. At times he does so by means of persecution; at other times his devices are more subtle. He may try to introduce false teaching in the pulpit, lethargic worship in the pew, or simply discord and dissension in the fellowship. How easily Satan is able to blind many Christians to the necessity of maintaining the peace and unity of the local Christian fellowship. Sometimes he appears as an angel of light (2 Cor. 11:14). Under the guise of a right principle, someone will cause disharmony in the church. Their concern will be stated as "truth" or "righteousness," but despite appearances the real motivation will be "self." This dissension will be rooted in pride, or lust for power and personal influence, or a refusal to submit to the principles of Scripture. The peace of Christ will not be allowed to rule despite the biblical prescription (Col. 3:15).

3. Satan is very skilled at introducing wrong thinking and doctrinal controversy into the church—deceitful teaching is always a mark of the Antichrist. So conscious was Paul of this that he warned the elders of the Ephesian church: "I know this, that after my departure savage wolves will come in among you, not sparing the flock. Also from among yourselves men will rise up, speaking perverse things, to draw away the disciples after themselves. Therefore watch, and remember. . . ."(Acts 20:29–31). If this could happen in the church where Paul, Apollos, John, and Timothy all served in ministry, can we doubt that it could happen in our church too? We must always be on our guard for the sake of the church of the living God because it is "the pillar and ground of the truth" (1 Tim. 3:15). Christ will build His church and not even the gates of hell will be able to stand against it. That divine decree does not prevent Satan's launching onslaught after onslaught on the church throughout the ages. The last days (that is, the period from the ascension of Christ and Pentecost until the return of Christ) will be punctuated by times of stress (2 Tim. 3:1). There will be those who reject the crucified Christ, seek to destroy the church, and resist the truth (2 Tim. 3:2–8).

These things will reach their climax in the days of the man of sin or lawlessness (2 Thess. 2:3–10). That final, future, apocalyptic figure and his actions have an older, deeper, more sinister origin. Antiochus's attack on these three features of life with God are not only reminiscent of the last days, but they are also rooted in the temptation of the first days. In the Garden of Eden, Satan sought to undermine that sense of self-denial that is fitting for us as God's children and servants. "Assert yourself, and deny God" was his blatant attack. He thus began to spread the seed of disunity in the harmony of the family-church to which Adam and Eve (and later their children) belonged. The parents were set against each other (Gen. 3:12, 16) and the children likewise (Gen. 4:6–8). At the root of all this, the truth of God was denied (Gen. 3:1–5). Indeed there is nothing new under the sun.

How then are we to live? "Be sober, be vigilant; because your adversary the devil walks about like a roaring lion, seeking whom he may devour. Resist him, steadfast in the faith, knowing that the same sufferings are experienced by your brotherhood in the world" (1 Pet. 5:8–9).

CHAPTER NINE—INSPIRER AND HEARER OF PRAYER
DANIEL 9:1–27

Scripture Outline
Inspired to Pray (9:1–3)
The Inspirer of Prayer (9:4–19)
The Hearer of Prayer (9:20–23)
The Seventy Weeks (9:24–27)

We have suggested that one of the reasons that the Aramaic section of the Book of Daniel continues in the second half is to underline the interconnectedness of the two sections. There are various ways in which this relationship can be envisaged. One possible way of thinking about the two sections is to see the first half of the book as a biography of Daniel. He sang the Lord's song in a strange land. In the course of these chapters we are also given intimations of his place on the larger scale of world history. In contrast, the final six chapters take us into the spiritual experiences that lay behind his public service. Here is Daniel in the presence of the God who reveals mysteries and who shares His secrets with His servants (Dan. 2:29; Amos 3:7). He is one of "the people who know their God," who are "strong, and carry out great exploits" (Dan. 11:32). The entire book is about the blessings of knowing God. Daniel himself is one of the great biblical models of what it means to know the Lord.

In this context, chapter 9 takes on special significance. There is an evangelical dictum—stretching back at least to John Owen, the great seventeenth-century Puritan writer: What an individual is in secret, on his knees before God, that he is and no more. Since this is so, it is in this chapter that we learn who Daniel really was and discover the secret of his usefulness in God's kingdom. He was a man of prayer. It is not only true that more things are wrought by prayer alone than this world dreams of, but to the truly discerning ear more would be revealed about us by our private praying than by anything else. Prayer is an expression of what we know of God and of ourselves. In public we may successfully disguise the truth about ourselves but not in private prayer—or in the lack of it.

Daniel, as we have seen (2:17–18; 6:10), was a man of prayer. He prayed in times of crisis, but such prayer was the expression of a life of regular, disciplined praying. Here in chapter 9 Daniel recognizes that a critical time has come for God's people, and that realization grew out of his regular times of study, meditation, and prayer. It is often so in the kingdom of God.

INSPIRED TO PRAY

> **9:1** In the first year of Darius the son of Ahasuerus, of the lineage of the Medes, who was made king over the realm of the Chaldeans— **2** in the first year of his reign I, Daniel, understood by the books the number of the years specified by the word of the LORD through Jeremiah the prophet, that He would accomplish seventy years in the desolations of Jerusalem.
> **3** Then I set my face toward the Lord God to make request by prayer and supplications, with fasting, sackcloth, and ashes.
>
> *—Daniel 9:1–3*

It was the first year of the rule of Darius the Mede. Belshazzar was gone. It was a time of transition, and Daniel was engaged in Bible study. He was looking for the answer to the perennial cry of the people of God in exile: "How long, O Lord?" (cf. 8:13; Is. 6:11; Rev. 6:10). He was reading the books of Jeremiah's prophecies to find an answer—which he did: "'And this whole land shall be a desolation and an astonishment, and these nations shall serve the king of Babylon seventy years. Then it will come to pass, when seventy years are completed, that I will punish the king of Babylon and that nation, the land of the Chaldeans, for their iniquity,'" says the LORD; "and I will make it a perpetual desolation'" (Jer. 25:11–12). John Calvin observed, "Although Daniel was an interpreter of dreams, he was not so elated with confidence or pride as to despise the teaching delivered by other prophets."[1] He was seeking to have his mind informed and his heart dominated by whatever God had said about his current situation. Now he felt that he understood the significance of those *"seventy years in the desolations of Jerusalem"* (v. 2).

Daniel's reaction is of great significance. It reveals his practical sensitivity to the biblical teaching on divine sovereignty and human responsibility. He knew what God had foreordained. Jeremiah's prophecy was not conditional in character (that is, God will do *x* if man will do *y*). It was an unconditional and specific statement of intention (*"the number of the years specified by the word of the LORD"* [v. 2]). Yet rather than say: "Well, if God is going to do it, there is no need for me to labor or pray for restoration," Daniel devoted himself to prayer. Nor was it ordinary prayer. His *"supplications"* were accompanied by the rigorous discipline and devotion of *"fasting, sackcloth, and ashes"* (v. 3). He uses one of the most beautiful descriptions of true prayer to be found anywhere in Scripture: *"I set my face toward the Lord God to make request by prayer and supplications"* (v. 3).

God's sovereign purposes are never revealed in Scripture as excuses for our personal indolence but as incentives for action. The fact that all authority in heaven and earth had been given to Jesus did not mean that His disciples could sit back and relax. To the contrary, it obligated them to go throughout the world with the gospel. So here, Daniel saw that since God had given this promise about the duration of the captivity, it was his responsibility to ask the Lord to fulfill His purpose. He recognized that God employs means to achieve His ends. The preaching of the gospel is the means by which Christ's sovereignty over the nations will be fulfilled; prayer for the restoration of Jerusalem—with all the labor that would demand—was the means by which the Lord's word through Jeremiah would be fulfilled.

What follows, as Daniel pours out his heart to the Lord, is one of the longest and most instructive prayers recorded in Scripture. Several general features of it call for comment before its content is discussed.

(1) *Why should Daniel have recorded this prayer at all?* We are enjoined by Jesus to pray in secret so that "your Father who sees in secret will reward you openly" (Matt. 6:6). Why, then, does Daniel make his prayer a matter of public knowledge? Jesus did not, of course, mean that we should never pray when others are present. He was contrasting prayer that is directed to men rather than to God with prayer that is truly God-centered and God-honoring. Daniel's recorded prayer obviously was God-centered and God-honoring—he set his face toward the Lord (v. 3).

One reason for Daniel recording his prayer was to testify that God does hear, honor, and answer secret prayer. The restoration did take place, not only as the fulfillment of prophecy, but also in answer to the cries of God's people. Daniel, a man of prayer, wanted God's people to see the intimate connection between their praying and the events of history.

The same connection is made in the New Testament apocalypse: "Another angel, having a golden censer, came and stood at the altar. He was given much incense, that he should offer it with the prayers of all the saints upon the golden altar which was before the throne. And the smoke of the incense, with the prayers of the saints, ascended before God from the angel's hand. Then the angel took the censer, filled it with fire from the altar, and threw it to the earth. And there were noises, thunderings, lightnings, and an earthquake" (Rev. 8:3–5). The supplication offered before the heavenly throne becomes the instrument of God's activity on the earth. This is the divine principle that Daniel's intercession unveils for us.

(2) *A second feature of this prayer is its similarity to the great prayer of the Levites in Nehemiah 9 when the people of the "first return" (Neh. 7:5) assembled before God.* Possibly these prayers are independent of each other, both being based on general biblical teaching. It is surely not idle speculation, however, to ask whether the character of the people's praying in Nehemiah 9 was not in part the fruit of Daniel's intercession and example in Daniel 9.

This is often how an awakening of prayerfulness takes place. A person devoted to the Lord becomes an example of prayerfulness and is subsequently used by the Lord to stir up others to lay hold of His promises in a similar fashion. The annals of periods of revival often trace the origin of the floodtide of blessing to one individual or a small group who set their faces toward the Lord to make request by prayer and supplication.

(3) *Daniel's ritual acts of self-denial were integral components of a disciplined prayer life.* Although the external rites of "fasting, sackcloth, and ashes" (v. 3) have been discarded by the church in the New Testament era ("when you fast, anoint your head and wash your face" [Matt. 6:17]), they represent a devotion of oneself to seeking the special blessing of God through self-denial. At the very least, life in today's busy world requires that we fast in relation to our use of time if we are to know God's Word and be stimulated to fervent prayer as Daniel was. That in itself may involve us in fasting in relation to food as well. In the Christian life especially there are no "gains" without "pains."

THE INSPIRER OF PRAYER

⁴ And I prayed to the LORD my God, and made confession, and said, "O Lord, great and awesome God, who keeps His covenant and mercy with those who love Him, and with those who keep His commandments, ⁵ we have sinned and committed iniquity, we have done wickedly and rebelled, even by departing from Your precepts and Your judgments. ⁶ Neither have we heeded Your servants the prophets, who spoke in Your name to our kings and our princes, to our fathers and all the people of the land. ⁷ O Lord, righteousness belongs to You, but to us shame of face, as it is this day—to the men of Judah, to the inhabitants of Jerusalem and all Israel, those near and those far off in all the countries to which You have driven them, because of the unfaithfulness which they have committed against You.

⁸ "O Lord, to us belongs shame of face, to our kings, our princes, and our fathers, because we have sinned against You. ⁹ To the Lord our God belong mercy and forgiveness, though we have rebelled against Him. ¹⁰ We have not obeyed the voice of the LORD our God, to walk in His laws, which He set before us by His servants the prophets. ¹¹ Yes, all Israel has transgressed Your law, and has departed so as not to obey Your voice; therefore the curse and the oath written in the Law of Moses the servant of God have been poured out on us, because we have sinned against Him. ¹² And He has confirmed His words, which He spoke against us and against our judges who judged us, by bringing upon us a great disaster; for under the whole heaven such has never been done as what has been done to Jerusalem.

¹³ "As it is written in the Law of Moses, all this disaster has come upon us; yet we have not made our prayer before the LORD our God, that we might turn from our iniquities and understand Your truth. ¹⁴ Therefore the LORD has kept the disaster in mind, and brought it upon us; for the LORD our God is righteous in all the works which He does, though we have not obeyed His voice. ¹⁵ And now, O Lord our God, who brought Your people out of the land of Egypt with a mighty hand, and made Yourself a name, as it is this day—we have sinned, we have done wickedly!

16 "O Lord, according to all Your righteousness, I pray,
let Your anger and Your fury be turned away from Your
city Jerusalem, Your holy mountain; because for our sins,
and for the iniquities of our fathers, Jerusalem and Your
people are a reproach to all those around us. 17 Now
therefore, our God, hear the prayer of Your servant, and
his supplications, and for the Lord's sake cause Your face
to shine on Your sanctuary, which is desolate. 18 O my
God, incline Your ear and hear; open Your eyes and see
our desolations, and the city which is called by Your
name; for we do not present our supplications before You
because of our righteous deeds, but because of Your great
mercies. 19 O Lord, hear! O Lord, forgive! O Lord, listen
and act! Do not delay for Your own sake, my God, for
Your city and Your people are called by Your name."

—*Daniel 9:4–19*

God's word through Jeremiah encouraged Daniel to pray. God
had promised the end of the desolation of Jerusalem. Yet Daniel
realized in the "first year of Darius" (v. 1) that this promise lay as
yet unfulfilled. God's infallible word must be fulfilled, and so
Daniel engaged in prayer. Notice, however, the kind of prayer that
Daniel offered: He confessed sin (v. 4). God's people had broken
His laws (v. 4), and they had ignored the solemn warnings of His
prophets (v. 6). He does not trivialize his relationship to God;
instead he acknowledges God's lordship and searches out the sin
of his people that has so grieved Him. Two things lie at the heart
of all mature praying: a recognition of God's "Godness" (He is the
covenant Lord) and a realization of the nature of our relationship
to Him (we are in covenant relationship to Him). Both of these
elements distinguish Daniel's prayer.

(1) *True prayer is based on the fact that God is a God who speaks.*
It was "the word of the Lord given through Jeremiah the
prophet"(v. 2) that drove Daniel to seek the LORD's face in the first
place. God had not been silent. He was a "God, who at various
times and in various ways spoke in time past to the fathers by the
prophets" (Heb. 1:1).

Throughout his prayer Daniel refers to God's word in a variety
of ways. It expresses His *"covenant"* and His *"commandments"*
(v. 4); it contains His *"precepts"* and His *"judgments."* It was written
by *"Your servants the prophets who spoke in Your name"* (v. 6). It is
"the voice of the Lord our God" (vv. 10, 11, 14) and contains His

"law" (vv. 10, 11). In it are found *"the curse and the oath written in the Law of Moses the servant of God"* (v. 11). They are God's own *"words"* (v. 12).

This is significant for our understanding of prayer because the basis for all prayer is what God has promised to do. The prayer of faith that James describes (James 5:15) is prayer that rests on what God has promised to do in His Word. In the same way this partic- ular prayer was inspired by the promise of restoration from exile that God had given in His Word. Furthermore, Daniel's prayer is an expression of trust in a God who keeps His word. This explains why Daniel constantly refers to what God has promised to do. He had already seen the fulfillment of the divine threats of judgment. Now he was praying that God would keep His promise of deliver- ance and restoration. In simple language, he spoke to God just as a child would speak to a parent: "Lord, you promised . . ."

Much has been said about the secret of prayer. Almost as much has been made of the prayer of faith. The secret of prayer is that we should ask in accordance with God's will. The prayer of faith asks in unwavering trust for what God has already promised to do. Faith is not a matter of looking within ourselves to see how much we feel capable of requesting. What faith does is search the Scripture to see what God has promised to do. That was what Daniel did. We should not do less than that; we dare not ask more than that.

The prayer of faith is the outworking of our covenant rela- tionship with God. This is why James chose Elijah as the classic Old Testament illustration. When his prayers closed and later opened the heavens, bringing drought and then producing rain, he was not working up his faith to see how much he believed God would do. The very opposite was true. He was beginning, like Daniel, with what God had promised to do. God had said He would close the heavens in response to the persistent disobedi- ence of His people (see Deut. 28:15, 23–24 for God's specific promise in His covenant with the people through Moses). Elijah had come to God and said, "Lord, You promised. I believe this is Your word. It must be so. Let it be so in answer to my prayers."

Daniel's praying was of the same order as his appeal to the *"righteousness"* of God eloquently testifies (vv. 7, 16). The Old Testa- ment term "righteousness" has a specifically covenantal orientation. The young Martin Luther could not see this when he struggled to understand what Paul meant by "the righteousness of God" (Rom. 1:17). Of course, Luther was not helped by the fact that his Latin

Bible translated Paul's Greek word *dikaiosune* (righteousness) as *justitia* (justice). Luther's mistake has sometimes been repeated by evangelical Christians. Often righteousness has been thought of merely as the equivalent of the just punishment of God. Preachers therefore may often accompany the use of the phrase "the righteousness of God" with the gesticulation of a clenched fist. It is clear even from this passage, however, that this is to reduce the full biblical meaning of God's righteousness. Daniel sees the righteousness of God both as the basis for God's judgment of the people (v. 7) and also as the basis for his own prayer for forgiveness (v. 16). How can this be? In Scripture, "righteousness" basically means "integrity." Sometimes it is defined as "conformity to a norm." In the case of God, the norm to which He conforms is His own being and character. He is true to Himself; He always acts in character.

God has expressed the norm of His relationship to His people by means of a covenant. He will always be true and faithful to His covenant and the promises enshrined in it. Plainly, God's righteousness is His faithfulness to His covenant relationship.

Daniel underlines God's faithfulness to His covenantal promise to punish the covenant-breaking of His people: *"O Lord, righteousness belongs to You, but to us shame of face. . . . Yes, all Israel has transgressed Your law, and has departed [from the covenant] so as not to obey Your voice; therefore the curse and the oath written in the Law of Moses. . . has been poured out on us because we have sinned against Him. . . . Therefore the* LORD *has kept the disaster in mind, and brought it upon us; for the* LORD *our God is righteous in all the works which He does, though we have not obeyed His voice"* (vv. 7–14). In contrast, the same righteousness of God is made the ground for Daniel's appeal for mercy because he knows that God has promised to receive His penitent people and to restore them to fellowship with Himself. His covenant righteousness holds out the hope of His forgiveness, and Daniel clings to this with his whole heart: *"O Lord, according to all Your righteousness . . . let Your anger and Your fury be turned away . . . because for our sins . . . Your people are a reproach to all those around us"* (v. 16).

Daniel trusted what God had said. He realized that God's word is a covenant word, and he prayed accordingly. That had been true of him in his youth when he had resolved not to breach his covenant with God. It remained true in these times of testing. It was true now toward the end of his life as he set his face toward the Lord in prayer.

(2) *True prayer always seeks the glory of God*. How little Daniel would have understood our pseudo-spiritual notions of prayer. Our age has come to believe that real familiarity with God is best expressed in a casual approach or in language that expresses how easily and informally we have entered His presence. Even the most cursory reading of this chapter should awaken us from such deception. The sad truth is that we do not pray like Daniel because we cannot pray like him. If we could we would know God as he did and live as he lived—to the glory of God.

Daniel's prayer is an anatomy of a heart conscious of the glory of the Lord and wholly devoted to Him. He appeals for mercy for the people because they bear God's own name (v. 19); he appeals for the restoration of Jerusalem because it is God's own city (vv. 18–19); he longs for the rebuilding of the temple because it is God's own sanctuary (v. 17). His prayer magnifies God and humbles himself. It is full of adoration and admiration of the character of God (what our forefathers called His "attributes").

The Old Testament word for glory (*kabod*) has the basic sense of heavy or weighty. The weight of an individual's riches was an expression of personal value or worth. God's worth or weight is expressed in the display of His attributes. Daniel's prayer reveals a mind dominated by the reality and splendor of these attributes. Only those who have meditated long and lovingly on God's character and have grown familiar with His glory could express themselves to God so naturally in these terms. To Daniel God is the *"great and awesome God"*; He who *"keeps His covenant and mercy"* (vv. 4, 18); He is a God of *"righteousness"* (vv. 7, 14, 16); one who shows *"mercy and forgiveness"* (vv. 9, 18–19); He confirms His word in holy judgment (v. 12); His word is *"truth"* (v. 14); He is a deliverer of the oppressed (v. 15).

Daniel's ultimate motive for prayer was the glory of God because it was his great motive for living. Daniel clearly saw the need of the people. His praying was clearly people-oriented, but it was God-centered. The bottom line of his heart cry was: "Save your people, Lord, *'for Your own sake'*" (v. 19). Only when that phrase is present in our hearts and not merely in our words have we been mastered by a true motive. Unfortunately, sin clouds our minds precisely at this point. We mistakenly think that God's glory and our blessing are incompatible. Daniel's spiritual vision was both stronger (he penetrated to the glory of God) and clearer (he saw devotion to God's glory was the only way of joy). God in His infinite glory, in His three persons, and in all His attributes has devoted Himself to the salvation of His people. Paul noted: "For all things are for your sakes, that grace, having spread through the many, may cause thanksgiving to abound to the glory of God" (2 Cor. 4:15).

(3) *True prayer appeals to the mercy of God.* Several decades had passed since the beginning of the Exile. Most of Daniel's generation rested with their fathers, albeit in the graves of an alien land. Exile must have seemed to many of the Jews to be "normal." They had learned to live with it. Perhaps some of them prospered. Yes, the Exile had been unfortunate, but once again they had made the best of a bad situation. They missed their homeland, but otherwise they had need of little.

How different was Daniel's attitude. To him the Exile implied "shame of face" (v. 8); it was the evidence of a divine curse (v. 11). It was an unparalleled *"great disaster"* (v. 12). It had brought *"desolations"* upon the people (v. 18). In the eyes of Daniel (as in the eyes of the Lord) the people were desperately needy. They dare not appeal to the righteousness of God for justice—that would involve their annihilation. The justice they deserved was destruction. So Daniel appealed to the covenantal righteousness of God for mercy: *"we do not present our supplications before You because of our righteous deeds [they had none], but because of Your great mercies"* (v. 18). God would surely respond to this plea because He was and is a God who "delights in mercy" (Mic. 7:18).

The covenant God is a Father. By His covenant He brings us into His family. As a Father He takes pleasure in the requests of His children when they appeal to His covenant character. Just as a father finds delight in his child's appeals to his honesty or generosity or faithfulness or love, so our God "delights in mercy."

Daniel knew that. He did not forget for a moment that he was in the presence of the Great King. That memory, however, made his appeal for mercy all the more poignant and all the more welcome by the Father. In seeking mercy from the God of heaven Daniel knew that he was touching the deep places of his covenant God. In His covenant God had promised to be merciful. Daniel prayed He would be so.

(4) *True prayer always expresses the needs of the people of God.* It never bypasses sin and its consequences in suffering and shame. So Daniel spreads before God the sin (vv. 5–6), shame (vv. 7–8), curse (v. 11), and humiliation (v. 16) that the people had experienced. All of this was their own responsibility. Daniel had also learned that the Lord is not indifferent to the self-caused needs of His people. He is a true Father.

Isaiah had recalled how, at the time of the Exodus, God said, "Surely they are My people. . . . So He became their Savior. In all their affliction He was afflicted" (Is. 63:8–9). Now in the second "exodus" that Isaiah had foreseen (Is. 40:1ff.), Daniel believed that God was still concerned to deliver and save His needy children. Like Hezekiah, he spread the needs of God's kingdom before Him and waited for a response (see 2 Kin. 19:14–19). God heard Daniel too. Such is our assurance that He will also hear us:

> Thy truth unchanged hath ever stood;
> Thou savest those that on thee call:
> To them that seek thee thou art good,
> To them that find thee, all in all.
> Our restless spirits yearn for thee,
> Where'er our changeful lot is cast—
> Glad when thy gracious smile we see,
> Blest when our faith can hold thee fast.
> —*attributed to Bernard of Clairvaux*

This is what it means to have faith in the covenant Lord and to know Him as the inspirer of prayer.

THE HEARER OF PRAYER

[20] Now while I was speaking, praying, and confessing my sin and the sin of my people Israel, and presenting my supplication before the LORD my God for the holy mountain of my God, [21] yes, while I was speaking in prayer, the man Gabriel, whom I had seen in the vision at the beginning, being caused to fly swiftly, reached me about the time of the evening offering. [22] And he informed me, and talked with me, and said, "O Daniel, I have now come forth to give you skill to understand. [23] At the beginning of your supplications the command went out, and I have come to tell you, for you are greatly beloved; therefore consider the matter, and understand the vision:

—Daniel 9:20–23

We reveal a great deal about ourselves by the point at which we open an exposition or commentary on a book of the Bible. Alexander Whyte, a nineteenth-century Scottish divine, had a standing order with his bookseller for commentaries on the Book of Romans. Whenever he received a new one he immediately turned to Romans 7:14–25 to see whether the author believed that Paul was there describing his Christian experience. If not, Whyte simply rewrapped the book and sent it back with a note: "This is not the book for me." To a certain extent Daniel 9:20–27 serves the same function for some Christians. Perhaps someone, somewhere, may even see this volume on a bookshelf and pick it up with one thought in mind: "What does he make of Daniel's seventy weeks?" Thus a whole exposition (alas, sometimes a whole ministry) may be judged on the basis of a passage universally admitted to be one of the most mysterious in the Bible.

This is a cavalier approach to Scripture for several reasons. (1) The section itself is relatively brief, almost obscure. No interpretation of the Book of Daniel should either begin or end with this section. (2) The New Testament nowhere clearly refers to the contents of this prophecy. Even the reference to "the abomination of desolation" in Mark 13:14 is from Daniel 11:31 and 12:11 and not strictly from 9:27. If the seventy weeks of this prophecy were fundamental to a biblical theology (as, for example, Isaiah 53 obviously is), there would undoubtedly be clearer exposition of the passage in the apostolic writings. (3) To look immediately for an explanation of the seventy weeks of verse 24 is to ignore the significance of the rest of this chapter. It is unfortunate in this context that controversy over the interpretation of these verses leads some commentators to devote more space to the last four verses than they do to the rest of the chapter.

This prophecy is set in the context of Daniel's further encounter with Gabriel (v. 21). While he was pouring out his heart in prayer (vv. 1–19), Gabriel was *"caused to fly swiftly"* to him (v. 21). This is doubtless the meaning of the enigmatic words "to fly" or "to be weary in weariness." The expression is an anthropomorphism of sorts to indicate the dramatic swiftness with which Gabriel was sent. His coming is full of significance.

(1) *The reality of God's hearing of prayer.* Daniel himself was amazed at the immediacy with which the Lord responded to his heart cry: *"Now while I was speaking . . . Gabriel . . . being caused to fly swiftly, reached me"* (vv. 20–21). Gabriel himself explained: *"At the beginning of your supplications the command went out, and I have come . . . therefore consider the matter, and understand the vision"* (v. 23). God always hears prayer immediately, even when His answer is long in coming. Why, then, was an assurance that his prayer had been heard given so instantaneously to Daniel? His prayer

seems to have been cut off in midsentence. Was it partly to assure him that all his prayers were heard by God as soon as they were spoken? If so, that was not the only reason.

(2) *The angel's coming is to facilitate Daniel's understanding.* What was there for Daniel to understand? Presumably he needed help in understanding verses 24–27. While Gabriel's greeting is enigmatic, it provides a major clue to this section. The reason for his appearance at that time was the way in which Daniel's prayer had focused on the end of the seventy-year period prophesied by Jeremiah. The Lord wanted His faithful servant to see those seventy years in a new and sharper focus. Spiritually, Daniel is like those whose eyes have been fixed on a mountain peak, which, as they approach it, has obliterated everything else from view. When they ascend that peak they discover they are not yet at the summit. There is a further peak to climb. In general terms Daniel already knows this (see Dan. 2 and 7). Now he is to see the path of ascent for the people of God with greater detail. He must look not at the seventy years described by Jeremiah but at the seventy weeks (that is, seventy sevens) prophesied by Gabriel.

A touching interchange takes place during the course of this conversation that illuminates a further reason for the angelic visitation.

(3) *A benediction of divine love is given by Gabriel.* Daniel is a man *"greatly beloved"* (v. 23). What gracious encouragement! Even in this brief section we are given some indication why Daniel was so greatly loved. Quite unconsciously he remarks that Gabriel came to him *"about the time of the evening offering"* (v. 21). That seems an unremarkable statement until we remember that it had been many decades since Daniel had been in Jerusalem where the evening offering was made (roughly midafternoon). Yet his thinking was still regulated by the life and worship of Jerusalem. This was the answer to the question of how one was to sing the Lord's song in a foreign land:

> If I forget you, O Jerusalem,
> Let my right hand forget its skill!
> If I do not remember you,
> Let my tongue cling to the roof of my mouth—
> If I do not exalt Jerusalem
> Above my chief joy.
>
> —*Psalm 137:5–6*

There is no more beautiful application of this principle of Daniel's life than that expressed by John Calvin:

> Already seventy years had passed away, during which Daniel had never observed any sacrifice offered; and yet he still mentions sacrifices as if he were in the habit of attending daily in the Temple, which was not really in existence. Whence it appears how God's servants, though deprived of the outward means of grace for the present moment, are yet able to make them practically useful by meditating upon God, and the sacrifices, and other rites, and ceremonies of his institution. If anyone in these days is cast into prison, and even prohibited from enjoying the Lord's Supper to the end of his life, yet he ought not on that account to cast away the remembrance of that sacred symbol; but should consider within himself every day, why that Supper was granted us by Christ, and what advantages he desires us to derive from it.[2]

Daniel was loved in heaven because he lived for God. His waking moments were dominated by God's covenant purposes. He lived to see God's city restored so that the Lord's name might be praised among the nations; he longed to re-experience the ancient sacrificial rites that reminded the people daily of their sin and their need for salvation, and the way by which God had promised to bring them forgiveness. Both in Old and New Testament teachings God dwells with such:

> For thus says the High and Lofty One
> Who inhabits eternity, whose name is Holy:
> "I dwell in the high and holy place,
> With him who has a contrite and humble spirit,
> To revive the spirit of the humble,
> And to revive the heart of the contrite ones."
> —*Isaiah 57:15*

> "He who has My commandments and keeps them, it is he who loves Me. And he who loves Me will be loved by My Father, and I will love him and manifest Myself to him. . . . If anyone loves Me, he will keep My word; and

My Father will love him, and We will come to him and make Our home with him."

—*John 14:21, 23*

Daniel's experience was nothing less than a foretaste of this.

THE SEVENTY WEEKS

24 "Seventy weeks are determined
For your people and for your holy city,
To finish the transgression,
To make an end of sins,
To make reconciliation for iniquity,
To bring in everlasting righteousness,
To seal up vision and prophecy,
And to anoint the Most Holy.
25 "Know therefore and understand,
That from the going forth of the command
To restore and build Jerusalem
Until Messiah the Prince,
There shall be seven weeks and sixty-two weeks;
The street shall be built again, and the wall,
Even in troublesome times.
26 "And after the sixty-two weeks
Messiah shall be cut off, but not for Himself;
And the people of the prince who is to come
Shall destroy the city and the sanctuary.
The end of it shall be with a flood,
And till the end of the war desolations are determined.
27 Then he shall confirm a covenant with many for
        one week;
But in the middle of the week
He shall bring an end to sacrifice and offering.
And on the wing of abominations shall be one who
        makes desolate,
Even until the consummation, which is determined,
Is poured out on the desolate."

—*Daniel 9:24–27*

The interpretation of this passage has been described as a dismal swamp by J. A. Montgomery. Like the earlier prophetic passages in Daniel, it has given rise to (or been interpreted in the light of) several schools of thought: (1) as applying to the period of

Antiochus; (2) as pointing forward first to the coming of Christ and then to the events of the end; and (3) as referring to the coming of Christ, the completion of His sacrificial work, and the destruction of Jerusalem that followed His rejection. The view adopted in this exposition is the last.

We have already noticed that the illumination given in Daniel is often of a progressive and cumulative nature, working from the general outline to the more specific details. That is equally true of these four verses.

(1) Intimation is given that the period in view is one of *"seventy weeks,"* or (literally) "seventy sevens" (v. 24). By the end of this period six things will take place.

1. Transgression will be finished
2. Sins will be brought to an end
3. Reconciliation will be made for iniquity
4. Everlasting righteousness will be established
5. Vision and prophecy will be sealed
6. The Most Holy will be anointed

It is almost instinctive to the New Testament Christian to see in these statements a prophecy of the work of Christ. He came to die for our sins that through Him we might die to sin and be raised to a new life of righteousness (Rom. 6:2, 18). It is because these things have been accomplished by Him that grace reigns "through righteousness to eternal life through Jesus Christ our Lord" (Rom. 5:21).

Christ does more than this. He came *"to seal up vision and prophecy"* (v. 24). He is God's last word (Heb. 1:1ff.). In Him all the promises of God receive their "yes" and "Amen" (2 Cor. 1:20). In Him alone is found the vision of God and His purpose; in Him. prophecy and prophet are united. How do the words *"anoint the Most Holy"* (v. 24) find fulfillment? The Most Holy is a reference to the holy of holies, the tabernacle and all the furniture of which were consecrated to God by careful ritual. Jesus came to fulfill all that the holy of holies represented. The fourth evangelist tells us He "became flesh and dwelt [literally, "tabernacled"] among us, and we beheld His glory [the shekinah glory of God which was manifested in the tabernacle]" (John 1:14). John's Gospel also records the remarkable words spoken by Jesus when, as our high priest, He entered into the presence of His Father to pray for us. As He did so, He said, "For their sakes I sanctify Myself" (John 17:19). Jesus Himself was and is the Most Holy.

(2) Gabriel further explains to Daniel the significance of these seventy sevens. From the time when the decree for the rebuilding

of Jerusalem was published (presumably God's decree given expression in the decree of Cyrus) until the coming of the Messiah, there would be sixty-nine sevens. These are to be thought of as two periods, one of seven sevens and another of sixty-two sevens (v. 25). During the shorter, earlier period, *"The street shall be built again, and the wall, even in troublesome times"* (v. 25). This is clear and genuine encouragement for Daniel. He longs for the restoration of Jerusalem and is told that it will be rebuilt despite considerable opposition and difficulty (as the Book of Nehemiah bears witness).

(3) The period of sixty-two sevens will be followed by the last week when *"Messiah shall be cut off, but not for Himself"* (v. 26). Gabriel uses the vocabulary of violent penal death (cf. Lev. 7:20). Here we are reminded of Isaiah's prophecy that the Suffering Servant would be "cut off from the land of the living; for the transgressions of My people He was stricken" (Is. 53:8). This event, mysterious to Daniel, becomes clear in the light of the Gospels. The Messiah would be crucified. During this same period of sevens, Jerusalem and the rebuilt temple will be destroyed. The entail will be *"desolations"* (v. 26).

(4) Verse 27 seems to refer to this same final week (that is, *"Then"*). Who is the one who *"shall confirm a covenant with many for one week; but in the middle of the week He shall bring an end to sacrifice and offering"*? If we are sensitive to the structure of this little section, the meaning may become a little clearer. In keeping with the general style in Daniel's revelations, it contains a progressive unfolding of the future. Each verse in verses 24–27 is set in the same overall time frame of seventy sevens:

Verse 24 covers the entire period;
Verse 25 divides the first sixty-nine sevens;
Verse 26 describes the final seven in indefinite terms;
Verse 27 describes the final seven in more detail.

If this understanding of the structure is correct, then the first half of verse 27 refers to Christ, the second half to the destruction of the city and the abominations involved in its downfall at the hands of Titus Flavius Vespasianus in A.D. 70. In the middle of the final week Christ died for His people. He brought all sacrifice to an end (as the Letter to the Hebrews underlines [whether or not it was written before the destruction of the temple]). Within four decades from the Messiah's rejection, the soil on which the temple was built, so beloved by Daniel, would once again be defiled by pagans. Jerusalem would again be desolate.

If this is the correct interpretation, it is not too difficult to see what it was that heaven was so anxious to communicate to Daniel, its representative on earth. It was right that he should long to see the people delivered from captivity; it was right that he should long to see Jerusalem rebuilt and the temple worship reinstituted. Yet the Lord wanted Daniel to see beyond these things to what they foreshadowed, however painful that might be. God's ultimate purpose was not a temple made with hands and a holy place entered but once each year. His Son was the place in which men were to approach God; His sacrifice was the one which would bring forgiveness. Then if men still clung to the shadows and symbols of the old order, rejecting what they symbolized, there was only one terrible prospect: judgment and destruction of the most terrible kind.

Daniel, for once, does not record how fearful this vision was to him. We are left to guess. He had climbed one mountain peak only to see another on the horizon. In the distance he saw the outline of a cross where the Messiah would suffer death, *"but not for Himself"* (v. 26). Beyond he saw the clouds of gathering gloom as the judgment of God rolled on to sweep away Daniel's beloved city. Did he now recall Nebuchadnezzar's dream of the stone that crushed the kingdoms built by human hands and grew until it became a mountain that filled the whole earth (Dan. 2:44–45)? Did he remember his vision of the Son of Man coming with the clouds of heaven to receive His kingdom from the Ancient of Days and to receive dominion over His people (Dan. 7:13)? Did he gasp with awe that his God should show him what his Savior-Messiah would accomplish for him—all to show him how much He loved him (v. 23)?

Perhaps there was a special reason why this message came to him "about the time of the evening offering."

NOTES

1. John Calvin, *Commentaries on the Book of the Prophet Daniel*, tr. Thomas Myers, 2 vols. (Edinburgh: Calvin Translation Society, 1852–53), 2:138–39.

2. Ibid., 2:191–92.

Scripture Outline
  Concern for the People of God (10:1–3)
  Vision of the Sufficiency of God (10:4–9)
  Conflict for the Kingdom of God (10:10—11:1)

Chapters 10, 11, and 12 constitute the final lengthy section in the Book of Daniel. Chapter 10 sets the scene of yet another heavenly visitation, while the closing two chapters contain a lengthy and detailed prophecy for the future. The book closes with a final greeting to Daniel himself. As we shall see, chapter 10 contains vital biblical insights into the nature of reality. It emphasizes that human causes and effects are not the only forces or influences operative in the history of the world.

A. W. Tozer once wrote an essay with the penetrating title, "God Tells the Man Who Cares." He noted:

> The Bible was written in tears and to tears it will yield its best treasures. God has nothing to say to the frivolous man. It was to Moses, a trembling man that God spoke on the mount, and that same man later saved the nation when he threw himself before God with the offer to have himself blotted out of God's book for Israel's sake. Daniel's long season of fasting and prayer brought Gabriel from heaven to tell him the secret of the centuries. When the beloved John wept much because no one could be found worthy to open the seven-sealed book, one of the elders comforted him with the joyous news that the Lion of the tribe of Judah had prevailed.[1]

This was one of the principles that governed Daniel's relationship to God. Here in chapter 10 God tells him something new and important which (rightly understood) will enable him (and us) to have peace and be strong (cf. v. 19).

CONCERN FOR THE PEOPLE OF GOD

10:1 In the third year of Cyrus king of Persia a message was revealed to Daniel, whose name was called Belteshazzar. The message was true, but the appointed time was long; and he understood the message, and had understanding of the vision. 2 In those days I, Daniel, was mourning three full weeks. 3 I ate no pleasant food, no meat or wine came into my mouth, nor did I anoint myself at all, till three whole weeks were fulfilled.

—Daniel 10:1–3

With the meticulous care of a civil servant, Daniel here recorded his final vision. It was in *"the third year of Cyrus king of Persia."* Once again there is much that is enigmatic about the revelation Daniel received, but he himself *"understood the message and had understanding of the vision"* (v. 1). Later in verse 4 he pinpoints the date of the experience. By "the twenty-fourth day of the first month" Daniel had been engaged in fasting, mourning, and praying for a period of *"three full weeks"* (v. 3). Since it was "the first month" (v. 4), that would include the days of Passover celebration and the Feast of Unleavened Bread that followed it (he was engaged in these spiritual exercises from the third to the twenty-fourth of Ahib [later Nissan (Neh. 2:1)]).

To anyone familiar with the chronology of this period, there is something almost jarring about what Daniel says. For one thing, Cyrus had issued a decree allowing the Jews to return home in the first year of his reign, a record of which is found elsewhere in Scripture:

Now in the first year of Cyrus king of Persia, that the word of the LORD spoken by the mouth of Jeremiah might be fulfilled, the LORD stirred up the spirit of Cyrus king of Persia, so that he made a proclamation throughout all his kingdom, and also put it in writing, saying,

Thus says Cyrus king of Persia: All the kingdoms of the earth the LORD God has given me. And He has commanded me to build Him a house at Jerusalem which is in Judah. Who is among you of all His people? May his God be with him, and let him go up to Jerusalem which is in Judah, and build the house of the LORD God of Israel (He is God), which is in Jerusalem. And whoever is left in any place where he dwells, let the men of his place help him with silver and gold, with goods and livestock, besides the freewill offerings for the house of God which is in Jerusalem.

—Ezra 1:1–4

Why did Daniel not return to his beloved Jerusalem? He specifically mentions that he was "by the side of the great river, that is, the Tigris" (v. 4). In view of the hints we have already received (cf. 6:10; 9:16–20), we would have anticipated that Daniel would have been in the vanguard of those who returned. Apparently he remained in Babylon. Was he simply too old for the journey? He was, after all, well into retirement age. Scripture provides no certain answer to this question, but knowing Daniel as we now do we must assume that the Lord had given him a deep conviction that he was to remain in Babylon. There may be a hint of an explanation in these opening verses. The rebuilding of Jerusalem would involve heavy labor, action, busyness, controversy, time-consuming activity. God had already raised up leaders in that area (Ezra and Nehemiah). What these leaders needed most (as Moses had done before) was someone who would engage in the hidden but strategic work of prayer for the defense and advance of the kingdom of God. It was apparently in this activity that Daniel was already engaged when he received a further heavenly visitation.

This in itself scarcely explains the rigors of Daniel's discipline. It was Passover, a time to celebrate the deliverance God had wrought. It was a time of restoration, a time to rejoice that a way of return to Jerusalem had been provided. Yet Daniel was *"mourning three full weeks"* (v. 2). Why? Presumably because he knew that only small numbers of people had taken the opportunity to return. Those who could not sing the Lord's song in a foreign land came to the point where they had no desire either to sing it in the Lord's land.

No doubt Daniel had also heard that there was strong opposition to the rebuilding program (described in detail in the Book of Nehemiah). It also seems that in the third year of his reign, Cyrus had gone abroad, leaving his son, Cambyses, to act as regent, and he had issued an edict forbidding the building of the temple.

Those who had returned to Jerusalem were easily discouraged. The work of restoration proved to be far more difficult than they had anticipated, the opposition far more concerted than they had imagined. Would the restoration fail? It would not fail if Daniel could pray the work of God through these days of crisis. With great self-discipline and clear discernment of the needs, he devoted himself to seeking blessing from the God of heaven.

What is so remarkable about Daniel here is the way in which he consecrated himself to the advance of God's kingdom, even though he was not directly involved in the rebuilding of the temple, nor would he live to see it. That is the hallmark of true faith and commitment. He believed but did not receive what was promised (cf. Heb. 11:33). He prayed for blessing he would never personally witness. What commitment his decision to remain in Babylon displayed!

The need for such Daniels has not diminished with the passing of time. Indeed, often in the history of the church it has been met by Danielles—women who sometimes in their latter years, like Daniel himself, have devoted themselves to fast, mourn, and pray for the church of God in their area and worldwide.

The church I attended as a student was reborn from such a womb. It has never grown to become a megachurch, but through its ministry multitudes of men and women have been sent to the ends of the earth, strengthened for Christian service and loved and prayed for constantly. Its pastor of more than forty years once wrote:

> I was minister . . . only a few months when an old lady sent for me. When I called, she said, "I have been praying for many years that God would send . . . a man a little bit 'out of the usual' to do a work for the Lord here. From what I hear, you are the answer to my prayer." She told me this: "I have been a widow for seventeen years. Formerly I had a Bible Class of over one hundred girls, many of whom have since gone to the mission field, yet it was only after my dear husband died, and I was by then rather frail and able only to sit at my own fireside and pray, that the Lord gave me this burden, and said to me, 'You have served me long with these girls, and in your local church; but this is the task of your life, reserved for you in your eighties: you have to pray for something in Aberdeen.'"[2]

We miss the point of the constant emphasis on Daniel's understanding, wisdom, and discernment if we fail to see that it led him to become a man of prayer. Yet this is constantly reiterated through-out the book (cf. 1:17, 20; 5:11–12; 9:22; 10:1). His recognition of his own role, his discernment of the weakness of the people and the opposition they faced, all drove him to commune with God. That was why his "words were heard" (v. 12).

The contemporary church has much to learn from Daniel in this respect. In many churches and Christian organizations, per-sonality is more highly prized than wisdom and understanding; weaknesses are resolved by new programs, not by faithful prayer; opposition is overthrown by growth in numbers rather than in depth and quality. The foundations are rarely examined because we are so engrossed in the business of creating visible activity (and often it is a "business" as well as "busy-ness").

Christian leaders like Daniel who devote their energy to seek-ing the word of God and the face of God rather than to seeking one-way tickets to Babylon might be people the affluent and busy twenty-first-century church would find difficult to understand. Daniel was committed to the long-term view of God's kingdom. The Lord had nurtured that spirit in him through the visions he had already received. Now as he prayed, he would not only receive further revelation of the future, but he would also be given an insight into what is involved in true, prevailing prayer for the church of God. E. M. Bounds observed that while "the church is looking for better methods, God is looking for better men. For people are God's methods."

VISION OF THE SUFFICIENCY OF GOD

4 Now on the twenty-fourth day of the first month, as
I was by the side of the great river, that is, the Tigris,
5 I lifted my eyes and looked, and behold, a certain man
clothed in linen, whose waist was girded with gold of
Uphaz! 6 His body was like beryl, his face like the appearance of lightning, his eyes like torches of fire, his arms
and feet like burnished bronze in color, and the sound of
his words like the voice of a multitude.
7 And I, Daniel, alone saw the vision, for the men
who were with me did not see the vision; but a great terror fell upon them, so that they fled to hide themselves.
8 Therefore I was left alone when I saw this great vision,
and no strength remained in me; for my vigor was turned
to frailty in me, and I retained no strength. 9 Yet I heard
the sound of his words; and while I heard the sound of

his words I was in a deep sleep on my face, with my face to the ground.

—Daniel 10:4–9

The psalmist speaks of God as "My glory and the One who lifts up my head" (Ps. 3:3). Daniel knew Him similarly in the majesty of His power and in the gentle intimacy of His grace. As he gathered with others (v. 7) *"by the side of the great river, that is, the Tigris"* (v. 4), his eyes were irresistibly drawn to the person who stood before him. Such was the majesty of this figure that although Daniel's companions *"did not see the vision"* (v. 7), they felt it with such force that they fled in terror (cf. the experience of Saul/Paul and his companions on the Damascus Road [Acts 22:9]). Daniel *"was left alone"* (v. 8). Overwhelmed with shock, he was overcome and fell before the figure, *"face to the ground"* (v. 9).

He struggled to find words to express the glory of the presence of this "man." He ransacks the vocabulary of precious metals, stones, and the natural elements to describe the inexpressible beauty he beheld. The figure is clothed in linen, and everything about him expresses power, beauty, majesty, glory, and honor. His *"waist was girded with gold of Uphaz! His body was like beryl, his face like the appearance of lightning, his eyes like torches of fire, his arms and feet like burnished bronze in color."* When he spoke, his voice sounded like a *"multitude"* (perhaps not only in its strength but also in its richness of tone) (vv. 5–6). He spoke, but Daniel seems to have been too overcome to hear more than *"the sound of his words"* (v. 9).

Who was this figure? Various answers have been given: Gabriel, Michael, or Christ in a preincarnate manifestation are popular interpretations. In favor of the last of these views is that the description of this figure and the impact of his presence on Daniel and the others far surpasses anything that is said of either Gabriel or Michael. Furthermore, there are similarities between this vision and other biblical theophanies or Christophanies (for example, Ezek. 1:26ff. and especially Rev. 1:12–15, where Christ is described in somewhat similar terms as He walks among the churches). Additionally, Daniel addresses the figure in terms of reverence not found in his conversations with the others. He calls him "my Lord" three times (vv. 16, 17, 19).

If a choice has to be made, there is much to be said for seeing this revelation as a Christophany. More important than identifying the figure—it was, aside from that indefinable reality, a vision

(vv. 7, 8)—is recognizing the impression the vision is intended to create. Even if the figure is not divine, Daniel's vision is still essentially theophanic in nature because it communicated to him a sense of the omnipotence and all-gloriousness of God. It reveals His absolute sufficiency to meet the needs of His people.

It would be a mistake to see each detail of Daniel's description as having a one-to-one point of reference in the character of God. Two features, however, must have caused certain associations for him. The first was that the figure was *"clothed in linen"* (v. 5). Linen garments were worn by the priests. In particular, the high priest wore linen when he went into the holy place (Ex. 28:42; Lev. 6:10; 16:4). This would have reminded the exiled Daniel of the temple sacrifices and the Day of Atonement, the way of forgiveness ordained by God.

The second outstanding feature was that the face of this figure was *"like the appearance of lightning"* (v. 6). This would, of course, suggest power and glory in general, but lightning is a frequent accompaniment to the coming of the Lord in Scripture (cf. Ezek. 1:13–14; Rev. 4:5; 8:5; 11:19; 16:18) and was so supremely at Sinai (Ex. 19:16; 20:18). Was it meant to be a reminder to Daniel here of the Lord's covenant faithfulness that he himself had confessed in the previous chapter?

God was impressing on Daniel that He was a God of forgiveness and faithfulness. Daniel was rightly concerned for the prospects of God's kingdom and mourned deeply over the sins and shortcomings of the people. His God, however, remained the same. He had not changed. The God of the past—of the covenant at Sinai and the sacrifices at Jerusalem—was still all-sufficient to meet the needs of His people. By reminding Daniel of the past, God was giving him encouragement to trust His adequacy for a future that looked increasingly bleak.

An important spiritual principle is enshrined here: Knowledge of God's work of grace in the past encourages us to trust Him and seek His blessing in the present and for the future. Think, for example, of the way in which Psalm 44 describes an individual in the midst of discouragement finding encouragement from the past. The prayer would be something like this: "You worked before, O Lord; work again in this time."

This illustrates the value of a knowledge of church history, whether it be of the apostolic or postapostolic church. Biblical Christians cannot canonize an individual or an age in the history of the church, but we can be stirred to pray and be excited and stimulated in our witness, service, study, and zeal by knowing what God has done in by-gone days. If we do not know of other days and experiences than our own, we will be in danger of living short-sightedly in a short-sighted society. We will fall into the error of thinking that our experience is normal and normative, not realizing how deficient we actually are. When we read of God's mighty works in the past, however, we are humbled and ashamed, yet excited to pray, "Lord, you did it then; do it again."

Daniel was given a great vision, but none may experience such intimacy with God without it leaving a mark on their lives. Think of the great Old Testament picture of Jacob limping away from his encounter with the Lord (Gen. 32:22–31). Daniel is no exception. The vision makes him prostrate himself; even when he is encouraged, he trembles (vv. 10, 11); when he is addressed, he is speechless and turns his face to the ground (v. 15). He is overwhelmed with a sense of sorrow and feels himself to be without strength (vv. 16, 17). When he is thus emptied of all confidence in his own resources, he is strengthened by grace (v. 18) and given the ability to be strong (v. 19).

Such people who have seen God's glory and grace can never be the same again. They have come to know who God is, and in His presence they come to know what they are themselves in their need and by His grace. They lose their taste for all that is trivial. They learn to live as Daniel did, near to God. They are never far from heaven because they know they are no longer distanced from it by the guilt of sin. Forgiven and cleansed, they have a presence about them. It is the presence of God.

CONFLICT FOR THE KINGDOM OF GOD

10 Suddenly, a hand touched me, which made me tremble on my knees and on the palms of my hands.
11 And he said to me, "O Daniel, man greatly beloved, understand the words that I speak to you, and stand upright, for I have now been sent to you." While he was speaking this word to me, I stood trembling.
12 Then he said to me, "Do not fear, Daniel, for from the first day that you set your heart to understand, and to humble yourself before your God, your words were heard; and I have come because of your words. 13 But the prince of the kingdom of Persia withstood me twenty-one days; and behold, Michael, one of the chief princes, came to help me, for I had been left alone there with the kings of

Persia. [14] Now I have come to make you understand what will happen to your people in the latter days, for the vision refers to many days yet to come."

[15] When he had spoken such words to me, I turned my face toward the ground and became speechless. [16] And suddenly, one having the likeness of the sons of men touched my lips; then I opened my mouth and spoke, saying to him who stood before me, "My lord, because of the vision my sorrows have overwhelmed me, and I have retained no strength. [17] For how can this servant of my lord talk with you, my lord? As for me, no strength remains in me now, nor is any breath left in me."

[18] Then again, the one having the likeness of a man touched me and strengthened me. [19] And he said, "O man greatly beloved, fear not! Peace be to you; be strong, yes, be strong!"

So when he spoke to me I was strengthened, and said, "Let my lord speak, for you have strengthened me."

[20] Then he said, "Do you know why I have come to you? And now I must return to fight with the prince of Persia; and when I have gone forth, indeed the prince of Greece will come. [21] But I will tell you what is noted in the Scripture of Truth. (No one upholds me against these, except Michael your prince.

11:1 "Also in the first year of Darius the Mede, I, even I, stood up to confirm and strengthen him.)

—Daniel 10:10—11:1

Daniel is asked a tantalizing question in verse 20: *"Do you know why I have come?"* It is intended to stimulate him to think over the message he has received and recognize its wider implications. As such it is the question with which our study of this section must begin: Why did Daniel receive the message of this heavenly vision? The answer lies in the earlier part of the chapter.

Daniel's spiritual exercises had been prolonged for three weeks before the heavenly figure appeared (v. 2). For his patience and persistence he was a *"man greatly beloved"* (v. 11; cf. 9:23). What was news to Daniel, however, was that *"from the first day [he] set [his] heart to understand, and to humble [himself] before . . . God, [his] words [of prayer] were heard"* (v. 12). The figure had come because of Daniel's words. It seems that Daniel had been praying for further understanding of God's purposes. Sixty-two of the seventy weeks of the previous chapter were still vague in his mind. What was God's plan, and how would it affect His people? It was not only the specifically messianic prophecies that Daniel sought to understand (1 Pet. 1:10–12). His mind ranged over all the counsel God had given him (cf. Acts 20:27). Nothing God revealed could ever be unimportant for him to study. In this too he is a model to believers in every age.

The figure had also come immediately as Daniel had begun to pray (v. 12). How then had it taken three weeks for him to arrive? Is earth three weeks away from heaven? To ask the question is to recognize how ludicrous it is. The figure himself explains: *"But the prince of the kingdom of Persia withstood me twenty-one days; and behold, Michael, one of the chief princes, came to help me, for I had been left alone there with the kings of Persia"* (v. 13). As he departs, he says further, *"And now I must return to fight the prince of Persia; and when I have gone forth, indeed the prince of Greece will come"* (v. 20). All this appears to have taken place because the heavenly figure had come to Daniel *"to make you understand what will happen to your people in the latter days* [that is, some time in the future, cf. Gen. 49:1; Num. 24:14] *for the vision refers to many days yet to come"* (v. 14).

Daniel's special concern had apparently been to understand the prospects of the people of God during the Medo-Persian kingdom and then during the Greek Empire. The heavenly apostle comes to reveal to him what will take place. Precisely because this will stir up Daniel (and perhaps others) to pray for the kingdom of God, that the gates of hell will not withstand it, opposition is mounted by the *"prince of Persia"* (v. 13). In view here is the "angel prince of Persia" (NEB). The conflict envisaged is not one with flesh and blood but against principalities, powers, the spiritual hosts of wickedness in the heavenly places (Eph. 6:12). This is why Daniel needs to be "strong in the Lord" (Eph. 6:10). Nor is this conflict a momentary one. It will be engaged again (v. 20). It is perpetual.

What significance did this have for Daniel and what importance does it hold for us? (1) The events of this world cannot be interpreted by the canons of the historian alone. The historian studies events and traces, as far as one can, the sequences of cause and effect. Here Daniel is introduced to material from the heavenly archives. It indicates that the events of human history are inextricably intertwined with events in heavenly places. Thus, wrote Abraham Kuyper,

If once the curtain were pulled back, and the spiritual world behind it came to view, it would expose to our spiritual vision a struggle so intense, so convulsive, sweeping everything within its range, that the fiercest battle ever fought on earth would seem, by comparison, a mere game. Not here, but up there—that is where the real conflict is waged. Our earthly struggle drones in its backlash.[3]

Nor is that heavenly world organized as a mirror of ours. In that world the guardian of lowly Israel may do battle with and conquer the angel prince of mighty Persia.

Daniel was learning that the ultimate power struggle was fought out in a realm of which most people know nothing. It does not lie between Washington, D.C., and Moscow; its central point is not to be found in the Middle East. Indeed, the world crises we identify with these locations are actually reflections of an older, more ruthless, perpetual conflict, namely, that between the city of God with its angelic host and the kingdom of darkness, which seeks to turn the direction of all history against God and against His people.

(2) Christians are inevitably caught up in spiritual conflict. Was it this that so amazed Daniel (v. 15)? He saw that his own activity in prayer had unwittingly but inevitably linked him to the cosmic confrontation with far-reaching historical and spiritual consequences.

The word "inevitably" is used advisedly. Involvement in spiritual conflict is not an option for Christians; it is the new environment into which they have been brought by entrance into God's kingdom. Paul tells us that we receive spiritual blessings "in the heavenly places in Christ" (Eph. 1:3). Later in the same letter he tells us that those heavenly places are the sphere in which the principalities and powers of darkness have to be engaged. Christian armor is the prerequisite for surviving the conflict.

Daniel had been praying for the people of God. Some intimation of the kind of events recorded in Ezra 4 must have reached him. It seems likely that he was praying that the Persian regent would be favorably disposed to the Lord's people. Now the curtain, beyond which his prayers traveled invisibly, was momentarily lifted, and he realized the drama of heavenly warfare in which his intercession had involved him. No wonder he was awe-struck by what he saw.

Paul saw this same principle had another application, that is, in our understanding of others' responses to the gospel. Why do they not believe? Each unbeliever will have an answer, one intellectual, another emotional. Paul, however, speaks of a more sinister reason: "But even if our gospel is veiled, it is veiled to those who are perishing, whose minds the god of this age has blinded, who do not believe, lest the light of the gospel of the glory of Christ, who is the image of God, should shine on them" (2 Cor. 4:3–4). Such spiritual causes can be dealt with only by employing spiritual weapons: "For though we walk in the flesh, we do not war according to the flesh. For the weapons of our warfare *are* not carnal but mighty in God for pulling down strongholds, casting down arguments and every high thing that exalts itself against the knowledge of God, bringing every thought into captivity to the obedience of Christ" (2 Cor. 10:3–5). No wonder he asks, challengingly: "Do you look at things according to the outward appearance?" (2 Cor. 10:7).

(3) Daniel's vision underlined for him the power of prayer. His intercession was influencing the events of history. Mary Queen of Scots is reputed to have said that she feared the prayers of John Knox more than she feared an invading army. Such power is itself an encouragement to pray.

We should notice, however, that to speak of the power of prayer is potentially misleading. Two things must be added in order to safeguard it from abuse. The first is that the power does not belong to the praying or to the prayer but to God. Prayer has no power in and of itself; prayer is wholehearted dependence on God. It is a confession that we can do nothing and that God alone can work. If in our self-sufficiency and folly we should think otherwise, a rereading of Daniel 10 should act as the cure. Here a man of prayer is mourning, has no strength in him, but finds his vigor has turned to frailty so that he retained no strength. This is what is involved in drawing on the divine power to aid us in our weakness. Spiritual treasure is kept in "earthen vessels, that the excellence of the power may be of God and not of us" (2 Cor. 4:7).

The second qualification is that the only prayer which has power in its effect is that of a righteous person (James 5:16)—like Daniel (Ezra 14:14, 20). With God there can be no disjunction between the way we pray and the way we live. Prayer is not a piece of magic, a secret trick that we can use because we have a secret knowledge irrespective of our manner of life. The only prayer that is powerful in its lasting effect is the expression of the life and desires of a righteous individual who walks in covenant fellowship with God.

(4) Daniel's vision reminds us that God's people are never alone. His angels are "all ministering spirits sent forth to minister for those who will inherit salvation" (Heb. 1:14). There is an indication of this here. As soon as Daniel's cry is directed toward heaven, it is answered and help is on the way.

There was an earlier indication of this in the deliverances of Shadrach, Meshach, and Abed-Nego from the fiery furnace and of Daniel from the mouths of the lions (Dan. 3:24–25; 6:22). Here the reason these things could happen is made a little clearer. There is a passage from this world to the heavenly world and vice versa. Not only did Daniel use it, he lived at the point of contact between the two through his communion with God.

Just as it was fitting that Daniel saw the rough shadow of the cross at the time of the evening offering (Dan. 9:21), it was fitting that during this—the climax of all the manifestations of God to him—he was "left alone" (v. 8); "Daniel alone saw the vision" (v. 7). Throughout the book he is obviously a man apart. Now he is a man alone, but the truth of the matter was that he was never less alone in all his life.

NOTES

1. A. W. Tozer, *The Best of A. W. Tozer: 52 Favorite Chapters,* comp. Warren W. Wiersbe (Grand Rapids: Baker Book House, 1978), 61.

2. William Still, *Feeding God's Flock* (forthcoming).

3. Cited by G. C. Berkouwer, *A Half Century of Theology: Movements and Motives,* trans. and ed. Lewis B. Smedes (Grand Rapids: Eerdmans, 1977), 196.

Scripture Outline
> Persia and Greece (11:2–4)
>
> The Wars of Northern—and Southern—Aggression
> (11:5–35)
>
> The Antichrist! (11:36–45)

The last three chapters of Daniel form a unity. Chapter 10 provides the context within Daniel's life for this final vision. He was helped to understand the moral and spiritual character of all historical reality. This was in preparation for the revelation he was about to receive. In many ways it is the most remarkable of all the visions in the book in view of the details it includes, albeit communicated in a veiled and enigmatic fashion. The veil, however, is relatively thin. Although there are inevitable difficulties in this passage, there is wide agreement among commentators about the general outline of the history to which it points.

This raises a major question. In view of the detailed preview of history given here, can we seriously believe that this information was received by Daniel so long before the events themselves? A negative answer to that question has characterized liberal studies of Daniel. They argue, as we have seen, that the Book of Daniel was a tract for the times, written to encourage God's people during the terrible persecution of Antiochus IV (Epiphanes). An examination of this passage from such presuppositions has led scholars to believe that they can date the writing of these chapters to within a year (between 165 and 164 B.C.). Its message, it is argued, is to assure the people of God in the second century B.C. that their Lord is also the Lord of history; He is never taken by surprise by the way events work themselves out.

It need not be denied that Daniel's vision is a remarkable description of the history that followed his own time, nor should it be questioned that knowledge of the future is impossible for us to possess. This view is consistent with the rest of the book. Its claim is that God reveals to His people secrets and mysteries that cannot be understood by others: "As for me, this secret has not been revealed to me because I have more wisdom than anyone living, but for our sakes" (Dan. 2:30). In principle, it is no less likely that this panoramic vision of history was given to Daniel than that he had knowledge of Nebuchadnezzar's dream without being told of it by the king.

What is at stake then is a vital issue: Does God so rule history and can He so communicate with us that His future purposes may be disclosed to us before the events? It is, of course, denied that this is the issue. Rather it is said that this unusually detailed account is one of the clues the Book of Daniel gives us that its contents are fictitious (or at best legendary); God is speaking through a well-established literary genre.

God does reveal His truth through different literary forms. Our Lord Himself used parables and analogies. Relatively few Christians feel themselves bound to believe that the passages which begin "A certain man had . . ." or "There was a certain rich man . . ." are in the form of newspaper reports. If the parables of the prodigal son or the good Samaritan or any other parables are fictitious, most Christians are not disturbed. Why? Because they recognize instinctively that Jesus used a certain style or rhetorical form in His preaching. Similarly, when Ecclesiastes begins, "The words of the Preacher, the son of David, king in Jerusalem," some of the most conservative Old Testament scholars believe there are good reasons in the book itself for understanding that this is a literary form and discount that Solomon was the author.[1]

In the same way, it is argued that what we have in the Book of Daniel is an accepted literary form. Those who first read it would not have been deceived by it. It is not historical, but rather fictitious—with a difference—it is a tract for the times, written in the second pre-Christian century.

However, conservative studies of Daniel disagree with this approach. What is of special significance in a study such as this, however, is that we press the question: Are you not in grave danger of saying with Nebuchadnezzar, "There is no God who can deliver men from a fiery furnace," or like Darius, "Is there a God who can deliver from the mouth of lions?" The special pleading of Daniel-as-literary-genre may mask practical atheism, that is, a rejection of the supernatural. The God who does not deliver men from the fire, shut the mouths of lions, and communicate His secrets to His servants tends to be a God who does not inspire Scripture, become incarnate in a virgin womb, rise from the dead, or return as the judge of the world. In turn, all these events become part and parcel of other literary forms. The plain truth, however, is that "if Christ is not risen, then our preaching is empty and your faith is also empty." Additionally, "we are found false witnesses" (1 Cor. 15:14, 15). Genre study is essential to proper, responsible biblical exposition, and that may provide considerable help in understanding the text of Scripture. The controversy does not lie there. The ultimate issue is better focused on the presuppositions that underlie genre study. Are they presuppositions of faith in the God who acts and speaks, breaking into the world in which I live in sovereign power and communicating truth about both past and future to His people?

Since these chapters are consistent with the rest of Daniel, and since the supernatural in Daniel is confirmed as historical in the New Testament (cf. Heb. 11:33–34), the position adopted in this exposition is that the Book of Daniel presents these chapters as a prophetic outline of future events.

Thus, understanding these chapters as genuine prophecy, how are we to approach them? We have already noticed two characteristics of the prophecies in Daniel. The first is the way in which he is given a broad vision of the forthcoming events of history; then the focus of attention will fall on one specific time period. In this way it is possible for the same ground to be covered again and again, with ever-increasing insight, detail, and application.

The second feature is that the kingdom of God and the kingdoms of this world are portrayed in a permanent state of conflict which breaks out in open hostilities from time to time. As Daniel ascended the hill of God's revelation and was brought nearer to the crisis points in that conflict, he inevitably found those peaks merging into each other, sometimes (to him at least and at times also to us) indistinguishably. It is not always easy for us to determine where the vision of an intermediate conflict merges into a vision of the last and greatest conflict.

Both of these characteristics are present in this final section. It traces in greater detail the flow of the future already outlined in chapter 8. It also seems to merge that flow into the final consummation of the conflict between darkness and light (toward the end of chapter 11) in a description that appears to transcend the events of ongoing history. It is in the light of this daunting prospect that the heavenly figure brings words of encouragement, restraint, and joy to Daniel.

PERSIA AND GREECE

2 And now I will tell you the truth: Behold, three
more kings will arise in Persia, and the fourth shall be far
richer than them all; by his strength, through his riches,
he shall stir up all against the realm of Greece. 3 Then a
mighty king shall arise, who shall rule with great dominion, and do according to his will. 4 And when he has
arisen, his kingdom shall be broken up and divided
toward the four winds of heaven, but not among his posterity nor according to his dominion with which he ruled;
for his kingdom shall be uprooted, even for others besides
these.

—Daniel 11:2–4

Daniel had been informed where future heavenly strategy lay. His visitor had recently been withstood by the angel prince of Persia (10:13). His plan was to "return to fight with the [angel] prince of Persia," but the conflict would continue thereafter with the angel prince of Greece. Verses 2–4 describe this in more detail but in the form of a sketch rather than a comprehensive description. This reminds us that prophecy is not history written in advance of the time; rather it is present or future history interpreted from the standpoint of God's Word.

The future of the Persian Empire is summarized by means of a familiar Old Testament style of speech: three, followed by a fourth (cf. Prov. 30:15, 18, 21, 29). Many commentators understand the prophecy to refer to Xerxes (the fourth Persian king following Cyrus, cf. 10:1). Xerxes does appear to have spent a great deal of his wealth raising an army *("through his riches, he shall stir up all against the realm of Greece"* [v. 2]). Jerome, one of the Church Fathers, speaks of him leading an enormous army against the Greeks. If Xerxes is one of the kings, clearly Scripture traces the decline and fall of the Persian Empire from the early years of the fifth century B.C. (Xerxes ruled 486–465 B.C.). The definiteness of the statements makes this interpretation more likely than the view that the four kings are representative of the Persian Empire.

The heavenly messenger had already advised Daniel that the Persian Empire would be followed by that of Greece. The *"mighty king . . . who shall rule with great dominion"* (v. 3) is clearly a reference to the "goat" of chapter 8. That Alexander the Great should be described in these animal terms may seem strange enough to the secular historian; that his life should be summarized here in a few words may seem to defy explanation. This prophecy, however, has its center in God's reign and its ultimate focus on God's people. In the light of that, the great empires and emperors of history are as a drop in the bucket to God (Is. 40:15). Even one who *"shall rule with great dominion, and do according to his will"* (v. 3) is dependent upon God for the ability to exercise that will.

Herein lies the difference between biblical prophecy and secular biography. One of Alexander's earliest biographers, Quintus Curtius, wrote that "he seemed to the nations to do whatever pleased him." Scripture agrees, on the surface, but sees the hand of God lying behind the day when *"his kingdom shall be broken up and divided toward the four winds of heaven, but not among his posterity"* (v. 4). Alexander could not even secure what every father desires, namely, that his children inherit his achievements. His two sons were soon assassinated, and, as we have already seen, his empire passed into the hands of several others (cf. v. 4). Scripture's judgment of Alexander is that he was a broken horn (Dan. 8:22).

We need this heaven-given and long-term perspective on the affairs of our own time. This is what gives peace and strength to live through the crises experienced by the kingdom of God (cf. 10:19). The people of God do not view the great ones of this world through the eyes of the media but through the spectacles of scriptural revelation. They know that:

> It is He [not great men] who sits above the circle of
>   the earth,
> And its inhabitants are like grasshoppers,
> Who stretches out the heavens like a curtain,
> And spreads them out like a tent to dwell in.
> He brings the princes to nothing;
> He makes the judges of the earth useless.
> —*Isaiah 40:22–23*

THE WARS OF NORTHERN—AND SOUTHERN—AGGRESSION

> [5] "Also the king of the South shall become strong, as well as one of his princes; and he shall gain power over him and have dominion. His dominion shall be a great dominion. [6] And at the end of some years they shall join forces,

for the daughter of the king of the South shall go to the king of the North to make an agreement; but she shall not retain the power of her authority, and neither he nor his authority shall stand; but she shall be given up, with those who brought her, and with him who begot her, and with him who strengthened her in those times. 7 But from a branch of her roots one shall arise in his place, who shall come with an army, enter the fortress of the king of the North, and deal with them and prevail. 8 And he shall also carry their gods captive to Egypt, with their princes and their precious articles of silver and gold; and he shall continue more years than the king of the North.

9 "Also the king of the North shall come to the kingdom of the king of the South, but shall return to his own land. 10 However his sons shall stir up strife, and assemble a multitude of great forces; and one shall certainly come and overwhelm and pass through; then he shall return to his fortress and stir up strife.

11 "And the king of the South shall be moved with rage, and go out and fight with him, with the king of the North, who shall muster a great multitude; but the multitude shall be given into the hand of his enemy. 12 When he has taken away the multitude, his heart will be lifted up; and he will cast down tens of thousands, but he will not prevail. 13 For the king of the North will return and muster a multitude greater than the former, and shall certainly come at the end of some years with a great army and much equipment.

14 "Now in those times many shall rise up against the king of the South. Also, violent men of your people shall exalt themselves in fulfillment of the vision, but they shall fall. 15 So the king of the North shall come and build a siege mound, and take a fortified city; and the forces of the South shall not withstand him. Even his choice troops shall have no strength to resist. 16 But he who comes against him shall do according to his own will, and no one shall stand against him. He shall stand in the Glorious Land with destruction in his power.

17 "He shall also set his face to enter with the strength of his whole kingdom, and upright ones with him; thus shall he do. And he shall give him the daughter of women to destroy it; but she shall not stand with him, or

be for him. [18] After this he shall turn his face to the coastlands, and shall take many. But a ruler shall bring the
reproach against them to an end; and with the reproach
removed, he shall turn back on him. [19] Then he shall
turn his face toward the fortress of his own land; but he
shall stumble and fall, and not be found.

[20] "There shall arise in his place one who imposes
taxes on the glorious kingdom; but within a few days he
shall be destroyed, but not in anger or in battle. [21] And in
his place shall arise a vile person, to whom they will not
give the honor of royalty; but he shall come in peaceably,
and seize the kingdom by intrigue. [22] With the force of a
flood they shall be swept away from before him and be
broken, and also the prince of the covenant. [23] And after
the league is made with him he shall act deceitfully, for
he shall come up and become strong with a small number
of people. [24] He shall enter peaceably, even into the richest places of the province; and he shall do what his
fathers have not done, nor his forefathers: he shall disperse among them the plunder, spoil, and riches; and he
shall devise his plans against the strongholds, but only for
a time.

[25] "He shall stir up his power and his courage against
the king of the South with a great army. And the king of
the South shall be stirred up to battle with a very great
and mighty army; but he shall not stand, for they shall
devise plans against him. [26] Yes, those who eat of the portion of his delicacies shall destroy him; his army shall be
swept away, and many shall fall down slain. [27] Both these
kings' hearts shall be bent on evil, and they shall speak
lies at the same table; but it shall not prosper, for the end
will still be at the appointed time. [28] While returning to
his land with great riches, his heart shall be moved
against the holy covenant; so he shall do damage and
return to his own land.

[29] "At the appointed time he shall return and go
toward the south; but it shall not be like the former or
the latter. [30] For ships from Cyprus shall come against
him; therefore he shall be grieved, and return in rage
against the holy covenant, and do damage.

"So he shall return and show regard for those who forsake the holy covenant. [31] And forces shall be mustered by

him, and they shall defile the sanctuary fortress; then they shall take away the daily sacrifices, and place there the abomination of desolation. [32] Those who do wickedly against the covenant he shall corrupt with flattery; but the people who know their God shall be strong, and carry out great exploits. [33] And those of the people who understand shall instruct many; yet for many days they shall fall by sword and flame, by captivity and plundering. [34] Now when they fall, they shall be aided with a little help; but many shall join with them by intrigue.

[35] And some of those of understanding shall fall, to refine them, purify them, and make them white, until the time of the end; because it is still for the appointed time.

—Daniel 11:5-35

The perspective from which history is assessed now changes. Until this point of the final section, the viewpoint has been from above. Now it is from the center. The long and complex prophecy from verse 5 onward sees the ensuing history as a conflict between the kings of the north and the kings of the south. But north and south of where?

The center of the compass used here is the Glorious Land (v. 16). The point from which history is now viewed is that of God's covenant people. The "Land" is glorious because there the promises of God's covenant were enshrined and His *shekinah* presence was made known. While, at least at first glance, this prophecy has to do with foreign nations and their conflicts, Daniel is learning that all human history is part of the fundamental conflict in which the object is the destruction of the city of God.

In one sense Daniel 11 is a mosaic or tapestry of historical events in which the connection between events is not always clear. Since most of us have a limited knowledge of ancient history, we consequently find it difficult to identify the events to which the vision points. We may therefore sympathize with the words of one scholar who commented on Daniel 11, "We do not see how it could be used for a sermon or for sermons."[2] The exposition of the passage becomes somewhat easier when we realize what lies behind it, and we are able to see the details as pieces of a larger design.

Our best procedure in exposition is to outline the history of which verses 5-35 speak. The *"king of the South"* (Egypt in v. 8) momentarily stands before us in all his strength (v. 5). Alexander the Great's empire was eventually divided into four sections: (1) Macedonia, ruled by Cassander; (2) Thrace and Asia Minor, ruled by Lysimachus; (3) Syria under Seleucus; and (4) Egypt under Ptolemy.

Seleucus was forced to flee from Syria, but with Ptolemy's help he recovered Babylonia in 312 B.C. and did, in fact, build an empire greater than Ptolemy's.

"At the end of some years" (v. 6), that is, later in these dynasties, a marriage alliance was attempted between the king of the North and the daughter of the king of the South. This seems to be fulfilled in the bigamous marriage between Antiochus II (grandson of Seleucus I) and Berenice (the daughter of Ptolemy Philadelphus). Shortly afterward, Ptolemy died, and Antiochus divorced Berenice, returning to his earlier wife, Laodice. Fearing the possibility of an eternal triangle, Laodice poisoned Antiochus and encouraged her son, Seleucus Callinicus, to murder Berenice and her child, thus leaving the way clear for him to inherit the throne.

The dynastic feud continued when Berenice's brother, Ptolemy III (Euergetes [meaning, "well-doer"]) arose *"in his place"* (v. 7), overcame the forces of the North, executed Laodice, and pillaged the Northern kingdom (v. 8—note the reference to gods that need to be carried). Some time later, Seleucus Callinicus regained power, marched against Ptolemy, and was defeated (v. 9). His sons, Seleucus Ceraunus and Antiochus III (later, the Great), continued the conflict (v. 10). Antiochus III then led an army *("a multitude of great forces"* [v. 10]) to Ptolemy's fortress.

Ptolemy IV (also called Philopator), now *"the king of the South"* (v. 11), angered by this movement of troops into his territory, made ready for war with Antiochus, in which he was victorious (the king of the North *"shall muster a great multitude; but the multitude shall be given into the hand of his enemy"* [v. 11]). Ptolemy inflicted a tremendous defeat on the North at Raphia, but, as verse 12 indicates, hinting at his profligate life-style, his ascendancy did not last. He did defend his kingdom against further invasions (in which apparently a number of Jews participated believing they were fulfilling prophecy [v. 14]). Eventually, however, Antiochus would be victorious. Not even the choice troops of Ptolemy could withstand him. Now Antiochus III also betrayed the hubris that characterizes great men without God in the Book of Daniel: he *"shall do according to his own will"* (v. 16).

All this, however, is but the preface and explanation for a statement of devastating force to Daniel: *"He shall stand in the*

Glorious Land with destruction in his power" (v. 16). Antiochus III now completed a marriage treaty by betrothing his daughter, Cleopatra, to Ptolemy V, apparently to give him a fifth column within the kingdom of the South *("to destroy it"* [v. 17]). She sided, however, with her husband—*"she shall not stand with him, or be for him"* (v. 17). Antiochus then turned his attention to the Mediterranean area *("the coastlands"* [v. 18]). He was, however, defeated in battle at Magnesia in 190–189 B.C. by *"a ruler,"* when the Romans, under Scipio Asiaticus, intervened. There was no place left to go but *"toward the fortress of his own land"* (v. 19). He was eventually assassinated while trying to rob a temple at Elam, thus fulfilling the words, *"he shall stumble and fall"* (v. 19). Antiochus III was succeeded by Seleucus IV (also known as Philopator) in 167 B.C. He sent his chief minister to take the treasures of the temple in Jerusalem, but, according to 2 Maccabees, he was prevented by a supernatural vision. Seleucus was assassinated shortly after this (*"not in anger or in battle"* [v. 20]).

The next figure to step onto the stage of history dominates the rest of the chapter. He is *"a vile person, to whom they will not give the honor of royalty"* (v. 21). This is Antiochus IV (Epiphanes). Since we have now reached the central section of this vision, it will perhaps be helpful to review the conflict between the kings of the South and the North. The two dynasties were as follows:

The South (Ptolemies—Egypt)	The North (Seleucids—Syria)
Ptolemy I (Soter) 323–285	Seleucus I (Nicator) 312–280
Ptolemy II (Philadelphus) 285–246	Antiochus I (Soter) 280–261
	Antiochus II (Theos) 261–246
Ptolemy III (Euergetes) 246–221	Seleucus II (Callinicus) 246–226
	Seleucus III (Ceraunus) 226–223
Ptolemy IV (Philopator) 221–204	Antiochus III (the Great) 223–1 87
Ptolemy V (Epiphanes) 204–181	Seleucus IV (Philopator) 187–175
Ptolemy VI (Philometor) 181–145	Antiochus IV (Epiphanes) 175–164

Antiochus Epiphanes was the brother of Seleucus IV. By careful intrigue he had gained the throne that should have belonged to his nephew, Demetrius. It has been suggested that Demetrius is the *"prince of the covenant"* (v. 22), because he was already loved by the people; others suggest Onias III, the high priest who was later poisoned. We should not be confused by the use of the term "covenant," which often carries special redemptive connotations in Scripture. It may be employed in the sense of alliance or treaty here as elsewhere in Scripture and points to someone who bore such a relationship with Antiochus IV.

Antiochus appears to have continued his intrigues by ingratiating himself to some of the Jews (v. 28), thus enabling him to *"enter peaceably"* (that is, into the city of Jerusalem [v. 24]). His lifestyle was quite prodigal: *"He shall disperse among them the plunder, spoil, and riches."* He made plans to invade *"the strongholds"* of Egypt (v. 24).

Antiochus made several attacks on Egypt (see the description of his attack in v. 29 as not *"like the former or the latter"*), two of which, with the ensuing consequences, are described in detail in verses 25–28 and 29–35. The first appears to have been incited by Ptolemy Philometor, who was to all intents and purposes the puppet of his advisers, Eulaeus and Lenaeus (*"those who eat of the portion of his delicacies shall destroy him"* [v. 26]). Antiochus was completely victorious in 169 B.C. and entered into an uneasy alliance with Ptolemy Philometor, in which neither displayed great integrity (*"they shall speak lies at the same table"* [v. 27]). Antiochus's plans, however, did not bear the fruit he intended. Daniel is given an interesting reason, a divine reason— *"for the end will still be at the appointed time"* (v. 27).

Antiochus returned from Egypt. A rumor had spread in Jerusalem that he had been killed. The news had been greeted with both rejoicing and swift action. The puppet high priest and his supporters had been slain. Antiochus's *"heart"* was *"moved against the holy covenant"* (v. 28). He invaded Jerusalem, looted the temple, and carried its treasures home to Antioch in Syria.

Once again, in 168 B.C., Antiochus set out to invade Egypt. This time, however, he was *"grieved"* [v. 30]) by the entry of delegates from Rome into the conflict (arriving in *"ships from Cyprus"* [v. 30]). It is reported that the Roman consul, Gaius Popilius Laenas, drew a circle around Antiochus and told him to decide on his movements before he stepped out of it. Deeply humiliated, Antiochus sought to strengthen his power base, and at the same time vented his anger on the people of God.

Returning to Jerusalem, either in person or through his representative, Antiochus conferred secretly with those Jews who were sympathetic to the Hellenization process then taking place around the Mediterranean (*"he shall return and show regard for those who forsake the holy covenant"* [v. 30]). Finding stubborn resistance to his plans, he drafted Apollonius, the leader of a group of mercenaries. He pretended to be disposed peacefully toward the Jews, but on the Sabbath he paraded his fully armed men and then proceeded to massacre those Jews who stood by as spectators. He ravaged the city mercilessly. No effort was spared to destroy the faith of the people of God. The sanctuary was defiled, the daily sacrifices abolished, and an altar or image of Zeus was set up and pagan rites were celebrated on the altar of burnt offering (*"the abomination of desolation"* [v. 31]).

Although there were those who apostatized, many remained faithful in the face of persecution— *"the people who know their God shall be strong, and carry out great exploits"* (v. 32). Leaders emerged to encourage the faithful while the persecution continued (v. 33). Military resistance was offered in the heroic deeds of the Maccabeans (recorded in the Books of the Maccabees in the Apocrypha). They faced the problem often besetting resistance movements: *"Many shall join with them by intrigue"* (v. 34). Among the faithful, some will prove unfaithful and will *"fall."* Even this illustrates a constant biblical principle: "There must be factions among you, that those who are approved may be recognized among you" (1 Cor. 11:19, cf. v. 35). Persecution will happen *"to refine them, purify them, and make them white, until the time of the end"* (that is, until God's purpose through such persecution has been fulfilled [v. 35]).

At this point in our study of Daniel 11 all teachers and preachers must face the inevitable question: How is such a passage as this "profitable for doctrine, for reproof, for correction, for instruction in righteousness" (2 Tim. 3:16)? Should we not simply accept the verdict that this section is valuable only as an outline of ancient history? The answer must be "No" for these two reasons:

(1) It is always important to cover passages of Scripture that contain material that is difficult to follow (whether because of our own lack of general knowledge or the inherent difficulty of understanding the passage). Why? Because it underlines the biblical teaching that studying Scripture is hard work ("a worker who does not need to be ashamed, rightly dividing [handling] the word of truth" [2 Tim. 2:15]) and that some passages of Scripture are "hard to understand" (2 Pet. 3:16). Until we grasp that the inspiration of Scripture does not mean

we will always be "inspired" when we read it, we will not make much headway as students of God's Word. On the other hand, when we or those we teach see the doctrine or instruction that can be gleaned from a passage like this, the value of such study will be obvious.

(2) No right-thinking communicator would present such material as this merely as a history lesson for one important reason: It is not history—it is prophecy. It foretells the future in a remarkable way. Understanding this should fill our hearts with fresh reverence for the wonders that are contained in God's Word.

What specific doctrine, reproof, correction, or instruction in righteousness do we find in this chapter? We must ask: What is the purpose or function of this passage? The purpose of Daniel 11 will be missed unless we remember that chapters 10, 11, and 12 are a unity. The chapter divisions mark the development within one single vision. In chapter 10, Daniel was taken behind the scenes of history to see both the nature of the heavenly, spiritual conflict that affects history and to learn the degree to which his prayers played a causal, if secondary, role in that conflict. The whole point of that revelation was surely to encourage Daniel to understand the significance of the rest of the vision and to teach him how he should pray and live in the light of the direction of world events and their impact upon the city of God. He was to see that there were certain recurring characteristics in the pattern of the activities of the kingdoms of the world. Knowing that, he could pray intelligently and confidently for the future of the city of God.

Four profitable lessons of this section may be mentioned. (1) Daniel's vision reveals the perennial instability of the kingdoms of the earth. Evil is always unstable because it is rooted in our following our own wills instead of God's will. God's will alone is stable and enduring; it alone will ultimately come to pass (Job 41:10; Rom. 8:28; Eph. 1:11b).

The kingdoms of the world are unstable because their gods are also unstable—being no gods at all. The heavenly visitor speaks about the king of the South having to carry away the gods of the king of the North (v. 8). Isaiah had spoken graphically of something similar:

Bel bows down, Nebo stoops;
Their idols were on the beasts and on the cattle . . .
[they] have themselves gone into captivity.
—*Isaiah 46:1–2*

Everything to which this world's kingdoms are devoted is ultimately ephemeral. That principle applies whether we are devoted to idols we call gods or simply idols of ambition, power, fame, and possessions. The kingdom that has no ultimate foundation is bound to crumble since it is populated by sinners devoted to their own ways; it contains the seed of its own destruction. Where there is self-seeking and pride, there will also be intrigue and deceit (vv. 6, 17, 23, 27, 32, 34). This is a moral universe. Under God's judgment evil will eventually destroy itself for it cannot control itself (vv. 28, 30).

(2) A second important lesson surfaces in verses 30–32. Here Antiochus, the symbol of earthly kingdoms, gains a foothold among the people of God. Historians believe that this double-dealing within Jerusalem was the reason for his success in Jerusalem. This illustrates another general biblical principle: Evil cannot gain a foothold in the city of God unless it finds a spirit of cooperation among the visible people of God. It is not inevitable that the church should be corrupted by the world; there must be a willingness or a blindness in the church before that happens. This is true at three levels of our lives: doctrinal, moral, and spiritual. Where there is compromise in any of these areas, weakness and failure follow. All three must be guarded with care. Antiochus (who, we will see, bears some of the marks of the final Antichrist) succeeded only because he found those in Jerusalem enamored with Hellenization, which involved a weakening of their doctrinal, moral, and spiritual vigor. That is no less of a danger for the church today.

(3) There is also much here to bring encouragement to God's beleaguered people. Daniel's vision describes wave upon wave of the activities of the worldly kingdoms. The vision's structure makes it clear that in the final analysis the aim of evil is always to destroy the people of God. The kingdom of darkness never learns the lesson: "Man proposes, God disposes."[3] It does not yield to God because it knows it is doomed to destruction. The believer, however, sharing Daniel's vision, knows this to be the case.

This assurance appears in a subtle but definite way in Daniel 11—in the number of times the word "but" is used (vv. 4, 6, 7, 9, 11, 12, 14, 18, 19, 20, 21, 25, 27, 29). It reveals a pattern: The worldly kingdoms plot their schemes; as they unfold, God brings them to naught. We make our plans, but God intervenes. He does so in various ways. His judgments are rarely recognized, but they are nevertheless real. The one who blatantly despises God's Word may arrogantly ask: "Where is the wrath of God when I do all these things and He does not even respond?" The sobering truth, however, is that enslaved devotion to "these things" is an indication that God's wrath is already revealed. God has given the despiser up (Rom. 1:18, 24, 26, 28).

God is a righteous judge. He will not be mocked. What the kingdoms sow, they must also reap. If they sow to self-interest, then the harvest will be their own corruption and disintegration. The people of God know this because they know God. Consequently they *shall be strong and carry out great exploits* (v. 32). Evil is *only for a time* (v. 24). There will be, in one form or another, divine judgment on the specific manifestations of evil we encounter and ultimately on the entire kingdom of evil.

(4) The final lesson of this section is that God is working out His purpose for His people in all the circumstances of their lives (cf. Rom. 8:28). They will taste "tribulation . . . distress . . . persecution . . . famine . . . nakedness . . . peril . . . sword" (Rom. 8:35). They know that through this, the Lord will *refine them, purify them, and make them white, until the time of the end* (v. 35).

If Daniel learned these principles, he would be able to pray, face the worldly kingdoms, and sing:

> Workman of God! O lose not heart
> But learn what God is like,
> And, in the darkest battlefield,
> Thou shalt know where to strike.
>
> —F. W. Faber

THE ANTICHRIST!

36 "Then the king shall do according to his own will: he shall exalt and magnify himself above every god, shall speak blasphemies against the God of gods, and shall prosper till the wrath has been accomplished; for what has been determined shall be done. 37 He shall regard neither the God of his fathers nor the desire of women, nor regard any god; for he shall exalt himself above them all. 38 But in their place he shall honor a god of fortresses; and a god which his fathers did not know he shall honor with gold and silver, with precious stones and pleasant things. 39 Thus he shall act against the strongest fortresses with a foreign god, which he shall acknowledge, and advance its glory; and he shall cause them to rule over many, and divide the land for gain.

⁴⁰ "At the time of the end the king of the South shall attack him; and the king of the North shall come against him like a whirlwind, with chariots, horsemen, and with many ships; and he shall enter the countries, overwhelm them, and pass through. ⁴¹ He shall also enter the Glorious Land, and many countries shall be overthrown; but these shall escape from his hand: Edom, Moab, and the prominent people of Ammon. ⁴² He shall stretch out his hand against the countries, and the land of Egypt shall not escape. ⁴³ He shall have power over the treasures of gold and silver, and over all the precious things of Egypt; also the Libyans and Ethiopians shall follow at his heels. ⁴⁴ But news from the east and the north shall trouble him; therefore he shall go out with great fury to destroy and annihilate many. ⁴⁵ And he shall plant the tents of his palace between the seas and the glorious holy mountain; yet he shall come to his end, and no one will help him.

—Daniel 11:36–45

A new phase of activity begins at verse 36 and introduces us to probably the most difficult section in chapter 11. The spotlight has been on Antiochus Epiphanes in verses 21–35, but it is widely recognized that the section that follows no longer focuses on him. How are we to understand this?

It has become a canon of critical scholarship that these verses intend to describe Antiochus because there is no change of subject from the previous verses. That these later verses are not consistent with what we know of Antiochus's later life is curiously regarded as a bonus for this understanding. It suggests that at this juncture the author ceased describing past events (of which he had already detailed historical knowledge) under the guise of prophecy and began to offer a little prophesying of the future himself. The point at which his "errors" begin pinpoints his time of writing. This view scarcely commends itself to those who are convinced that the Book of Daniel contains both history and prophecy. How then are these verses to be understood?

Clearly the concluding phrases of verse 35 are ambiguous. If we read only to the end of the verse, the phrases the "time of the end" and "the appointed time" appear to signify the end of the period of persecution. The description of the king's blasphemy, however, follows, suggesting that these phrases may refer to the final consummation of God's purposes in history. Thus the "then" of verse 36 points to some period between the days of Antiochus and the last day of history. During that time there will be apostasies and refinings among the visible people of God.

Such a view is certainly consistent with the way in which the New Testament views history and the experience of the church in particular (Mark 13:8–13). It is also consistent with the way in which Jesus seems to have seen the description of Antiochus's activity as foreshadowing the future. Jesus speaks of an "abomination of desolation" (v. 31) that was yet to come (Mark 13:14).

The question, therefore, is: To whom do these verses refer if not to Antiochus? Numerous answers have been proposed ranging from the Roman Empire (as John Calvin believed) to Herod, to Mohammed, to the papacy (as many Protestants held in the early years of the Reformation), to the view that is held by many of today's interpreters, that the reference is to the final Antichrist. There is good reason to adopt this view. The king in view clearly transcends in wickedness any figure in history. Then the time in view, "that time" (Dan. 12:1), appears to be related to the final resurrection (Dan. 12:2).

Two important principles will enlarge our appreciation of this section. The first is that Daniel himself did not fully understand the vision he received. Later he confessed, "Although I heard, I did not understand" (Dan. 12:8). Yet it was intended that he share the consolation implicit in its teaching. The same can be true for us even when we cannot fully understand the details of these verses. It ought to be added that a confession of ignorance about the precise significance of some of these statements is nothing of which to be ashamed. Adding a dogmatic assurance to one's interpretation of a passage of Scripture is no guarantee that the interpretation is correct.

The second principle is equally important. If indeed these verses do refer ultimately to the personification of enmity against God in the figure of the Antichrist, then there will inevitably be many foreshadowings of his character. Those who were united to Christ through faith before His coming bore many of His gracious characteristics. In a nontechnical sense, they were types of Christ. The same is true of the Antichrist. History is frequently punctuated by those who share his kingdom and whose lifestyles resemble what his will be. No wonder that precursors of the antichrist have been taken to be the final Antichrist (cf. 1 John 2:18).

What are the features of the final Antichrist and all interim Antichrists? A number of features stand out in Daniel's vision.

(1) The most basic is the quest for autonomy: *"the king shall do according to his own will: He shall exalt and magnify himself"* (v. 36). We have already seen this spirit emerge in various figures in Daniel (cf. 3:15; 4:30; 8:25; 11:3, 12, 16). It will emerge in full-blown form at the end in the final conflict between the kingdoms. It does so inevitably because it is the crux of the conflict. Its foundations run back into the origins of history and beyond into the mists of eternity. The tempting words "you will be like God" echo through the ages from a whisper in the Garden of Eden to a clamor at the end of time.

(2) Coupled with this is blasphemy and inhumanity. *"The king . . . shall speak blasphemies against the God of gods"* (v. 36). He will lack and despise any sense of loyalty, even to parental religion—a mark of appalling decadence in the world of Daniel's time and still in many places of our world today. *"He shall regard neither the God of his fathers nor the desire of women"* (v. 37).

The "desire of women" is sometimes taken to refer to Tammuz, the pagan deity whose death the goddess Ishtar mourned and summoned others to mourn also (cf. Ezekiel's dismay at this abomination [Ezek. 8:13–14]). The phrase, however, may be taken in a narrow literal sense (think, for example, of the way in which those who have borne some resemblance to the Antichrist have shamefully and shamelessly treated the women in their lives—mothers, sisters, wives, and others). A wider sense may be in view. God has made humanity as male and female, interrelated and interdependent, to reflect His glory. There is nothing more basic to human life, biologically, psychologically, emotionally, and socially, than the male-female distinction-within-unity. The "love of women" (2 Sam. 21:6) is synonymous with deep and lasting affection and devotion. For this the Antichrist has no regard. It is no surprise that empires that bore some of his traits should be painted in the Book of Daniel as beasts.

(3) The doctrine of the Antichrist is "might is right." The god whose glory he advances and honors is *"a god of fortresses"* (v. 38). Here the metaphor is military but the principle applies to all circumstances of life in which power is possessed. What we have here is simply a thumbnail sketch of sin grown to maturity. Wherever we see these elements we know there is enmity to the kingdom of God. That may be in the society in which we live; it may even be in our own hearts.

Having described the character of the Antichrist, Daniel's vision went on to describe his progress. Here again caution is required because inevitably the vision of the future is presented in terms of the experience, knowledge, and events of the present. He refers again to the conflict between the king of the South and the king of the North. Many Christians read these verses with complete literalism or "literalistic-ism." This is probably to miss the intention of the vision. Taken in a literal fashion, these verses suggest that chariots, horsemen, and ships will be the weapons of conflict in the last days. This fails to see that prophetic visions view the future in terms of the contemporary. The understanding of them requires the recognition of symbolism.

Verses 41–45 present us with a picture of the final struggle. The king of the North (antichrist) prevails over the king of the South (v. 40) and establishes himself in the Glorious Land (v. 41). The only nations to escape (*"Edom, Moab, and the prominent people of Ammon"* [v. 41]) are the age-old enemies of Israel. All his enemies and their allies (Egypt, Libya, and Ethiopia [v. 43]) *"shall follow at his heels"* as prisoners (v. 43).

Curiously, the narrative is cut short. The king will hear of trouble and plan to destroy it (v. 44). He will set up his headquarters *"between the seas [plural although perhaps the Mediterranean is in view] and the glorious holy mountain"* (v. 45). His defeat will be as inauspicious as his rise to power was meteoric. There is a devastating—presumably deliberate—anticlimax to the progress of evil. In fact, "The Lord will consume [him] with the breath of His mouth and destroy with the brightness of His coming" (2 Thess. 2:8). Christ will simply blow him away. It will be as anticlimactic as that. If we may parody T. S. Eliot's "The Hollow Men":

> This is the way the antichrist ends
> Not with a bang, but a whimper.

Conservative interpreters believe that these words will have complete fulfillment in the future. Few, if any, however, would interpret them *All pied de la lettre.* Even among those who favor a generally literal interpretation, it is not uncommon for the kingdom of the North to be interpreted as one of today's superpowers and for chariots and horsemen to become tanks. We should remember that such exegesis already assumes that the language here has been understood symbolically, not literally.

Given this principle, it is a mistake to assume that the conflict involved is to be understood exclusively in military terms. To do so draws our attention away from the fact that the real war for our souls is never fought on the battlefields of history but elsewhere. The principle "might is right" is as often manifested in financial, intellectual, and moral terms as it is in military terms. We must never forget that the weapons of our warfare are not and never will be carnal—they must always be spiritual. This at least was the conviction of Paul who believed that the Antichrist would be destroyed not by might, nor by power, but by the Spirit or breath of Christ. The implication he drew was:

> Finally, my brethren, be strong in the Lord and in the power of His might. Put on the whole armor of God, that you may be able to stand against the wiles of the devil. For we do not wrestle against flesh and blood, but against principalities, against powers, against the rulers of the darkness of this age, against spiritual hosts of wickedness in the heavenly places. Therefore take up the whole armor of God, that you may be able to withstand in the evil day, and having done all, to stand . . . praying always with all prayer and supplication in the Spirit, being watchful to this end with all perseverance and supplication for all the saints.
>
> —*Ephesians 6:10–13, 18*

After all is said on this difficult chapter, we should not lose sight of the fact that its whole function was to encourage Daniel to faithfulness in prayer. By showing him that the real conflict lying behind world events is spiritual (cf. ch. 10), the Lord was teaching Daniel that the real weapon of the church is prayer. Fail in the work of prayer, and we fail to understand this great vision.

NOTES

1. E.g., E. J. Young, *An Introduction to the Old Testament*, 2d ed. (Grand Rapids: Eerdmans, 1964), 347–49.

2. H. C. Leupold, *Exposition of Daniel* (Grand Rapids: Baker Book House, 1969), 525.

3. Thomas à Kempis, *The Imitation of Christ*, 1.19.

CHAPTER TWELVE—FROM HERE TO ETERNITY
DANIEL 12:1–13

Scripture Outline
The Hope of Glory (12:1–4)
Living with Unanswered Questions (12:5–13)

The third and final section of Daniel's vision fittingly provides the conclusion to all that we know of his life. In keeping with the thrust of the book, chapter 12 contains both revelation of God's future purposes and application to Daniel's life in the present. It also provides further illustration of the eschatological ethic that characterizes all Scripture.

In every epoch of revelation, God's people have been encouraged to live in the light of what He has promised for the future. That was true in the Garden of Eden when Adam and Eve were given God's commandment not to eat of the tree of the knowledge of good and evil. Apparently He intended that one day they would eat of it (Gen. 3:22; Rev. 2:7). In a similar way the heroes of the faith lived in the light of the future: "And all these, having obtained a good testimony through faith, did not receive the promise, God having provided something better for us, that they should not be made perfect apart from us" (Heb. 11:39–40). What distinguished those Old Testament characters in general was specifically true of Daniel. God told him that while he had done much already, the time of His kingdom's consummation was "not yet." Daniel and others with him (including us) must wait with patience for the final inheritance (v. 13).

Chapter 12 divides into two sections: Verses 1–4 conclude the prophecy that had begun in 10:20; verses 5–13 contain Daniel's own record of the final moments of his visionary experience.

THE HOPE OF GLORY

12:1 "At that time Michael shall stand up,
The great prince who stands watch over the sons of
your people;
And there shall be a time of trouble,
Such as never was since there was a nation,
Even to that time.
And at that time your people shall be delivered,
Every one who is found written in the book.
² And many of those who sleep in the dust of the
earth shall awake,
Some to everlasting life,
Some to shame and everlasting contempt.
³ Those who are wise shall shine
Like the brightness of the firmament,
And those who turn many to righteousness
Like the stars forever and ever.
⁴ "But you, Daniel, shut up the words, and seal the
book until the time of the end; many shall run to and
fro, and knowledge shall increase."

—Daniel 12:1–4

The heavenly visitor had described the rise of Antiochus Epiphanes (as the fulfillment of his prophecy indicated). The description of his blasphemous activities seemed to serve as a springboard for describing a more sinister figure yet to come, to be known in the New Testament as the final antichrist or the man of sin. He now once more explains *"the time of the end"* (v. 4, cf. 11:40).

Scripture promises us that the last days (that is, the period between Pentecost and the return of Christ [Acts 2:16–17]) will be punctuated by times of special stress and danger (2 Tim. 3:1). This will reach a climax at "the time of the end": *"there shall be a time of trouble, such as never was since there was a nation, even to that time"* (v. 1). Daniel, however, must not allow himself to be overwhelmed with despair because God will provide His people with protection, specifically in the work of Michael.

Michael (meaning, "Who is like God?") has already been mentioned in 10:13, 21. He is "one of the chief princes," that is, an archangel (Jude 9). Indeed, he is *"the great prince"* who acts as the guardian of all God's people ("your prince" [10:21], the one who *"stands watch over the sons of your people"* [v. 1]). His task is to bring deliverance to all those whose names are written in the book of life (v. 1).

Two explicit references to Michael and his ministry appear in the New Testament. In Jude 9, his restraint is set before us as an example: "Michael the archangel, in contending with the devil, when he disputed about the body of Moses, dared not bring against him a reviling accusation, but said, "The Lord rebuke you!" Michael did not underestimate the power or perversion of Satan. He did not imagine that he could tangle with evil in a cavalier fashion, but he instead trusted in the Lord to rebuke the evil one. What is significant for our purposes is that Michael here is seen in the fullest possible sense as the guardian of God's people until the resurrection. That is why he contended with the devil over the body of Moses.

The allusion in Jude is to an extrabiblical apocalyptic work, The Assumption of Moses, in which Satan claims Moses' body as his own on the grounds that Moses had been a murderer in earlier life. Jude's use of a nonbiblical Jewish work should not cause us any more difficulty than Paul's citing pagan poetry in Athens (Acts 17:28). He is drawing on an extrabiblical story to illustrate a point he wishes to make. That extrabiblical story, however, simply underlines the point that Michael is the guardian angel of the Lord's people.

The final reference to Michael is found in Revelation 12:7, in which he is seen as the leader of the heavenly host making war on the dragon and his angels (who sought to destroy the male child). Here again, Michael is seen as the one who battles on behalf of God's cause. Daniel learns that through him "[his] people shall be delivered" (v. 1). All those whose names God has written in the book of life will be preserved.

Nothing more is known directly of this grand figure. It is interesting to ask whether Michael may not also be the angel mentioned in Revelation 20:1 (the one who binds the dragon for a thousand years) since he was already instrumental in the dragon's being cast out of heaven (Rev. 12:7-9). In that case, there may also be good reason for believing that Paul's obscure and much-debated reference to "what is restraining" and "he who now restrains" the man of sin (2 Thess. 2:6-7) is also a reference to Michael and his ministry. This not only provides biblical content to Paul's allusion, it also explains how the dragon once again is allowed to deceive the nations while Michael's influence is withdrawn.

The references in Daniel to the ministry of Michael and other angelic figures reminds us that we do not live in an impersonal universe. God's providence is never a matter of impersonal forces somehow sustaining the development of history. Conscious experience of angelic intervention was doubtless rare, even in biblical times (Heb. 13:21), but the reality of their guardian work is plainly affirmed: God "shall give His angels charge over you, to keep you in all your ways. In *their* hands they shall bear you up, lest you dash your foot against a stone" (Ps. 91:11–12). The people of God have been preserved by angelic intervention times beyond number. Only the final, heavenly unraveling of the plan of God in history will unveil the extent of their work.

In any event, these verses point out that Michael's influence will once again be exerted. The "time of trouble" (v. 1) will be brought to an end, and the resurrection will occur.

Daniel is assured that *"many of those who sleep in the dust of the earth shall awake"* (v. 2). A clearer reference to the hope of the resurrection scarcely seems possible, but how do we understand the words "many of those who sleep"? Will not all who sleep be raised, either to salvation or condemnation? Some commentators understand these words in a universal sense ("many" = "all," which it may do in Scripture). Others take the expression here to refer to many but not all, without necessarily excluding all; that is, those concerned are those who have been put to death in the great tribulation just described. This latter view seems preferable. Not even the terrible time of suffering can destroy the certainty of the resurrection.

Throughout the Book of Daniel people are divided into two groups. The last judgment perpetuates that division. Some will awaken *"to shame and everlasting contempt"* (v. 2). Raised from the dead, they will be forever excluded from the city of God. The annihilation of the wicked is not envisaged here, but rather a perpetual state of guilt and separation from God.

As elsewhere in Scripture, the description of the blessedness of those whose names are *"written in the book"* (v. 2) is both fuller and richer. They will shine like the sun and display a splendor like the stars (v. 3). The "saints of the Most High" (Dan. 7:27) will reflect the glory received by the One like the Son of Man (Dan. 7:13–14). They will be changed into His likeness (2 Cor. 3:18; 1 John 3:1–3). Nothing will then be able to undo that final transformation. It will last *"forever and ever"* (v. 3).

Already in the Old Testament we see that the goal of the hope of believers is not individual death. It is the resurrection and the transformation (or glorification) that will accompany it. Believers do not look forward merely to dying but to the destruction of death (which is not so much the last enemy but "the last enemy that will be destroyed" [1 Cor. 15:26]). They see the fulfillment of God's grace not in release from the body but in total transformation, body and soul, when they share in the triumphant glory of the kingdom of God.

In view of this great prospect, there is something that Daniel must do. He must preserve the revelation he has received, *"until the time of the end"* (v. 4). It must be on record for God's people so that the events of the end will not take them by surprise. Later believers who are familiar with God's Word will not only be equipped for every good work (2 Tim. 3:17) but also will be kept trusting the Lord and living stable lives even in the troubles that precede the end. They may not have access to the details of God's planning, but they know that God has a plan and that He is faithfully fulfilling it. All that they have learned thus far from the Book of Daniel helps them to "sing the Lord's song in a strange land." Because believers will be different there and then, they learn to be different here and now.

The difficult statement that follows (v. 4) is best understood as a further contrast between the life-style of the citizens of God's city and that of the citizens of the city of destruction—not only in the long term (vv. 2–8) but also in the short term. While believers are able to rest secure in the knowledge of God they receive through God's Word, unbelievers are agitated in their search for the truth— *"many shall run to and fro"* in the quest for reality. As a result of their quest, *"knowledge shall increase"* (v. 4). Apart from the knowledge of God's Word, that increased knowledge will simply be in vain. There seems to be an echo here of the statement in Amos:

> They shall wander from sea to sea,
> And from north to east;
> They shall run to and fro, seeking the word of the
>   LORD,
> But shall not find *it*.
>
> —*Amos 8:12*

It is a picture of those who reject God but who are driven to seek for what God alone is able to give. When truth is rejected for lies (Rom. 1:25; 2 Thess. 2:11), we cannot find contentment. We must live as though we have been branded with the mark of Cain

(Gen. 4:12); as gypsy wanderers without homes, we are driven from one home to the next, seeking a place of rest. In the process we discover many things but find no sense of peace (think of the explosion of knowledge in the past century, accompanied by the increased anxieties and the restlessness of our society). "'There is no peace [shalom, health, wholeness of life],' says my God, 'for the wicked'" (Is. 57:21). How different is life in the city of God, the heavenly Jerusalem, the city whose maker and builder is God and whose very atmosphere is "salem" (=shalom, peace).

LIVING WITH UNANSWERED QUESTIONS

5 Then I, Daniel, looked; and there stood two others, one on this riverbank and the other on that riverbank. 6 And one said to the man clothed in linen, who was above the waters of the river, "How long shall the fulfillment of these wonders be?"

7 Then I heard the man clothed in linen, who was above the waters of the river, when he held up his right hand and his left hand to heaven, and swore by Him who lives forever, that it shall be for a time, times, and half a time; and when the power of the holy people has been completely shattered, all these things shall be finished.

8 Although I heard, I did not understand. Then I said, "My lord, what shall be the end of these things?"

9 And he said, "Go your way, Daniel, for the words are closed up and sealed till the time of the end. 10 Many shall be purified, made white, and refined, but the wicked shall do wickedly; and none of the wicked shall understand, but the wise shall understand. 11 "And from the time that the daily sacrifice is taken away, and the abomination of desolation is set up, there shall be one thousand two hundred and ninety days. 12 Blessed is he who waits, and comes to the one thousand three hundred and thirty-five days.

13 "But you, go your way till the end; for you shall rest, and will arise to your inheritance at the end of the days.

—*Daniel 12:5–13*

As Daniel's vision begins to fade, he finds himself returning to an active role in the revelation. The heavenly visitor has been describing God's future purposes. Daniel now catches sight of two other figures, one on each side of the river (v. 5). He overhears one of them questioning the giver of the revelation, *"the man clothed in linen, who was above the waters of the river"* (v. 6). It is the very question Daniel himself (and not only Daniel) would like to ask: *"'How long shall the fulfillment of these wonders be?'"* (v. 6).

The answer is one of the most solemn moments in the vision, indeed in the entire book. It is reminiscent of the solemn oath of the Lord Himself in Moses' great psalm at the conclusion of the exposition of the divine covenant (Deut. 32:40). The One who is *"above the waters"* (v. 7) raises both hands to heaven, as if taking a sacred oath, and affirms in the name of the Living God that *"it shall be for a time, times; and half a time"* (v. 7).

We have seen before that this expression has a rather general numerical significance (see the discussion on 7:25). It conveys a sense of extended periods of time, but it also conveys something of God's sovereign control over all events. By His own power He is able to cut short apparently inevitable historical developments. All these things will be finished, adds the heavenly figure, *"when the power of the holy people has been completely shattered"* (v. 7). When the powers of darkness have done their worst against the kingdom of God, and the truth of God has been set at a final devaluation, God will act.

Once more, Daniel heard alarming news by way of divine revelation. Like ourselves, instinctively, he wanted to know more because he *"did not understand"* (v. 8). His great concern was to know when and how all this would come to an end.

It was not for Daniel to know. He was commanded: *"Go your way"* (v. 9). The mysterious prophecy he had been given will be understood only as God unravels history in the unseen future. The important thing for Daniel to know is that the Lord's people will be purified and refined through these events; whereas those committed to the destruction of God's influence will harden their hearts even more and remain in their wickedness (v. 10). Despite their worldly wisdom, they will not understand God's ways. In contrast, for all the apparent confusions and contradictions of history, the wise—those who know that the fear of the Lord is the beginning of wisdom—will understand (Prov. 9:10). They know that if God is for them, nothing can ultimately be against them. He works everything together for the good of those who love Him (Rom. 8:28). The assurance that God has a purpose, that He uses the sufferings of His people to fulfill it, is all we need to know in order to trust Him fully.

Daniel receives his final word of encouragement. He is given fresh insight into the more immediate climax of the persecution of God's people. From the time when *daily sacrifice is taken away . . . the abomination of desolation is set up"* (v. 11), that is, in the days of Antiochus Epiphanes, *"one thousand two hundred and ninety days"* (v. 12) must pass. The period is approximately three and a half years. It perhaps suggests that this nearer period of suffering is a miniature or microcosm of the future period of *"a time, times, and half a time"* (v. 7). The nearer period is measured in days, however, in order to underline that it has been carefully measured and is completely controlled by God. It will not last forever. It will, however, be extended briefly for another forty-five days (v. 12; cf. Rev. 2:10; 11:3, 9, 11; 12:6 for a similar use of "days"). All this serves to emphasize that God alone changes the times and seasons (Dan. 2:21).

To Daniel, all this lies in the future. It should be remembered that the chief reason for his receiving this grand and mysterious vision was to lead him into a new dimension of spiritual understanding and, apparently, to encourage him as a man of prayer. It is not necessary for him to know more. Insofar as he is also the mouthpiece of God to the church in all future ages, it is well that his visions are not given in the form of history written in advance. Much of the meaning of Daniel's vision will become clear only when it is fulfilled. It is to be received by faith in such a way that we continue to live by faith, and not by sight.

What then should Daniel do? No doubt, like the Gadarene demoniac, he wanted to be with his Lord to learn the intimate details of His plans. Instead, he is told, *"Go your way"* (vv. 9, 13). In the light of the preview he has been given of God's future purposes, his primary task is to live now for God's glory.

This is the constant application of all biblical eschatology. In one form or another, every New Testament passage that points to God's future plans carries with it the application: "Therefore, since all these things will be . . . what manner of persons ought you to be in holy conduct and godliness, looking for and hastening the coming of the day of God?" (2 Pet. 3:11).

The biblical response to the promises of God's coming kingdom is always "Live for that kingdom now—recognize His reign now—be obedient now—fulfill your present responsibilities now." Then you will one day hear your Master say, "'Well done, good and faithful servant; you were faithful over a few things. . . . Enter into the joy of your Lord'" (Matt. 25:21). If this chapter teaches us anything it is that because God's people will be different then, they are different now. Indeed that is the challenge of this entire book.

Daniel was given the encouragement of a beautiful, personal promise. It forms not only a fitting conclusion but a vital application of our study of this great book: *"But you, go your way till the end; for you shall rest, and will arise to your inheritance at the end of the days"* (v. 13).

> Praise to the Lord,
> who o'er all things so wondrously reigneth,
> Shieldeth thee gently from harm,
> or when fainting sustaineth;
> Hast thou not seen
> How thy heart's wishes have been
> Granted in what he ordaineth?
> *—Joachim Neander (1650–80),*
> *tr. Catherine Winkworth*

BIBLIOGRAPHY

Anderson, Robert A. *Signs and Wonders: A Commentary on the Book of Daniel.* International Theological Commentary. Grand Rapids: Eerdmans, 1984.

Baldwin, Joyce G. *Daniel: An Introduction and Commentary.* Downers Grove, Ill.: InterVarsity Press, 1978.

Bulwin, J. M. "The Identification of Darius the Mede." *Westminster Theological Journal* 35 (1972–73): 247–67.

Calvin, John. *Commentaries on the Book of the Prophet Daniel.* Translated by Thomas Myers. 2 vols. Edinburgh: Calvin Translation Society, 1852–53.

Collins, J. J. *Daniel, with an Introduction to Apocalyptic Literature.* The Forms of Old Testament Literature, vol. 20. Grand Rapids: Eerdmans, 1984.

Hartman, Louis F., and Alexander A. Di Lella. *The Book of Daniel.* Anchor Bible, no. 23. Garden City, N.Y.: Doubleday and Co., 1978.

Keil, C. F. and F. Delitzsch. *The Book of the Prophet Daniel.* Biblical Commentary on the Old Testament, vol. 23. Translated by James Martin et al. Edinburgh: T. & T. Clark, 1872.

Lacoque, A. *The Book of Daniel.* Translated by David Pellauer. Atlanta: John Knox Press, 1979.

Leupold, H. C. *Exposition of Daniel.* Grand Rapids: Baker Book House, 1969.

Luthi, W. *The Church to Come.* Translated by D. H. C. Read. London: Hodder & Stoughton, 1939.

Mickelson, A. Berkeley. *Daniel and Revelation: Riddles or Realities?* Nashville: Thomas Nelson, 1984.

Montgomery, James A. *A Critical and Exegetical Commentary on the Book of Daniel.* The International Critical Commentary on the Holy Scriptures of the Old and New Testaments, vol. 22. Edinburgh: T. & T. Clark, 1959.

Olyott, Stuart. *Dare to Stand Alone.* Welwyn Commentary Series. Welwyn: Evangelical Press, 1982.

Philip, James. *By the Rivers of Babylon: Studies in the Book of Daniel.* Aberdeen: Didasko Press, 1971.

Poythress, V. S. "Hermeneutical Factors in Determining the Beginning of the Seventy Weeks (Dan. 9:25)," *Trinity Journal* 6 n.s. (1985): 131–49.

Rushdoony, R. J. *Thy Kingdom Come: Studies in Daniel and Revelation.* Philadelphia: Presbyterian and Reformed Publishing Co., 1971.

Taylor, William M. *Daniel the Beloved.* New York: Harper, 1878.

Veldkamp, H. *Dreams and Dictators: On the Book of Daniel.* Translated by T. Plantinga. St. Catherines, Ont.: Paideia, 1979.

Wallace, Ronald S. *The Lord Is King: The Message of Daniel*. Downers Grove: InterVarsity Press, 1979.

Wilson, Robert D. *Studies in the Book of Daniel: A Discussion of the Historical Questions*. New York: G. P. Putnam's Sons, 1917.

Studies in the Book of Daniel: Second Series. New York: Fleming H. Revell Co., 1938.

Wiseman, D. J., ed. *Notes on Some Problems in the Book of Daniel*. London: Tyndale Press, 1965.

Wood, Leon J. *A Commentary on Daniel*. Grand Rapids: Zondervan Publishing House, 1973.

Daniel: A Study Guide. Grand Rapids: Zondervan Publishing House, 1975.

Young, E. J. *A Commentary on Daniel*. Grand Rapids: Eerdmans, 1949.